Persian Mosaic

CARL,
THANK YOU FOR YOUR
INTEREST. IT IS HARD
TO BELIEVE IT HAS
BEEN 30 YEARS SINCE
THANKSGIVING IN
ZAHEDAN, '72.

David
Dev

Persian Mosaic

Getting Back to Iran
After 25 Years

David Devine

Writer's Showcase
San Jose New York Lincoln Shanghai

Persian Mosaic
Getting Back to Iran After 25 Years

Writer's Showcase
an imprint of iUniverse.com, Inc.

For information address:
iUniverse.com, Inc.
5220 S 16th, Ste. 200
Lincoln, NE 68512
www.iuniverse.com

ISBN: 0-595-19258-0

Printed in the United States of America

For my parents who provided me with the opportunity

CONTENTS

Acknowledgements ix

Introduction xi

1998 1
   Searching for Sarkis *3*
   Palaces and Tombs *19*
   Half of The World *30*
   The Streets of Shiraz *40*
   Fire and Light *55*
   Coming Clean *65*
   Back to Baluchistan *76*
   Going South Again *94*
   A View Across The Gulf *109*

1971 115
   Going There *117*
   Getting Acquainted *124*
   Bus Ride to Zahedan *136*
   North to Zabol *144*
   Flying South to Charbahar *153*
   Settling in *171*

1972 179
   Jamal and Fatima *181*
   Rain *187*
   Spring Break to The East *196*

Life in The Desert 219
Postcard From Corfu 225
Sarkis 232
Social Visits 235
The News 244
Christmas in Kerman 250

1973 255
Johnny Walker Black Label 257
Work 261
Breakup 266
Another Spring Break 269
North for The Weekend 275
Leaving Home 283
West from The East 292

ACKNOWLEDGEMENTS

This book would not have been possible without the support of my wife, Susie Morris. Her encouragement and backing, along with detailed criticisms of an earlier draft of this work, were necessary to make it happen.

Also offering advice and assistance on the style and content of the book were Ralph Kingery, Felicia Sanders-May, and Tim O'Connor. Their comments and suggestions were greatly appreciated.

Gerry Emmerich provided not only helpful ideas for making the book better but also pointed me in the right direction for obtaining a travel agent in Tehran when I told him of my plans for returning to Iran. Without that assistance, I would not have been able to take the trip in 1998.

Parvaneh Farzad and her husband Firooz Mahdavi both lent me their advice on the manuscript. In addition, she helped me refresh my memory of the Persian language I once knew. Bringing back at least some of those words helped me immensely in understanding what was happening around me in modern-day Iran. Parvaneh's and Firooz's patience, friendship and help will always be remembered.

Special thanks needs to go to Pat Toth for reading two versions of earlier drafts and making comments which resulted in the book becoming much more understandable. Her timely assistance was very helpful.

Thanks also to Tom Bergin for his art direction and layout for this book. Using my photographs, Tom did a marvelous job.

I am, of course, totally responsible for the contents of this book. While every attempt has been made to verify the statements and comments made in it, any errors or mistakes are my responsibility.

Some peoples' names, for both then and now, have been changed to protect their privacy. While Iran today is not the police state it once was under the *mullahs*, one never knows. Some other names have been invented because I simply forgot what they really were.

With those exceptions, it is my hope that the descriptions and details provided in this book accurately portray life in Iran, both now and then.

David Devine
June, 2001

INTRODUCTION

"Mister, you must come visit us. We are waiting for you."

By May of 1973, after two years in Iran, I was ready to leave. My Peace Corps tour of service was over, I planned on heading west overland through Europe, and I was going to enter graduate school in Tucson, Arizona in a few months. Like Dorothy in "The Wizard of Oz", I wanted to go home.

I had spent most of my time in Iran working as an urban planning volunteer in the small desert town of Zahedan, capital of Sistan and Baluchistan province. Located in the far eastern corner of the country about 25 miles from the border with Pakistan, the experience had offered me a close-up look at the Iranian male lifestyle. My Persian roommates and the tribal maid we employed had exposed me to a completely different way of living than I was accustomed to.

The house we rented had arched ceilings made of mud brick, it didn't have a television or a telephone, but did have a hole-in-the-floor toilet which had to be squatted over. The house was built along a narrow dirt alley just off one of Zahedan's main streets and a deep and always dry riverbed ran nearby.

My work at the provincial engineering office had shown me a great deal about the way another culture did business. Even though there was enormous poverty in Zahedan, the highest ranking local government officials weren't very interested in changing the situation.

Those officials, however, were extremely anxious to please the ruling dictator of the country. Reza Pahlavi, shah of Iran, or Persia as it had once been known, lived a lavish lifestyle and constantly talked of the great future for the country. While his words promised prosperity for all, many of Zahedan's 25,000 people lived in flimsy shacks, had no jobs, and survived on a day-to-day basis.

Despite that, I had enjoyed my stay in Iran but finally it was time to go. I packed my belongings into an old cardboard refrigerator box and sent them on a truck off to Tehran over an unpaved, rough road. Following a tearful farewell with those I worked with at the engineering office, I left for the capital.

After more than a week, the shipped possessions still hadn't arrived at the freight company in Tehran. Wondering what could have happened, I walked down Ferdosi Boulevard from my Peace Corps friend Gerry's apartment to the central telephone exchange building. I called Sarkis, my co-worker, roommate and best friend in Zahedan, to ask for his assistance in finding out where my things were. "They told me they would be here by now Sarkis, but the company manager says he has no record of them."

"I'll check here and find out what happen, Mister David. They must be there someplace."

The following day I called back. Sarkis told me the goods had been sent to a different freight office than the one originally planned. But, he said, they were in Tehran. Then he added, "Mister David, we miss you already. Everyone here wishes you would come back."

I located the refrigerator box and asked that the things be repacked into a sturdy wooden crate for shipping by sea to America. It was to be addressed to my hometown, Madison, Wisconsin, U.S.A.

A few weeks later, upon my return to Tehran from touring the western and southern provinces of Iran, I checked to make sure that had been done by the freight company. It had, so I was ready to leave the country. I called the railway station to inquire if a ticket was available for that night's train to Istanbul. When I learned there wasn't, I hurried to the bus station to catch an overnight ride to Tabriz. From there I was going overland through Europe.

As the bus left the suburbs of the capital, the schizophrenic nature of the place struck me again. People could eat hamburgers, drink beer and dance to western music at nightclubs in the northern part of Tehran. In the southern sections of the city, however, life was lived as it had been for centuries. Covered women fetched water from communal faucets and donkeys carried wood for burning. The American Embassy was located in the center of Tehran, and the city and its people were divided into two worlds.

Early the next morning I was on a bus from Tabriz to the Turkish border. We went by farms and fields of green, machinery doing most of the agricultural work. The bus eventually stopped at a small village with tightly stacked mud brick homes protruding from a hillside. I asked someone where the border crossing station was, and they pointed up the slope.

A building at the top of the hill marked the line between Iran and Turkey. Two Persian guards were sitting alone in a large room waiting for customers when I entered. After a brief search of my bags and a look at my passport, they silently waved me on. I thanked them in Farsi, their own language, and they wanted to know how I knew it and where I had come from. After a few minutes of chat, I left the country, the language and the culture behind.

The Turkish side of the border was a barren landscape of endless vistas and high mountain ranges. Vast expanses of dry emptiness were backed by tall peaks, including Mount Ararat. A van was waiting to take paying passengers west to the city of Erzurum. It was surrounded by about a dozen world travelers, members of a sub-species of Europeans and Americans that were commonly seen throughout the east from Turkey to India. They were usually young, barefoot, often stoned, and almost always filthy. Their primary pleasure in life came not from seeing exotic sights or experiencing different cultures, but from traveling as cheaply as possible. Saving every cent they could, even if it meant having to endure some real hardships, was the world travelers' principal credo.

The people standing around the van were mostly European college-aged kids who had been to the east and were now returning home. In their long wavy robes, dirty hair, bare feet and with money purses hanging around their necks, they looked strangely out-of-place. Some of them stood outside the van complaining about the $3 fare for the almost 200 mile ride while others were already inside, ready to go.

After a few hours of waiting, and a handful of more young travelers joining the crowd, the van driver announced he was leaving. He said those who were interested in going should get in. While most of us quickly did, a few people stayed behind. They claimed they wouldn't pay the "rip off" $3 price, that they'd get to Erzurum cheaper. How they expected to do that from a remote, little used border crossing wasn't clear, but a group of five was left standing in the dust as we drove away.

Going west through desolate countryside, I heard the travel tales of three of my companions. They were from Belgium and had gone off to see the east on the often followed overland circuit of young world travelers. It was Istanbul, Tehran, Mashad or maybe Zahedan, Afghanistan, India and then to Katmandu and the free flowing drugs of Nepal.

"We were having a good time and seeing some wonderful things," one of them said. "Iran was pleasant and Pakistan O.K., but when we got to India, things changed. The heat was oppressive and the poverty overwhelming. It was not at all what we were expecting."

"But we were still going to Nepal," another of them interrupted, "until we took a third class carriage on a train in India. The press of bodies, the chance of disease and the unbearable heat were just too much. So we turned around."

"You didn't make it to Katmandu?"

"No. We were all remembering the nice things about home too much. So Belgium is where we are going. But we're still taking our time in getting there."

These men also emphasized the importance of the speed of the van. The night train from Erzurum to Istanbul was scheduled to leave at 10 p.m. We had departed the border at 2 p.m. and it was suppose to be an eight hour trip, so there was no time to spare if they were to make the train.

"Why do you want to catch the train?" I asked innocently.

"Because it is by far cheaper than the bus," they explained, wondering what I could have been thinking.

After three hours of bouncing along the dirt road, we stopped at a village for tea and to pay the fare. Everyone immediately handed over their money except for a few passengers who loudly protested that they thought it should be cheaper. A Turkish gentleman of some sinister appearance was seated at the tea house and when he heard those complaints he got up out of his chair. Accompanied by a man with a rifle, he walked over to the van and said, very politely, "Pay the fare, please". Money changed hands rapidly and we were soon back on the road.

The trip had gone slower than expected and we didn't arrive in Erzurum until 11 p.m. I bought a ticket for the next morning's overnight bus to Istanbul and left the three boys from Belgium sitting on the floor of the station, talking about what they were going to do. I went to find a room to try and get some sleep.

In the heat of the following afternoon, the bus for Istanbul stopped in a remote area at a roadside restaurant. The large central dining hall was filled with hundreds of people, yelling at waiters and pushing and shoving to get tea from a passing tray. A man came to take my order but, not knowing Turkish, I simply pointed at the rice and greens that a fellow customer near me was eating. The waiter brought my food and shoved it in front of me with a grunt. That, I knew, was certainly not the kind of treatment a visitor received in Iran.

After three days and nights of almost continuous travel, my mind was foggy as the car ferry the bus was on crossed the Bosporus. Old parts of the city climbed up the hillsides on both sides of the straits while small boats and cruise ships made their way into the docks. The tall towers of the Hagia Sophia mosque loomed above us as the ferry unloaded on the other side, the European side, of the water.

Near the bazaar two days later I met the three travelers from Belgium. They had caught the train the same day I had left Erzurum but had just arrived in Istanbul. True to their culture however, one said, "We saved money by taking it".

A few minutes later I ran into a Peace Corps couple from Iran who had been on the same train when it left Tehran. After enduring two days of riding in a compartment for eight but filled with 18, they had gotten off and flown the rest of the way. The world travelers from Belgium would not have approved of that.

The next several weeks I spent slowly moving westward. A flight to Athens got me on a car ferry to Italy. After seeing Rome and Florence again, I went to Venice where a pigeon pooped on my head. A few days in Munich and Brussels convinced me to finish my European travels with a long stay in London.

A week before my charter flight to New York was scheduled to leave from England, I went to the airline company office to confirm my reservation. They told me to check back with them the day before departure. When I returned to the office as instructed, the girl at the counter looked at my ticket, made a strange face, and asked me to wait. After conferring with her boss she said nervously, "Your flight left yesterday. You were supposed to re-confirm with us 72 hours before the scheduled date. But we will see what we can do about getting you on another plane. Our next opening is in 8 days. Come back tomorrow morning and hopefully we'll have something worked out."

Swallowing hard, but keeping my temper under control, I walked out into the August afternoon sunlight. I only had about $100 left in my wallet and still needed some money to get from New York to Madison.

In the morning I was in front of the airline office 15 minutes before it opened. Another guy, however, had gotten there ahead of me. After the agent unlocked the door, he stood talking to her in low whispers and then quickly left. I moved to the counter and she remembered me. "Good luck" she exclaimed excitedly. "The man who was just here had a ticket on a flight from Dublin to JFK in three days. He doesn't want to use it, so if you like, here is a ticket on tonight's ferry train to Ireland and an airplane ticket to New York." Relieved, and thinking how things sometimes do work out, I went to spend my last day in London.

The night train to the coast was full of Irish families standing in the aisles in order to keep cool on a very warm night. Working men were drinking from cases of beer and singing songs while their wives tended to the children. By dawn, as the sun rose above the Irish Sea, most of the singers had passed out on the deck of the ship, while babies cried in their mothers' arms.

A few days later, the plane to New York was packed with Irish students going back to college in the U.S. There was free liquor on board and the talk was of future plans. My seatmates were headed for Tucson, where I was also going in two weeks to enroll in the urban planning program. They told me to expect a warm, dry, desert climate in a nondescript city. Sounded sort of like Zahedan, only much larger.

In the customs line at JFK, an immigration officer was intensely talking with a head shaved American dressed as an orange robed Buddhist monk. He had a large oriental doll and wanted to bring it into the country. Another agent waved me over to his line and by the time I departed the head was off of the doll, the search for hidden drugs continuing.

A month after arriving in Tucson, I sat on a small Persian rug in my dorm room, peeling an orange with the Swiss army knife I had bought in Tehran two years before. In front of me lay a letter from Sarkis, written in simple English.

He wanted to know when I was coming back to Iran. "Mister," he wrote, "you must come visit us. We are waiting for you." It was twenty-five years before I could return.

1998

ARMENIA
AZERBAIJAN
TURKEY
CASPIAN SEA
TURKMENISTAN

TEHRAN
QOM
IRAN
IRAQ
ISFAHAN
AFGHANISTAN

YAZD

YEZDIKHAST RAFSANJUN KERMAN
ABARKUH ZAHEDAN
BAM
SHIRAZ
PAKISTAN
PERSIAN GULF
IRANSHAHR

CHARBAHAR
GULF OF OMAN

1998

SEARCHING FOR SARKIS

The telephone jingled my mind awake from a half-sleep at 8 a.m. It had been four and one-half often disturbed hours of mostly semi-rest since I had arrived at the hotel in Tehran.

In broken English the voice on the line said, "Mister David, this is Reza, your driver. I waiting down stairs for you." I mumbled that I would be with him in ten minutes and tried to shake thoughts of the pillow out of my head.

At the same time, memories of how I got to Iran kept emerging. Having family and friends, who knew little about the world or its ways, repeatedly tell me the trip would be highly dangerous. Responding with a hearty laugh to my American travel agent's request that I sign a statement certifying I had read the U.S. government's pronouncement on Iran before she would send me my Tucson-Frankfurt-Tehran airline tickets. "The Department of State warns all U.S. citizens to defer travel to Iran…There is…evidence that hostility to the United States remains in some segments of the Iranian population and some elements of the Iranian government."

Danger wasn't the problem with going back to Iran, obtaining permission for the trip from the Iranian government was. Potential terrorism didn't frighten me, but possible long delays caused by Persian bureaucrats did.

An attempt I had made on my own to get a visa for a trip in 1997 had gotten no response from the Iranian government. Then after I discovered a travel agency in Tehran I could work with, I still had to wait 3 months for an entry visa and didn't know if I would secure one until it actually appeared. When it finally arrived from the Interests Section of the Islamic Republic of Iran, care of the Embassy of Pakistan, Washington, D.C., numbered 852, it was very satisfying.

To help with obtaining the visa, and to make arrangements for traveling around the country, I had been in communication with the tour company in Tehran for many months. My young female contact spoke English far better than I spoke Farsi and after several small glitches, we worked out an itinerary. I also wired the agency the cost of the trip in advance to pay for hotel rooms, meals, and a government required driver. That way I wouldn't have to be carrying large amounts of cash with me.

As the waiting area in the Frankfurt airport for the Tehran bound flight began to fill with Persian speaking people, my decision to return to Iran made sense to me. I was traveling back to the place that in large part had made me the person I was. I wanted to see how it, and I, had changed.

When I first flew off to Iran in 1971, I had been a semi-alcoholic college kid that didn't know anything about the world. In my two years there I found the people friendly and the desert beautiful. Now I was a year away from my fiftieth birthday, had visited dozens of countries on five continents, and seen death up close. It was time, I decided, to go back.

Iran twenty-five years ago had been an American backed dictatorial monarchy which tried to imitate western ways in lifestyle, dress and architecture. Alcohol was legal and widely consumed and drugs of all types were easily obtainable. Now, however, the country is a fundamentalist Islamic republic controlled by religious mullahs and alcohol is banned. While the ruling clerics had totally shunned the West for most of the last two decades, recently some of them seem to be slowly deciding that they want to forget past animosities.

The former shah of Iran had used a secret police force to keep people in fear of him. SAVAK, as it was known, was rumored to be everywhere. The current regime also has a secret police force, along with a militia and morality police, to insure that the goals of the religious revolution are followed and to enforce their views of Islam. From what I had read, however, the role of the morality police in dictating people's lifestyles appeared to be gradually diminishing.

The traditional architecture of Iran created beautiful cities made of mud brick. Arches, domes and narrow alleyways were the long standing way of building communities throughout the country. That, however, was beginning to change for the worse to modern European designs in the 1970s.

Twenty-five years ago most women outside of the major cities in Iran covered themselves with veils. Many women in the wealthy parts of central and northern Tehran as well as other large urban areas, though, were western in their dress. Despite their modern appearance, under the shah the role of women in the business world and society in general was severely limited. While one woman did have a cabinet level post in the early 1970s, all of the businesspeople and top level government administrators I encountered were men.

Today modesty in dress for women is a legal requirement. They must either cover themselves completely with veils or wear scarves and long, heavy trench coats. But in certain respects, according to American news reports which I had heard, under the fundamentalist government women have made strides toward a greater role in the economy. Some women now own their own businesses while others have more importance in the day-to-day operation of the companies they work for.

Iranian men, as I quickly learned when I moved to Zahedan, used the services of prostitutes frequently. Many men that I knew were very juvenile in their approach toward sex. Their views of women and the role of fidelity in marriage just weren't like those professed publicly in the western world.

Women were classified into two groups by many Iranian men. Mothers, wives, sisters and daughters were held to a high standard of behavior and mostly hidden away from society to insure they met that standard. Other women, however, such as prostitutes, foreigners and Iranian women trying to succeed in the business world, were "girl friends". They were considered fair game for any type of behavior by a man. Males had their needs and these women, whether they wanted to or not, could satisfy them according to some of the Persian men I knew.

The population of Iran exploded with the clerics rise to power in 1979. It went from about 25 or 30 million people when I lived there to an estimated 65 million today. Much of the small middle class of the country fled because of the fundamentalist revolution, and the new emerging middle class is being pinched by economic difficulties now.

Americans knew little about Iran in the early 1970s, but two and a half decades of oil embargoes, hostage takings, Middle East wars, and death threats against author Salman Rushdie have changed that. Today the country is generally recognized by people in the U.S., if it is recognized at all, as a supposedly ardent enemy of ours because that is what they hear the State Department repeatedly say.

The friendliness of most Iranians, however, is not known in the U.S. When I lived in Zahedan, it was the kindness and hospitality of the people which left the deepest impact on me. But most Americans, even though they know next to nothing about the country except its name and the "terrorist state" tag put on it by the American government, are terrified of Iran. A friend of mine told me as we rode to the airport in Tucson on my way to Germany, "You'll be killed when you go to Iran. They'll eat you alive. They are fanatic and never forget a grudge."

I knew from experience that was nonsense. From what I had read in newspaper accounts about other Americans' recent trips to Iran, I concluded that our State Department knew as much about the country now as it did back in the 1970s, which in my opinion was almost nothing. The Nixon administration had wanted U.S. diplomats to be ignorant of the history, culture and language of Iran, incorrectly assuming that what they heard from the shah and his allies was totally accurate. Under Carter, continuation of that philosophy would lead to the United

States being surprised by the Iranian revolution and then not anticipating the U.S. Embassy takeover with its prolonged holding of American hostages.

As I thought over these changes between now and then, Iranian women in the Frankfurt airport's waiting area were joking about whether to don their coverings before or after they got on the plane. Several Persian children were running around, one wearing a Batman t-shirt, another lugging a "Scooby-Do" suitcase.

By the time the late afternoon flight was called, most of the older women were covered. The younger ones, however, were just pulling on long coats and wrapping their heads in white, patterned or black scarves, but the conformance with modesty regulations couldn't hide the Nike swoosh on their shoes.

Sitting next to me on the plane, a German businessman who had first flown to Iran shortly after Ayatollah Khomeini's 1979 return warned that I should expect a different country. "Right after the revolution things looked promising for democracy. Then the mullahs took control and they dealt with their opponents ruthlessly. Plus," he added, "the traffic is so bad now in Tehran that it is best to drive at night."

"But the current diplomatic and military tensions with Afghanistan shouldn't cause you any problems in the eastern part of the country," he said. "During the war with Iraq, I was down in the area near the fighting and when we approached the war zone the soldiers just told us to be careful because there was shooting up ahead."

As Persians sitting near us finished their beer, wine or Johnny Walker scotch, the scattered lights of Iranian villages appeared below the plane. We were soon approaching Tehran, the huge golden dome and four towering minarets of Khomeini's tomb passing underneath us in the moonlight. Twenty-five years before, the city had ended many miles north of the religious shrine, but now Tehran's lights stretched almost all that way south.

A portrait of an old, wrinkly faced Khomeini with white beard, black turban and fierce, piercing eyes looked down on tired passengers waiting to clear passport control and enter the country. Even though it was well after two in the morning, the airport lobby was crowded with a human gauntlet of relatives, pushing and shoving to be the first to welcome arriving travelers. No one, however, seemed to be waiting for me.

After a few minutes of unsuccessfully looking for someone from the travel agency who was suppose to meet me, I began negotiations with a private driver. He wanted $20 to take me to my hotel, I offered five and we settled on $8. As we walked to his car, I knew the lessons I had taken to refresh my memory of the Persian language or Farsi had already paid off.

Just outside the airport, the shah's now ironic 1971 giant white monument to the 2,500 anniversary of the Persian monarchy was bathed in bright light. Speeding past a small newsstand, the middle-aged driver pointed out the displayed photograph of one of the five Iranian diplomats recently slain by the Taliban army in Afghanistan. He shook his head and exclaimed that something would have to be done about it. Then he said proudly "The population of Tehran is now 12 million people. When you were here it was what, 3 or 4 million? There is so much traffic now. And all the streets have changed their names from that time."

"Things have gotten so expensive since you were here. Automobiles cost very much now. And gas. When you and I were young, it was only a few pennies. But now it is 15 cents a gallon."

"Where is your wife? In Germany! Why? Drinking wine! Do you have children? Why not? I have two."

As we drove by the hotel where I had spent my first night in Iran in 1971, he told me the name had been changed from the Atlantic to the Atlas. Just down the street, the grounds of the former American Embassy were dark and looked foreboding behind a high brick wall.

I had to wake the night clerk at the Mashad Hotel by banging on the front door, but he soon appeared. It was 3:30 a.m. and it had been more than 30 hours of almost continuous travel before I finally got to lay my head on a pillow. Over me, an arrow painted on the wall pointed the direction toward Mecca for the Muslim faithful who wanted to pray in the hotel room.

Traffic noise from below the sixth floor room woke me at dawn. The sky was a clear but faded blue because of smog, and the towering gray mountains to the north of the city were visible only through a haze of pollution. My alarm clock showed 6 a.m., so I lay back down and tried to sleep until the telephone woke me again.

One of the first things my driver Reza said when we met was, "I at airport. I look all over for you. I wait until everyone has gotten off plane. Then I have information desk page you. But you weren't there. I ask at taxi stand. They say nobody go to Mashad Hotel. So I call hotel. They tell me you are resting."

An hour later, sleep still pushing at my brain, we were on the street looking for Sarkis. Since he was a Christian in a country where almost everyone is a Muslim, I assumed trying to find him would be uncomplicated. Using a phone book was out of the question since they were completely out-of-date and inaccurate. But a personal search, I hoped, would produce results.

Our first stop was the Hazrate Sarkis Armenian Church, a large and modern complex of white buildings floating on an ocean of believers in Islam. With some difficulty we found a parking space only a few blocks away and Reza wrapped a very heavy chain around his steering wheel and secured it with an enormous ancient metal lock. He then put his briefcase, containing all of the money he would take to pay for our expenses on the upcoming trip, into the trunk and carefully locked it, double checking to be sure.

"I pay for taxi from airport. How much you pay?" Reza asked as we walked down the street. He was a short man of about 50 who was losing his hair and gaining weight around the middle. He had to move quickly to keep up with my long strides.

"Too much, so forget it," I replied.

Having to cross a major thoroughfare, we waded out into traffic just like in the old days. The Persian pedestrian steps into a moving stream of usually slow moving cars and then keeps going, crossing a street anywhere he wants. The total lack of obedience toward traffic rules by motorists can make the job somewhat challenging. Some vehicles may slow down a little, but if they don't, those on foot have to stop in the middle of the street to wait for a break in the flow.

We found three fully bearded, elderly priests dressed in black robes talking quietly in the hallway of the church office building. They directed us to speak to the chief administrator, who saw us immediately. After looking at the photograph I had of Sarkis from 26 years ago and thinking for a moment, he said, "My best guess, because of his last name, is that he was an Assyrian, not an Armenian. There are two small Assyrian churches in Tehran. One is not far away. You should try and go there."

After weaving through the one way streets of central Tehran, Reza stopped near a small shop to ask the storekeeper where the church was located. The merchant pointed down an alley and we found a side gate and rang the bell. A cleaning woman opened the door, showed us in and went to get the woman in charge. She was in her 40s and after seating us in her office, she quickly excused herself to go get her overcoat.

The walls of the room were dirty and needed painting and the rug on the floor was old and frayed. After explaining to her about Sarkis, I handed her the picture I had of him. It showed a very short man in his early 30s with graying hair. He was standing in the courtyard of our house in Zahedan, posing sternly for the camera.

She looked at the photograph for a minute and said she didn't know him, but she immediately reached for the phone to call the other Assyrian church to ask if they did. As she dialed, she inquired how long it had taken for me to get a visa. "Three months isn't too bad. That is about what it takes us to get permission to leave the country for a trip," she said.

No one was at the other church, so she told me to call back after 4:00. Searching for a pen with which to write her telephone number, she couldn't find one. I gave her a pencil I had and after jotting down the number, she put the pencil gently down on her desk and didn't offer it back to me. I remained silent, since she needed it more than I did.

With the church search at a standstill, I tried another approach. For years I seemed to remember in the back of my mind that Sarkis had once told me his parents lived in Tehran on "Kuchey Abrahimi" near the Pepsi-Cola bottling plant. The building was a familiar fixture in the capital in the early 1970s since it was on the main road to the airport. It was also well known because the company was thought by many people to be owned by a member of the Bahai faith.

Bahais believe in religious freedom, oppose racial and sexual discrimination, and promote international peace through governmental unification. The religion had been founded by a Persian in the 19th century and its followers had been persecuted as heretics in Iran ever since its inception. Under the shah in the early 1970s the religion was not an officially "recognized" faith so members had to practice it secretly. It was commonly believed, though, that the Pepsi bottling plant was owned by a Bahai.

Even the small degree of tolerance permitted by the shah, however, was unacceptable to the clerics when they took control of the country in 1979. During the revolution, 400 Bahais were among the 4,000 people quickly executed by the new regime. Many other followers of the faith joined the more than one million Iranians who fled Iran to escape the fundamentalists and their enforced way of religious life. Over time, as political assassinations and public unrest mounted during the war with Iraq, the *mullahs* in charge would murder another 2,500 people in order to retain their control of the country.

The Pepsi plant was still there, now called Zam-Zam, with the bottling process happening behind a large window. All around the plant new commercial structures had risen, so it was now just another nonde-script building in a miles-long strip of them.

South of the plant, narrow residential streets and alleys, or *kucheys* in Persian, were filled with parked cars. The streets crossed each other at regular intervals and slow moving automobiles and pedestrians had to make room for one another to pass. Reza asked in a shop where Kuchey Abrahimi was and then inquired of an old man who was walking by if he remembered the family. "The area has changed a lot in 25 years," he said, "with most people who were here moving further north and new families moving in. I don't remember the family but check with the real estate agent on the corner."

Outside his small office, the middle-aged agent stood watching the world go by as he slowly moved stringed prayer beads in his right hand. Over his head, a street sign in Persian and English pointed out the three block long Kuchey Ebrahimi, the spelling of my memory not having been too far off. He had been in the area a long time, the agent said, but didn't recall the family. "Only three families have lived here for 25 years and they aren't one of them. But try walking down the kuchey and see if anyone remembers where they went."

The asphalt alley was lined by three and four story row houses built on narrow lots. At one address, a new concrete and glass home was under construction to replace a demolished structure. The small paved front yards of these houses, like many in Tehran, had once been used for washing and drying of clothes and other outdoor activities. Now the space was needed for parking of automobiles.

A young woman veiled entirely in black was standing in a doorway, watching her two small children play in the alley. She didn't know the family, she said, but recommended we talk to the merchant at the end of the street who had been in business a long time.

His mouth full of gaps from missing teeth and wearing a short gray stubble on his chin, the storekeeper said he couldn't remember the fam-ily. "The area has changed a lot," he explained.

These roadblocks to finding Sarkis weren't unexpected. The enormous growth in the size of Tehran meant that people could have moved several times over the past 25 years. Plus the revolution had resulted in many entire families leaving the country. Large Iranian communities developed in Turkey, Germany and Los Angeles and perhaps Sarkis now lived somewhere else besides Iran.

"Maybe church can help later," Reza offered hopefully as we drove from the area. Huge banners showing men killed in the 1980s war with Iraq lined the main streets and enormous murals of Khomeini and current religious leader Khamenei dotted downtown buildings. Glass and metal highrises rose where once six or seven story buildings had been and the redevelopment process was continuing on other recently cleared lots.

"Now I want to go to the travel agency," I decided as we slowly made our way through heavy central city traffic. Reza questioned why I would want to do that and I replied that I had some unfinished business to complete. That was true, since I still had to pay a small amount for the trip. But I also wondered what the company's relationship with the government was. I thought I just might find something out during an unannounced appearance.

My visa hadn't cost me the standard $50 because I had booked my trip through the agency. They had also been able to secure approval for me to visit the country when my own attempt to obtain the required permission had failed miserably. I considered that strange and wanted to see if I could learn anything about a possible connection between the agency and the government.

At the tour company office I was introduced to my English speaking contact. I had made several late night phone calls to her about my travel plans and faxed her information numerous times. She was a Iranian woman in her 20s sporting lime green fingernails and wearing platform sneakers. A piece of glitter shown on her nose and her veil hung loosely around her head.

While Reza remained in the lobby, she and I went into a small conference room to talk about my trip. She was at one corner of the table
and I sat at the other end opposite her. After handing her some cash to
cover my remaining costs for the trip, I inquired, "How will my hotel
rooms and eating expenses be paid for?"

"Your driver will take care of everything. If you need anything, just
ask him," she said.

"And if we have any problems, what should I do?"

"Hopefully you won't. But if you do, just call me."

"One final thing. I would like to thank you for all of the assistance
you and your company have given me. Without you, I wouldn't be here.
To show my appreciation, I brought you a box of chocolates from
Germany."

"You didn't have to do that, but thank you. Now let me go get the
receipt I owe you."

No one at the agency had offered us the once customary tea upon
our arrival, so while I waited for the receipt, Reza insisted I be given
some. As I sipped it, I couldn't see any obvious links to the government
around me. It was just a typical Persian office with colorful travel
posters hanging on the wall and a few old metal desks crammed into a
too small space. Some ancient equipment sat on one of the desks and
another was covered by a computer terminal that looked unused.

Later, as both of us yawned over a lunch of rice and fried mutton,
Reza told me something about himself. "I learn English when I live in
Oklahoma and San Antonio. Live there in late '60s. Was fighter pilot in
training. Have been driving tourists for over 4 years. Have two sons 4
and 2. Only been married five years. We live in north part of Tehran."

Heading back to the hotel so we could both get some sleep, I asked
about the 25 year old proposal to build a subway system in Tehran. "The
subway went away," Reza chuckled, even though I learned later that a
short line was under construction. What, I inquired, had happened to
the bowling club, a once famous landmark of music, dance and drinking

in the far northern part of the city. It had become a recreation center for youth, he said.

"I see you in morning," Reza said when he dropped me off. "If you ever need anything, you call me at home. Here is my phone number."

After a long nap, I called the church about Sarkis. "No news today," an unknown male voice informed me. "We keep trying. Call back tomorrow at this same time."

Disappointed, but not surprised, I went for a walk. Nearby Ferdosi Boulevard, which honored a great 10th century Persian poet, had not changed names from 25 years ago. It was still tree lined and bordered by small shops selling handicrafts, rugs, and dry goods. At one major inter-section, many men dressed in sport shirts looked for shady spots in which to stand on a warm afternoon. They each held a large wad of paper currency in their hands, the bills tightly wrapped by a rubber band. As I passed them, one after the other said, "Change money?". But Reza had warned that was illegal and most of the men probably worked for the police. I silently nodded at their inquiries and kept walking.

There was obvious idleness on the street, with some men just stand-ing around doing nothing. That had been a common sight under the shah also but the number of beggars along Ferdosi seemed to be less than before. Poor people sitting on the sidewalk selling large colorful lottery tickets on the street had been a very common sight in the 1970s. But now they were completely gone because gambling was forbidden.

A kiosk offered several newspapers, including three English language Iranian ones. There was also a "Time" magazine, dated 1985, with a cover story on South Africa. The staff at a nearby "Fair and Store of Self Sustain Productions of Komite Emdad Emam Khomeini" which had handicrafts from around the country wasn't very interested in helping a foreigner buy something.

Down the street, the British Embassy lay hidden behind a very high brick wall and a sign on the gate directed visa applicants to enter the compound through Bobby Sands Avenue. Further along, the former multi-story department store which was a fixture on Ferdosi and once offered such exotic items as peanut butter looked abandoned. This store had been a major attraction to westerners in the 1970s because of its set prices and wide selection of items, but now it appeared to be deserted.

Searching for postcards, I dropped in at several shops but couldn't find any. Finally I came across a store that had a few unattractive ones showing in the window. As I twirled the display rack around, looking for something more colorful than a picture of the shah's stark white monument, a man in his late 30s wearing a sport coat stood near me. He was saying softly in Farsi, "He is looking at postcards". Selecting a few cards, I went to pay and the man, who had dark features and a rather large pointed nose, followed me to the counter. Asking how much they were, both the man and the shopkeeper exclaimed in unison, "He speaks Persian!".

The store owner told me that learning English for him was made easier by watching CNN received from a signal picked up on a illegal satellite dish. After I repeatedly urged him to tell me the truth, he reluctantly admitted there had been a great celebration in Tehran following the Iranian victory over America in soccer at the World Cup in June. He quickly added that the U.S. would get better with more experience. He obviously hadn't considered it hospitable to tell me about the victory party so his comments about the future of the sport in my country helped equalize things in his mind.

The other man followed me out onto the street and said he was a dry goods importer-exporter from Mashad. He had been in town for 10 days trying to obtain a visa to attend a business conference in Germany and thought he'd have it in another ten. He hoped, he said in slow but firm words, that he could walk with me and practice his English.

As we moved up the congested sidewalk, passing vendors sitting on the curb selling gum, flip-flops or neatly piled nuts, he said that before the revolution he first learned English from Mr. Carter. Now he was trying to remember it because "it is the universal language".

"I want to go to Germany for the conference and think that taking the train to Istanbul is the best way. But how much it cost from there to Germany by bus and ship I don't know. Do you?" I told him of my experience 25 years ago but suggested that flying might be the fastest and easiest way to travel. "Oh no! By land is the cheapest way to get there. I think will take 7 days maybe, but will save me money."

Having exhausted that subject, he nervously began a new one. "Some weeks ago, I meet doctor from New Orleans here in Tehran. He told me he lost all his money and credit cards and tickets. So got him $300 from Swiss Embassy and I lent him $300 more. But then I find out he spend money Embassy give him on luxury hotel room. He say he pay me back my money when he return to U.S. But it is 25 days since he left. Do you think he pay?"

"Did you get his address?"

"He give me note with address and promise to pay. He say he take bus and ship back to United States because is cheapest way. That will take long time, so maybe he not back yet. But do you think he pay?" I didn't want to answer so I changed the subject again and we soon parted near the former American Embassy.

Behind the compound's high walls, large pine trees still grew on the 27 acre estate which became a computer training center for Iran's Revolutionary Guards. Two men in guardtowers watched the empty sidewalk along the street, but nothing was happening there. "We will make Americ a face a severe defeat" had been written in slightly improper English on the wall but the paint had peeled from age and the slogan was hard to read. Two banners fluttered in the breeze, one showing a soldier holding a grenade which looked very much like a soda bottle and the other was of three soldiers and a veil-covered woman. At the corner of the property, "Down with U.S.A." had been painted in tall letters.

Across the street, in the front windows of high priced shops were displayed handicrafts and fine art items made of gold, silver and bronze. Salesmen stood around inside, no customers in the stores.

Later, while eating a $1.50 supper of soup, ice cream and soda in the hotel's 7th floor dining room, I watched the setting sun lengthen the shadows cast by the pine trees at the nearby former American Embassy. Traffic on the streets below had decreased and at least some of the cars had turned their headlights on.

An English language newspaper I was reading reported that at the previous day's funeral for the Iranian diplomats killed in Afghanistan, people had chanted "Down with Taliban" and "Down with the U.S.". I found that an odd mixture of villains, one radically Islamic, the other completely western.

Another story indirectly addressed the recent shutting down of a newspaper because it had been somewhat critical of the government's handling of the Afghan issue. The article failed to specifically mention the closing of the paper, however. Instead, it had a series of interviews with editors about the responsibility of the press toward society and what needed to be done to improve it.

A long graduation speech by Supreme Ruler Khamenei in which he discussed the difference between eastern and western meanings of freedom was reprinted in its entirety. He said, "in Western liberalism, on the basis of its philosophy and philosophical grounds, the limits on freedom are materialistic, not moral. However, in Islam, there exist moral limits on freedom. In Islam, there exist moral and spiritual limits beside material limits."

The next afternoon I called the church to find out about Sarkis. This time the female administrator was on the line. I heard her say as if from a long way away, "I think they must have gone out of the country. No one knows him. We are a small congregation and someone would have heard of him."

Palaces and Tombs

Northern Tehran, built on the foothills of the Alborz Mountains, was where the affluent lived, shopped and played in the 1970s. Its tree-lined streets were bordered by high priced restaurants that offered Continental cuisine and fancy stores which sold the finest European-style furniture. Its homes were on larger lots than those in the rest of the city and because of the rise in elevation, even the temperature was ten degrees cooler than in central and southern Tehran.

This part of the city was also where the shah lived. Police presence on the street would get thicker the higher in elevation, and the nearer his house, one went. After awhile, no one was allowed past the security checkpoints except for the other wealthy people who lived in the area.

Today northern Tehran is still home to the wealthy. They live in large, bunker-like concrete houses hidden behind high gated walls while guard dogs protect them from the outside world.

But now the shah's mansion, and the expansive tree covered estate which surrounds it, is a museum open for public inspection. As Reza paid for our entry tickets, a Japanese tour group arrived, some of the women in their hair coverings looking as if they had just stepped out of a rice paddy.

The palace, surprisingly, was a not-that-large 1950s two-story neo-classical style structure. Its interior was ornate but did not contain the expected opulent extravagance. There were sculpted ceilings, and huge, high quality carpets covered the wood floors in every room. European furnishings abounded and a "gambling" room, which seemed to consist of a pool table, was on display. Four large murals of scenes from an epic poem by Ferdosi covered one ceiling while western art adorned many of the walls, but for a family worth billions of dollars, it was something of a letdown.

Outside the front door had once stood a large metal statue of the shah's father, Reza Shah. The revolution, however, had resulted in the figure getting cut off at the knees. Today, two enormous riding boots, very much resembling a pair of giant beer mugs, greet visitors to the shah's former home. As we departed, seven black-veiled girls crunching on chips sat on the grass nearby, looking like a string of crows.

Reza Shah's own residence, the "Marble Palace", is also on the property and has a dramatic view of the expanding city below. Both architecturally and in decoration it is more interesting than his son's. The house has color-coded rooms, a room with walls completely covered in small mirrors, and a room with a carpet whose design is matched in the mirrored ceiling.

The European and American furnishings of the house reflected Reza Shah's interest in turning the country to things western. As a soldier he always slept on the floor, even after replacing the previous ruling family and assuming power in the 1920s. The large bed in one room, our guide told us, was installed by his son only as a showpiece.

In her 1931 book *Conflict:Angora to Afghanistan*, prolific British traveler writer and novelist Rosita Forbes recounts her very adventurous solo journeys throughout Iran. She hitched rides with truck drivers and others going in her direction and had to constantly endure the advances of men wherever she went.

But she also had a conversation with Reza Shah in his Marble Palace. He told her, "Persia must learn to do without foreigners. I hope that in five or six years it will be unnecessary to employ any but Persian officials...Of course, we shall employ foreign specialists in industry, agriculture and public works, in fact wherever they are needed, but Persia must learn to run her own affairs. Remember, she has inherited considerable experience for she once ruled an Empire."

Reza Shah also offered his views on world issues. "The two great evils from which a country can suffer" he told Forbes, "are foreign control and Communism, and if Persia had to choose between the two I should be the first to put myself at the head of a Communist army."

Ironically, it was Communist troops entering the country in 1941 which forced Reza Shah to abdicate his throne. He was seen as too sympathetic to the Third Reich and was replaced by his son after Russian and British soldiers invaded Iran. He would die three years later in South Africa.

As we were leaving the grounds, the old woman at the bag checkroom asked Reza for a tip. At one time, that would have been considered a very forward and un-Persian-like thing to do, especially for a woman, but Reza quietly slipped her a few coins.

Descending toward the city, we slowly drove by boys standing in the street selling both newspapers and band-aids to passing motorists. "What you do for work?" Reza asked as he gingerly maneuvered his car this way and that through traffic, ignoring lane lines just like everyone else was doing.

"I was an urban planner but now I write for a newspaper."

"You earn good salary writing for newspaper?"

"No, but we don't need the money."

"Which pays more, city planning or writing for newspaper?"

"City planning."

"Then why you not do that?"

"Because I got bored with it."

The maze of expressways, overpasses and thoroughfares of modern Tehran had me disoriented and confused as we drove south. The traffic was very thick and we had to park over a mile away from the bazaar in a metered space occupied by a wooden crate. When we stopped nearby, an elderly man appeared from the sidewalk, waved us over, moved the crate and was given 30 cents for his trouble. Nobody pays the meters, I was told, because they don't work.

When Reza unlocked the trunk to put his briefcase away, I noticed a small natural gas tank inside. "Why do you have that?" I wondered. "Everyone must use it in Tehran," he told me. "It helps the air. But car run on regular gas also."

Walking toward the bazaar, we passed an old man in tattered clothes who whispered to me, "Good whiskey?". At a major intersection, a slow moving motorbike just missed hitting a pedestrian and both men were shouting obscenities at each other as the human wave of walkers using the street flowed on. Near the Post Office, which was the first place outside of the Atlantic Hotel I had ventured in 1971, there were none of the letter writers looking for illiterate clients that had been so prevalent long ago. In the next block, boy soldiers with big guns now stood guard outside federal government buildings.

The dark, cave-like entrance to the bazaar was crowded with bodies and we immediately dove in. The dim, narrow main corridor of the bazaar was jammed with people slowly moving along as they looked at stalls selling produce, fruits, appliances, hardware, clothing and everything else a household could need. The arched ceiling of the structure rose high above the walkway and fluorescent light combined with some sunshine to illuminate the way. Side aisles branched off the main corridor in a maze of walkways and all were packed with shoppers.

The Iranian bazaar has always been mass consumerism for the general public. The press of flesh on this day contrasted sharply with the luxury stores still selling a different lifestyle to a very few that we had just seen in the northern part of the city.

Two young salesmen quickly attached themselves to us and both wanted to show me fine hand woven carpets. As we slowly made our way along, passing tiny stalls selling plastic jugs and machine made rugs featuring a Bugs Bunny motif, I kept telling them I wasn't interested. In halting English, they insisted I should look at their selections. I didn't have to buy anything, just take a look. But I already had all the carpets I needed, I replied in Persian, and my house was very small. Finally they gave up and as he departed one of them said in an apologetic tone, "Excuse me, mister, but I am just doing my job".

We walked by one merchant who was sitting in front of a small display of metal kitchenware, the shiny pots and pans reflecting the images of the passing throng. He asked where I was from and, when told replied, "Oh, our President is in New York now for a meeting at the U.N. about the crisis with Afghanistan". Around a corner were four porters, crouching in a walkway with their heads down and eyes shut. They were waiting to be hired to pick up their wooden back braces and carry something out of the bazaar. Later, we passed a man relieving himself on a wall. The traditional practices of public male pissing and crotch scratching certainly didn't seem to have diminished in twenty-five years.

Stopping at one store, Reza introduced me to a merchant friend of his and said he sold the best tea from India. The man invited us into his tiny shop where cans, jars and canisters were stacked to the ceiling and an old scale rested on the counter. On the floor sat large sacks of various varieties of dark-leafed tea. The shopkeeper pulled out two wooden stools from a back room, found an empty spot to put them, asked us to have a seat, and offered us tea. As we drank the steaming strong brew, he and Reza discussed our upcoming trip. Reza inquired about what the man knew about the road from Zahedan south to the coastal town of Charbahar, but his friend was very noncommittal in his response. He did, however, recommend a restaurant in the bazaar for lunch.

The very popular place had recently opened and had semi-fast food service selling the typical four or five rice and mutton dishes found in most Iranian restaurants. While Reza went off to order two ground mutton lunches, a waiter deposited small cellophane wrapped metal plates with flat bread, raw onions, and silverware in front of me.

Throughout the restaurant, people were pushing and shoving to find a seat at one of the long communal tables or to place an order with the cashier. The idea of protecting women from male aggression in the dense mob was out of the question. Gender simply didn't matter as bodies jammed together.

Reza returned with tokens for our meals. He also had two bottles of *dough*, the salty yogurt drink I had tried once many years before and detested, but it didn't taste too bad this time.

"In 1979 I go back to U.S." he told me over the din of the lunchtime crowd. "I visit man in Wichita Falls, Texas, and Iranian doctor friend of mine in Frankfort, Kentucky. He tell me I should leave Iran and move to United States."

"I have American girlfriend when I live in U.S. in '60s, so I call her house in San Bernardino, California. A little girl answer phone. I don't know who is it. But then woman answer and I say, 'This is Reza'. 'Who?' she asks. 'Reza, from Iran'. 'Oh, I thought you had been killed in the revolution' she says."

"I fly out to see her. She married since I knew her. But they break up. It was her daughter on phone. I stay one week. I fly back to Iran day before U.S. Embassy taken. If it happen two days earlier, I could stay in America."

After lunch, Reza had a shopping list of things to get for his wife and sons and I was looking for a scarf for my mother. So we slowly made our way out of the covered bazaar and walked to the "Kuwaiti" bazaar, a narrow street of shops with no roof over it.

Outside its door, one small store had scarves on a display rack, so we went in and I looked over the selection. "How much?" I asked the boy of twelve behind the counter and he said $5. Reza wanted several things and bought them from the boy's father without bargaining. When they had finished, I asked again about the scarf and the man said $3. "Sold," I shouted as the boy protested that it should cost more.

Walking back toward the car, we stopped to see the Iranian crown jewels. They were on public display, as they had been in 1973, in a bank vault not far from the bazaar. The glitter of precious stones and artistry of craftsmanship in creating the thrones and crowns, swords and jewelry was only diminished by the piercing alarm which kept going off. In the dark room containing hundreds of millions of dollars worth of baubles from the Persian monarchy, the thought of the thick vault door suddenly locking was somewhat scary, but fortunately that didn't happen. Instead, the high pitched bell just kept on ringing periodically.

Abandoning our precious parking space, we headed further south and came upon a minor traffic accident. Both drivers were in the middle of the street screaming at each other, wanting to fight. A crowd, however, had formed and passersby were pushing the men back toward their vehicles, telling them to drive away.

Searching for a large park which my Peace Corps friend Gerry had helped design, we drove around the area south of the bazaar. Years ago, this section of Tehran had looked like a huge village. Today it is dominated by expressways, midrise apartment houses, and pedestrian overpasses spanning multi-lane roads.

A woman driver wrapped in a black veil and wearing white gloves pulled up along side our car, waved at us to stop, and asked directions. Reza also repeatedly had to inquire of people on the sidewalk or in other vehicles which way to go to find the park. Some of the advice we got actually turned out to be accurate. Driving slowly along, we almost hit a young girl dashing across the street as the car's outside mirror clipped her arm, but Reza didn't even notice.

In the tree-covered park, clusters of veiled women were having picnics on the grass. Carnival-like equipment was being used, but it was definitely in need of some sprucing up. Swans and ducks swam in a small lake while girls in long coats and scarves swung on swing sets. A group of young boys played on a concrete fountain which cascaded down a short hillside.

"This was only desert before it became a park 26 years ago," an old caretaker told us. "The amphitheater over there was built for dancing but it was closed after the revolution since dancing isn't permitted."

Nearby, several men sat under tall shade trees and invited us to join them for tea. They had yogurt and cucumbers in a plastic container and asked us to share it. One man said he had a message about the park for Gerry, "Tell the American that he built well."

Walking by a day care center with cartoon characters brightly painted on its walls, I asked Reza why so many children were in the park. "School begin next week, so they still on holiday."

Later, I returned to the northern part of the city for dinner at an outdoor restaurant. I was the guest of a man who wanted to introduce me to his family. He was 58, very short, and had lived in Europe for almost 30 years. When he spoke of his 43 year old wife, his pride in her appearance was obvious. She was much taller than he was, which didn't bother him in the least. Plus, "She has green eyes and a fair complexion, not like Iranian women at all," he said proudly as we drove up through an 8 p.m. traffic jam into the cool night air of northern Tehran. When we parked, he also locked his steering wheel to the car, even though the area was well patrolled by attendants.

In the restaurant we reclined on pillows under trees with color-turning leaves. All around us female customers could be seen wearing make-up, ankle bracelets, and showing off painted toenails. Islamic, or non-alcoholic, beer was on the menu and in many respects the establishment was much the same as it would have been under the shah.

Our conversation was about mundane things like what I did for a living and what I wanted to see in Iran. As we spoke, long forgotten Persian words kept popping into my head. "Ice cream" appeared, then "stamps", and finally "Good health to you" which we always said before drinking a cold beer.

"It is the quality of life, not the length of life, that is important," my host's physician cousin said, smiling broadly under a bushy mustache. "And I just love cigarettes," he loudly proclaimed as he lit another one. While taking a long drag, he dropped a piece of meat for a wandering cat, but the feline turned up her nose at the offering.

After dinner, a five piece band played traditional Iranian music, desert sounds originally composed by nomadic peoples. Listening to those wailful tunes, I had to wonder if this city, with its huge apartment blocks, dirty air and clogged expressways is in any way related to the inseparable relationship between land and people which was once historic Persia? If Tehran's traffic jams or high-rise buildings under construction with colorful steel girders and beams which look from a distance like tinker toy materials is somehow linked to that past?

Between songs, my host asked why I had no children after 22 years of marriage and why I married someone 3 years older. Being tired, and not wanting to answer this personal line of inquiry, I excused myself and was driven back to the hotel. As we sped down now deserted streets and passed the former American Embassy, he said, "It is my fervent hope that the U.S. will again have an embassy here".

In the morning, as Reza and I began our cross country trip, I asked him to stop at Tehran's cemetery on the far southern edge of the city. A thick layer of filthy air lay over the capital, blocking out even a view of the towering mountain ranges as we drove south along the road which leads to Qom and Isfahan.

The cemetery is a huge city of the dead, with hundreds of thousands of graves. A sign at the entrance said that these people had not died, but had gone to be with Allah. It was not the hysterical, fountains with blood red water kind-of-place once portrayed by the western media. Instead, wide tree lined streets, vast expanses of grass, and water flowing over globe shaped fountains gave it the feeling of a park.

Those from Tehran who were killed in the war with Iraq, "martyrs" Reza called them, were buried in one section of the cemetery. Row upon row of tightly packed graves filled the space. Above each tomb was a small metal stand which held a photograph of the deceased along with a few personal mementos. From their pictures, it was apparent that many of the slain had been only boys when they had died. Some of the cases had tiny white curtains to signify that the soldier had been unmarried at the time of his death. "I have many friends buried here," Reza said quietly as we walked slowly along.

His father rested under a tree in another part of the cemetery. Among all of the closely spaced tombstones Reza found it with only a little difficulty. "He was storekeeper. We move to Tehran when I just a boy. He was good man."

Having brought a jug, Reza filled it from a nearby faucet and gently washed the dirt off the marble surface of the tomb stone. As he doused the grave with water several times, stroking it with caresses and carefully running his finger down its crevices, he said softly in a voice that was breaking with emotion, "I not here when he die in 1982. But I write this poem when I return," pointing to the inscription on the stone. "It say, 'Earth, be friendly towards my father, he was good man.'"

"Where were you?" I asked softly. "Out of country," was the whispered reply. Standing silently over him as he knelt next to the grave, I wondered about his decision to leave Iran. It must have been difficult, I thought, but out of politeness didn't ask him to explain.

As we departed the cemetery, two funerals were starting and flower arrangements could be purchased near the entrance. Just down the road in the enormous but mostly empty parking lot for Ayatollah Khomeini's tomb, directional signs were sponsored by a chain of stores. The gigantic onion bulb domed building covered acres of ground and was surrounded by four minarets and four smaller domes. Two very large structures were also being added at each end of the complex.

Shoes had to be removed upon entering the dark interior space of the building. Then a guard frisked us. Inside, the structure resembled a giant warehouse with exposed steel beams and huge metal air ducts. Children were running around and sliding on the shiny marble floor, their screams reverberating throughout the building.

The tomb was a simple metal cage which enclosed the coffins of the Ayatollah and one of his sons. Their photographs were displayed and around the edge of the cage was a foot high pile of Iranian paper currency.

A few people, separated by sex, touched the tomb while praying silently, but most of the small crowd sat on the floor talking as they watched their children play.

As we drove toward Qom later, passing a modern international airport under construction, Reza said plans were to develop a new town near the cemetery and Khomeini's tomb. Then he added, "I was fighter pilot and flew F-5 Tigers. I leave country for 10 years, but then I come back. I get married, even though I like single life. But people tell me, you need someone take care of you in old age. My wife is doctor. She doesn't say anything about my job taking me away from Tehran. But her family complain about it."

Half of The World

A six lane toll road, where twenty-five years before a two lane highway had been, ran through the desert to Qom. A solitary herd of sheep was being watched over by a shepherd in one place and the adobe colored rolling earth was mostly barren of plant life. A series of long religious sayings proclaiming the greatness of God bordered the road for miles. Placed on rock outcroppings and hillside embankments, the stark white slogans, written in either chalk or cut stone mosaics, scrambled across the landscape.

Looking for a place to eat in Qom, we drove into the center of the city. Near the gold domed shrine of Fateme, sister of Imam Reza who is buried in Mashad at Iran's holiest site, Islamic clerics of all descriptions were trying to jump through traffic. In their brown and black robes, the mullahs had to move quickly to avoid being hit by speeding cars.

After Reza stopped to ask several people where a restaurant was, we found one on the way out of town. It was a new place with small tables, ceiling fans which moved the still air, and shiny glass and metal cooler cases filled with soda bottles. A large family presided over by a gray bearded patriarch talking on a cell phone were the only other customers. While we ate our rice and broiled chicken lunch, Reza told me that he understood plans were to bring water the entire 100 or so miles from Tehran. "Water here very salty," he said.

A back road out of Qom took us through a desolate landscape of deep red gorges and distant gray mountains. In one place a small but flowing stream ran alongside the road, and dark green trees lined the riverbed. Pomegranates and other fruits were for sale at dozens of wooden roadside stands watched over by poor men dressed in tattered clothes who had pitched tiny canvas tents next to the pavement.

In the mid-afternoon heat of 100 degrees and intensely bright sunshine, Reza was fidgeting as he drove. He constantly rubbed his eyes or held his left hand out the window for a few seconds and then pulled it back in. Twice he crossed to the wrong side of the road and had to swerve to avoid oncoming traffic. Eventually we stopped for tea in a little town, and after drinking it he announced with a laugh at my obvious anxiety that he was fine.

The desert in one place eventually revealed a dry salt lake of bleached white color contained within an enormous depression in the earth. Vast vistas of beige-toned emptiness opened in other directions and the four-lane divided highway we were on had a heavy stream of trucks and cars speeding along at 70 m.p.h.

Driving into Isfahan, a city which now has over 1 million residents, we passed a stylish distant suburb of large homes and wide streets. "That where Americans live before," Reza said. "It very nice."

"I know about Bell Helicopter being here," I replied. "They wanted me to teach English after I left the Peace Corps, but I decided not to."

"Why not?"

"Because out here it would have been like living in America, not Iran."

Immediately after our late afternoon arrival, I decided to visit the main square and bazaar. They had always been two of my favorite places in the country and I wanted to get back to them as soon as possible. Today the city may have spread out in all directions, but I wanted to see if its center had remained intact.

As we entered the ancient covered bazaar by a side portal, bearded carpet dealers were sitting around drinking tea, discussing the day's business. A motorbike carrying a rolled up room-sized rug on its back rack tried to squeeze by us in the narrow passageway. In one place a shaft of light rained down from a hole in the mud brick ceiling, illuminating a perfect circle on the concrete floor.

Emerging from the semi-darkness of the bazaar, the bright sunlight showed off the enormous main square. On the left side, the beautiful blue tiled dome of Sheikh Lotfollah's Mosque was nestled above a long string of two story mud-colored buildings. Across the grassy mall and large wading pool, the seven-story Ali Ghapu palace looked down on the square. At the far end, the tall, arched, angled entryway and towering minarets of the immense Imam Mosque was highlighted by a backdrop of the rugged peaks of a nearby hill. The name of the mosque may have been altered from the earlier Shah, but the beauty of it hadn't changed in 25 years.

People were mingling around the square, watching their children play in the pool. Window shoppers looked in at the many stores which ring the space, comparing prices of the metal work, block prints, inlaid wood and painted miniatures for which Isfahan is famous. Only a few beggars were present, mostly older people and far fewer than I remembered from before. A line of horse drawn carriages waited to give rides around the almost 1 mile circumference of the mall.

The nearby columned reception hall of Chehel Sotun had been built during the 1588-1629 reign of Shah Abbas I to hold formal functions. Its interior walls are covered by six large paintings showing scenes of royal parties and play-making. For several years after the revolution, three of the works were covered to shield the public from their depictions of debauchery, but today all of them can be seen again.

Four men in their early 20s wanted their photograph taken next to the large but shallow pool in front of the hall. It is the water's reflection of the reception hall which provides twenty of the forty columns that give Chehel Sotun its name in Persian. After snapping their picture, the men asked for one which included the American.

Returning to the hotel, we sat in the lobby looking over a map of the country. A German tourist group was checking in, and the television was showing Iranian President Khatami at the U.N. On the wall was a small plaque with a quote from a local man who had been killed in the war with Iraq. It read, "It had to be done to protect Iran's Islamic way-of-life."

After scanning the map, Reza announced that he had a problem with my itinerary for the trip. "When we in Kerman, we must go to Mahun and Bam one day. Then go back to Kerman. Next day we drive to Zahedan."

"But that makes no sense," I said. "Bam is three hours on the road to Zahedan."

"But we in Kerman for 2 days."

"We will go on the way to Zahedan."

"Then we must start very early in morning."

After that was decided, Reza said with concern, "I think Charbahar 1,000 miles from Zahedan. That what looks like on map. We must go through Iranshahr to get there."

"And that," I said with some playful glee, "is one of the hottest places on earth. So hot, people live underground there in the summertime." Reza shook his head in disbelief and worry, never having visited Sistan and Baluchistan province before. As it turned out, however, the actual travel distance to Charbahar would be less than half his estimated mileage.

We were soon joined by a friend of Reza who ran the small gift shop in the hotel. They discussed the trip from Zahedan to Chahbahar and how long it would take. While they talked, I noticed that over our heads was a sculptured ceiling depicting two lovers in an embrace. Neither Reza nor his friend had ever been in the southeastern part of the country, and the map didn't offer much information. It did show that the roads weren't first rate, however.

Almost seventy years ago, Rosita Forbes had found Isfahan a very different kind of place than it is today. It was a city of only 80,000 people, and she wrote, "In the days of its glory Isfahan was the capital of Shah Abbas. It had a population of nearly a million. Its circumference was twenty-four miles, 1,500 villages flourished in the neighborhood and its proud inhabitants boasted that 'Isfahan is half the world.'"

"Today, its dim, vaulted bazaars and its gardens, which keep their secrets behind twenty-foot mud walls, are strewn over a third of the original space, and the polo ground of Shah Abbas, 560 yards long, is to be converted into a public park."

Early the next morning I walked alone back to that park, today's main square. The sepia tones of dawn were slowly fading as a few men slept on the sidewalk along the city's major boulevard. A solitary woman wrapped in black sat on a bench in the middle of the street, waiting for something. Thin white blocks of ice had been placed in front of several small grocery stores and restaurants for later use inside. The ice was gradually melting, narrow bands of water running toward the curb.

Turning off the boulevard, I walked down a deserted road lined by locked tourist shops and several shoe stores. After a few blocks, the narrow street opened into the great square.

An old, gray bearded man neatly dressed in worn clothes was lying on a small red rug spread out across the mall's sidewalk. Resting among his worldly possessions, he wished me a good morning and asked for help. "Let's go eat breakfast at the tea house," he said. Next to him, three sleeping college-aged boys on a pre-school trip from Tehran began to stir. Standing up, the old man informed me that, "Your country has many things. Airplanes! Railroads! Trucks! Give me some help please."

The smiling and yawning college boys were watching us as the old man proudly displayed his things for me. He had a few plastic jugs, one of which he held up to show that it was filled with sugar cubes. Some empty plastic bags and his much prized rug were also lying there.

"Are you married? Yes. Thank God for that. And children? No? Is this strong?" he questioned, quickly grabbing my crotch.

"How old are you?" I asked repeatedly, but he ignored me. The boys indicated that the man was crazy as he kept muttering away. Finally he turned, looked at me intensely, and said, "I am 150 years old. I have children and grandchildren. I am from Shiraz and your country is very good. Please give me some help."

I went off to take pictures instead as the rising sun was very slowly drying the washed blue tone of the Imam Mosque into a bright, sharp shade. One section of the tiles on the dome had been removed, a restoration project underway. Exercising men were walking around the square while a few covered women rinsed dishes under running faucets next to the pool. Men preparing to pray were also cleaning themselves off. Crows were fighting over crumbs left by some of the few dozen people who had bedded down around the mall the previous night.

The old man soon appeared nearby and very carefully began to wash his rug. Over and over he ran it under a faucet, making sure to hit every spot. I gave him 20 cents, and he thanked me profusely, but said I should also buy him breakfast. Instead, I asked to take his picture. He agreed and straightened himself up. Then he bent over and slowly washed his hands and threw water on his face, arranged his rug on the sidewalk to dry, washed his hands again, then stood erect in front of me for his portrait. With the Ali Ghapu palace in the background, he looked serious and solemn for the camera. As I departed the square, he wished me well.

By the time I returned to the sun drenched main boulevard, it had filled with traffic. A city bus drove by, standing men crowded in front and black veiled women sitting in back. At a major intersection, large banners depicted some of the local men killed in the war with Iraq. It was the 18th anniversary of the start of that terribly bloody conflict, and cities throughout the country were commemorating it. Most of Isfahan's largest street corners displayed the 15-foot tall banners, which had a drawing of a killed soldier along with a scene of fighting.

After a self-serve buffet breakfast, Reza and I drove to the Friday mosque. He told me that part of the historic building had been bombed in the war. I thought that incredible, and he said, "Wait. I show you."

While every major city in Iran has a traditional Friday mosque as the primary place for the faithful to gather once a week, Isfahan's is renowned for its beauty. The complex of buildings which comprise it epitomizes the "I can do better than you" philosophy. One Persian ruler after the other kept adding to the structure, building new prayer rooms and study halls, trying to out-do their predecessors. The result is a hodge-podge of styles and forms which somehow mesh into a beautiful whole.

In the far corner of the mosque, Reza pointed out the section which had been destroyed by bombs. It had recently been rebuilt, and a display case had a magazine article about Ayatollah Khomeini's belief in the importance of preserving Iran's historic monuments.

Fortunately, no such damage had been inflicted on the great Imam Mosque. Standing in front of it later, a carpet salesman told me, "We remember the Americans from when they lived in Isfahan and hope they will come back." Inside, a large, heavy-set elderly bald man missing several teeth and wearing a stocking cap acted as unofficial guide. Looking for a tip, he showed us around the echo chamber in one of the mosque's huge alcoves and then pointed out an alabaster column which read in part, "If a man does not believe in God, that man is no good." After Reza gave him some money, they chatted for a minute about their shoes, both pairs American-made and with a lot of years on them.

Upon leaving the mosque, we walked around the square and were soon approached by an elderly woman beggar. Reza gave her a coin and she sarcastically said, "This is very little". Reza was astonished at her response but could only blurt out, "Little?" as we moved on.

While I looked over the merchandise in a wood working shop, the storekeeper and his adult son asked me questions. When I said I was an American, the old man proclaimed, "We can be friends with the Americans because we all believe in one God. We may call him by different names, but he is one God."

As I purchased a small inlaid box, the son said it had been very hard on business without the Americans. Then he asked who the box was for. "My friend," I said.

"I hope he like it."

"No, it is for a woman."

"Oh, your girlfriend."

"No, my friend."

"Yes, your girlfriend," he laughed.

When I made by way alone back to the bazaar later in the afternoon, I passed a small newsstand. An English language paper had a headline that read, "Khatami will not meet with U.S. officials at U.N.".

With dusk approaching, the bazaar was full of people slowly moving along its crowded narrow corridors. I wanted to try my bargaining skills after all these years, but the merchant selling the miniature painting I decided on didn't seem interested. Instead, he declined my offers in a gentle fashion before half-heartedly agreeing to knock $1 off the $9 asking price. That was much different than the aggressive give-and-take which I had once been familiar with.

After I returned to the hotel, Reza and I went for a drive. Twenty-five years ago, the Zayande Rud River was a mostly dry stream of sand which cut through Isfahan. Today, a wide swatch of water in the channel is the center strip of a riverside park development. The city's two famous ancient bridges are highlights of the area, along with amusement rides, picnic spots, and mile after mile of trees and grass.

On the lower level of the 17th century Khaju bridge, groups of people were relaxing in the cooling night air. Among the row of mud brick arches on the upper level, a couple was having their picture taken. She had her veil thrown open to show off the fashionable dress she was wearing.

A woman with her veil, and pant legs, pulled up to her knees waded into the water in front of the Sio Se Pol, or thirty-three arched bridge, built in 1602. The bridge's walkway was crowded and in the misty dark

eerie silhouettes would materialize from the shadows and then trans-
form into human shapes as people walked by us heading in the other
direction.

On our way to the Abbasi Hotel, I noticed that most cars had their
headlights on. Reza, however, along with some other drivers, continued
the Iranian tradition of only turning running lights on in the dark.
Fortunately, the streets were very well lit.

Before dining at the luxury hotel, we visited the shop of the "Tile
Engineer", the old man who was supervising the restoration work on
the Imam Mosque dome. After chatting for a few minutes about the
beauty of his tiles and the number of projects he was working on, he
said, "Everything about America is good". Trying to be amusing, I said
our soccer team wasn't. That set him off on a five minute lecture about
why America will assuredly improve in the sport. Iran was lucky to win
the game, he insisted, and they had played much better in a qualifying
match against Australia than they did while beating the U.S.

The Abbasi Hotel had been named the Shah Abbas in the 1970s. Built
in a caravanseri, or historic travelers' guesthouse, the hotel was famous
for an ornate lobby and the architectural beauty of the arched walkways
which surround a lush interior courtyard garden. The restaurant service had been poor 25 years ago, and since the revolution had only gotten
worse according to reports. But on this night the waiters were prompt,
the food well prepared, and the experience enjoyable.

While we were eating, a sandy colored cat wearing a coat patterned
after a Persian carpet approached us. He was looking for a handout and
appreciated what he got, but when he went begging at another table, an
Iranian boy of about 12 became terrified and chased him away.

During dinner, Reza showed me the United States Air Force ring he
wore. "I train in Enid, Oklahoma. Had many friends there. One time we
swim laps. My American friends say not to swim fast, but I do. So they
hold me under water for minute. Another time, in winter, we run laps

inside. They say not to run fast, but I do. So one of my friends puts leg out and I fall. I break leg. In snow was hard to get around on crutches."

"Did you report him?"

"No, he was my friend."

The Streets of Shiraz

South of Isfahan a divided highway ran through a desert of pebbles and small green shrubs. Mountains painted red, brown and tan constantly loomed in the distance. Stopping in Shahreza to search for a gas station, we found both sides of the city's main street lined by parked cars. All the roads and alleys of the town seemed to be paved, and large crowds packed the sidewalks. Reza said this was one place where it hadn't been possible for the fundamentalists to remove the word "shah" from a name; it was just too traditional.

Heading further south, I wanted to visit the town of Yezdikhast. I had read about the ancient hillside community in English travel books from the 1920s and '30s, but Reza had never heard of the place. The city turned out to be a typical small settlement of modern concrete block buildings built along the main highway. In response to our request for directions at a tiny store, we were told to keep driving over the crest of a nearby hill. When we did, the old city appeared before us, crumbling in ruins.

Around 1930, Rosita Forbes wrote of this place, "It was dark when, averaging twelve-and-a-half miles an hour, the overloaded truck jolted into Yezdikhast, which means 'God willed it'. This amazing village consists of mud-built hovels projecting from either side of a boat-shaped rock some hundred and fifty feet high, which stands in the middle of a ravine, once the boundary between Fars and Iraq. It is a gash in the earth, perhaps a hundred feet deep and two hundred and fifty yards across. Entrance to the houses which hung like bird-cages far above our heads, is obtained by a bridge of rafters from the 'mainland'. This can be drawn up at night and it admits to a single tunnel-like street, between the crazy houses, which are rapidly falling down, and off which, in a high wind, children are continually blown."

Today's children are safe. The hillside houses have long been abandoned, and the mud brick is slowly melting back into the earth. As we stood looking at the disappearing structures, an old man leading a small white donkey loaded with long shafts of green grain came up the steeply inclined highway. I asked if I could take his picture in front of the ship-wrecked ruins and he stopped for a moment. The donkey, though, just kept on going up the road, heading for town.

As I photographed the man, an elderly, almost toothless woman dressed in rags was calling to us from across the road. She wanted some money, "because we have nothing here," she yelled. After Reza gave her something, and she posed for a picture, she explained that in her 70 or so years she didn't remember anyone living in the old houses on the hill.

Driving on at over 60 m.p.h., the car was filled with silence. Even though my arm was covered with sun tan lotion, I had to keep moving it to prevent getting burned by the desert heat. Around noon we looked for a tea house in the town of Abadeh and Reza also found a music store. He had forgotten to bring any cassettes, including his favorite Andy Williams tape purchased in the United States long ago, so we had been tuneless until now.

While Reza looked over the store's selection, I stood on the sidewalk in front. An old man with a crutch came hobbling up, stopped to clap along with the music playing in the shop and asked where I was from. "America is very good. My son went to Baltimore once. He was a student at the University of Tehran when he was killed in the war with Iraq." With that the old man limped away.

A nearby storekeeper had been listening in on our conversation and asked which was better, Iran or America. I said that for carpets and soccer, Iran was. Reza appeared with a cassette in hand, and the man proudly announced, "He says Iran is better than the U.S.".

"Not for cars or basketball," I disagreed as we all laughed. "We have Michael Jordan."

Tearing the plastic wrapping off of the cassette as he drove, Reza said he really liked this Iranian singer. In a low, melodic voice, the man sang about everything and everybody being drunk on life. Speeding along the highway, we passed intercity buses, some of which had "Remember God" stenciled on the rear window. A few large trucks had their backs decorated with two very long lashed, enormous doe-looking female eyes.

While the singer wailed away, Reza told me of his recent trip to Germany to visit his sister. "I jog near military base in Wiesbaden. American military there always friendly to me. But Germans, no. They are unfriendly."

"My sister never marry. She spend money on buying things. She has very nice things. But she robbed once. Lose many things. I ask her, who take care of you when you old? She says she has friends. That she move into home. But that is not good."

After listening to the tape a few times, we left the desert behind. Earlier we had seen some biblical scenes of men leading donkeys and shepherds with herds of sheep and goats settled near small nomadic camps made up of what looked like army surplus tents. When we entered the Kur Rud River valley near the ruins of Pasargadae, however, there were combines and tractors in use and fields of corn, sunflowers, and a variety of other crops spread across the landscape.

Three children were sitting under a tree next to a tiny stream which flowed in front of the ancient, sun drenched tomb of Cyrus the king, the main attraction at Pasargadae. They were waiting to beg while most of the kids in the village were attending school. After being asked for money, Reza handed out apples instead, and insisted they be washed before being eaten.

The former royal community of Pasargadae, dating to 550 B.C., today displays the scattered remains of a few small palaces on a flat, windswept plain. The 2,500 year old white stone tomb of Cyrus, how-ever, has been completely restored on top of a twenty foot high stepped platform. A family, ignoring the low metal chain around the site, had climbed the steps. The woman had somehow managed to crawl between metal bars and was looking out at us from the shadows of the tomb itself. Reza told them they shouldn't be on the monument, and the man asked him abruptly, "Where are you from?". On our way out, Reza complained to the custodian about the family and how they could harm the ruins. In response, the man in charge said only that they had no staff to guard the place.

Toward Shiraz the valley narrowed as mountain cliffs tightened in toward the river and the entire landscape became farmland. This was a perfect spot for a royal residence and it is the site of Persepolis. The once grand palace of Darius and Xerxes sat in its ruined majesty off to the side of the highway as we sped by.

In front of our hotel in downtown Shiraz, Reza backed the car into a *jube*, one of the omnipresent open storm drains which border streets throughout Iran. With the assistance of a newspaper vendor, we were able to get the car out without much difficulty.

Inside the hotel, the man at the desk looked at my passport and said, "It is just good to be able to touch an American passport". Then he asked after my country's president. "How is Mr. Bill? I think he has many problems."

"With his pants," I replied as we both chuckled.

Just after sunrise the next morning, I went for a walk. Hundreds of wall posters of Ayatollah Khomeini were prominently displayed along the main street. One had been torn off so only the piercing eyes remained. That look, I thought, could put the fear of God into almost anyone.

A large pack of dogs was running through a wide, mostly dry riverbed as I stood on a bridge above them. Five of the animals were slowly trotting in a tiny garbage strewn stream, their footsteps causing shards of reflected sunlight to break off from the water's surface. Nearby, a kindergarten wall was decorated with a mural of the seven dwarfs and Snow White, who was wearing a veil.

A green grocer was chopping vegetables in preparation for the day while a short line of people waited outside a nearby bakery to buy their morning bread. Inside, one man pounded the off-white dough into low mounds while others pushed it into a shiny metal oven, then later pulled out the hot flat loaf. A tribal woman in a pink blouse, multi-pleated white skirt and small veil passed me on the sidewalk.

Kids on their way to school were stopping to buy candy spread out across a sidewalk table. Shrimp swam in a large bowl of ice water on the floor of a small shop. Two men were looking at a current movie's promotional photos, one of which showed a veiled woman holding a gun to protect her child.

Tents containing books, photographs and other material about the war with Iraq had been set up on the sidewalk along the main street. A bicyclist adorned in full spandex gear and jet stream helmet went racing by them. Two old women sat on a carpet laid out on a tree-shaded sidewalk waiting for a building to open. Their tea service was arranged in front of them as an old man squatted a few feet away, working his prayer beads intently.

At breakfast, when I told him about my walk, Reza strongly insisted he must go with me everywhere. "It can be very dangerous. There are many thieves in Shiraz. Last night I see man steal something and he run away. Police run after him but he get away. So I must come with you."

As a graduate of the Bogota, Columbia school of street crime prevention for tourists, however, I wasn't going to listen to him. My biggest fear, frankly, was running out of toilet paper and having to ask for more. I wasn't certain that I knew the proper words in Persian for a little used commodity in Iran.

Later, when we returned to walk the streets of downtown Shiraz together, a crowd of men had gathered around a series of display cases showing scenes from the war with Iraq. Most of the photographs were of corpses, some with black, burned faces staring out with unseeing eyes.

The war left at least one-quarter of a million Iranians dead and many more injured. It also cost the country tens of billions of dollars to repel the Iraqis from its territory and then to try and inflict punishment upon Saddam Hussein. A Vietnam Memorial type wall for the war, if built proportionally to the population of Iran and the number of people killed, would have to be almost 2.5 miles long, not the 490 feet found in Washington, D.C.

American, European and United Nations response to the 1980 Iraqi invasion that began the war was very restrained. U.S. hostages were being held in Tehran, a fundamentalist revolution that was seen as a threat to stability in the region was still working itself out, and Khomeini was constantly calling America "the Great Satan".

While the war dragged on over the next eight years, the world saw a return to the trench warfare tactics of World War I. To defend itself, since it had great difficulty in buying new weapons or securing replacement parts for the military equipment it did have, Iran fought using human waves of "martyrs". With the high number of casualties, most Iranians must have known a soldier who died or the family of someone slain.

Near the war's end in 1988, while the U.S. navy patrolled the Persian Gulf to insure that oil shipping lanes remained open, the American cruiser *Vincennes* shot down an Iranian civilian aircraft. All 290 people on board, including 66 children, were killed and Washington's response was basically, "Whoops. How much do we owe you?".

Two years later, Iraq invaded neighboring Kuwait. The world quickly agreed this was a situation that would not be tolerated. Saddam Hussein was labeled a madman who threatened global peace. Under American-led forces, Kuwait was soon liberated, and the country returned to its pro-western dictatorial rulers.

Iranian reaction to the American hypocrisy concerning these two events is understandable. While they held our 52 hostages for 444 days, for eight years Saddam Hussein, with the apparent blessing of the U.S., used chemical weapons and other means to kill tens of thousands of their sons.

After looking over the photographs of the war dead, we visited an ancient public bath undergoing renovation. It had faded scenes of love and glory painted on its deteriorated mud brick walls and arched ceilings. The rehabilitation work which needed to be done to fix the place up was obviously very extensive.

Then we went searching for a religious school built in 1615 by Gholi Khan, former governor of the province. As we walked along, Reza told me that he had taken the haj, or holy pilgrimage to Mecca, five years ago. After that experience, he said, he got married.

Winding our way through twisting alleys, we passed two women beggars sitting on the sidewalk. One had dark empty eye sockets, wrinkled spotted skin and a skeleton-like look which indicated she wouldn't be among the living much longer. The other was completely wrapped inside her black veil, only a shrouded hand emerging from the bundle to ask for alms.

"I know where is," Reza kept insisting about the centuries-old school as we went on. He asked directions repeatedly, and people pointed this way or that. Finally a man overheard his question and told us to follow him. Retracing some of our steps, we walked through narrow passages of light and dark, by tall brick walls and tiled mosaic entryways. Above our heads, a black cat went racing by, running along the top of a high wall.

We were led to the school where the ancient wooden front door was closed, but from the interior an old man pushed it open in response to our knock. Inside were a few brown or black robed Muslim clerics, *mullahs* in Persian, sitting around talking in a large formal garden of trees and flowers. Surrounding the courtyard were small rooms recessed into individual arched alcoves which were tiled in patterns of blue. Time had done considerable damage to the mud structure, but repair work didn't appear to be in progress.

The nearby complex of buildings containing the tomb of Sayyed Mir Ahmad has attracted pilgrims from throughout the Islamic world since it began to be developed in the 14th century. He was the brother of Imam Reza, the Shiite sect of Islam's eighth successor to the prophet Mohammed. Reza's brother Sayyed died or was killed in Shiraz in 835 A.D., and today the large garden and numerous buildings which comprise the sacred compound remain a much visited place.

In the mid-morning heat, hundreds of people were standing and sitting in the shade provided by tall trees and brick walls. Inside a building with an egg shaped dome, the tomb of the holy man was enclosed within a fully mirrored room. A few tinted windows let in a little light which bounced off the mirrors and ran in a colorful spectrum across the walls. While men and women silently prayed in separate rooms, they came together in front of the grave to touch it and show their belief.

Ceiling fans quietly twirled overhead and children were running around playing, but not loud enough to disturb the faithful. When Reza went to pray at the shrine, I sat on the floor in a cool space, watching people depart by always facing the tomb so they wouldn't have to turn their backs on the holy man.

From across the street, the sound of a loudspeaker-amplified sermon could easily be heard as we left the holy compound. The area's leading *mullah* was preaching to a seated congregation in the open courtyard of a large mosque as we walked by.

On our way back to the hotel a teenager asked where I was from. "America? Oh, freedom," he said. We later passed a very thin man totally bent over at the waist as he slowly made his way down the street on all fours.

In front of the hotel, Reza stopped to talk to someone he knew about the best route to take on his return trip to Tehran from Zahedan. Next to them, a short, silver-haired man in black pants, white shirt and gray vest was washing the sidewalk. He carefully doled out handfuls of water from a jug, spreading it with sweeping strokes across the pavement.

Later in the day we left the city to take the 35 mile drive out to Persepolis. On my two previous trips to the ruins, the road had gone through farm fields and small towns, but today much of the highway is lined by urban development.

The remains of the huge palace Darius began constructing in 512 B.C. and which was burned by Alexander the Great 180 years later are built on a platform at the base of a hill. They rise above the surrounding valley and provide an outstanding view of the countryside. As we walked around the hall of 100 columns and other parts of the enormous complex, Reza explained the significance of the common relief depiction of a priest giving the king a large ring. "It show power of king come from God," he said. He also wanted me to see the many rooms where the women lived. "The king go there for kissing ladies. Very good."

Persepolis' tall sculptured columns which once supported massive stone capitals and its series of beautiful reliefs that show bearers bringing gifts to the king remain magnificent. The long, impressive entry staircase, the great halls, a small reminder of his 1870 visit etched in stone left by Henry Stanley, and the entire ruin is still as majestic as ever. They will always be the first great archeological site I ever saw. But after visiting Ankor Wat in Cambodia, and experiencing the magnitude of the monumental building of the Khmer kings, my reaction this time was, how can Persepolis compare?

Hidden among a grove of trees at the base of the hill upon which Persepolis rests sit the rotting remains of the tents the shah had built for his 2,500 anniversary party of the Iranian monarchy. Held in 1971, the celebration was attended by dignitaries from around the world who stayed in the tents, feasted on food flown in from France, and toasted his majesty with the finest imported wine.

Today, as custodians play soccer in the abandoned streets of the development, the tents are wasting away. A handwritten sign on the main tent where the celebration's banquet was held says that prayer is the answer. As we stepped over broken glass and other debris which littered the grounds, Reza mentioned that while he was a fighter pilot, he had shaken the shah's hand several times.

Many of the tents have turned to rubble, only their steel frames remaining. Of those that still stand, the tent material has ripped in many places, and unrepaired flaps now blow in the harsh desert wind. The cheap particle board interior walls of these tents have been stripped of their coverings and plastered with graffiti. One, scrawled in neat handwriting said, "A kingdom like this can not last".

As we walked among the graveyard of tents, I told Reza what I remembered about the shah's celebration. While V.I.P.'s watched from a viewing stand built near the steps of Persepolis, men costumed to resemble soldiers from Persia's military past marched by in procession. "I was one of them," he informed me. "I wear beard and costume and was in parade."

I told him I had watched some of it on TV and the party was not good. "Why not?" he wanted to know.

"Because there were many poor people in the country," I replied.

After leaving the disappearing tent city, we drove by the three large but hidden-from-the-highway ancient rock carvings at Nakshi-Rejeb. Despite my chuckling suspicions, Reza insisted they were named after a man who sold tea on the spot 70 years ago. I found that hard to believe of the centuries old reliefs, but he said it was true.

In the middle of a flat, barren field near the series of massive reliefs carved in stone at Naghshe Rostom, we saw a small cluster of nomadic tents. I asked Reza to stop so I could take a picture of the people. As we approached on foot, two women stood next to a pot of bright red boiling tomato juice, watching us carefully.

When we got closer, a male voice from inside one of the tents called out forcefully, "What do you want?"

"The foreigner wants to take your picture," Reza replied as an unshaven man in his 50s along with a few younger men emerged from the tent.

"Why does he want a picture of how we live? You will have to send us copies. Plus, you'll have to pay."

"That's O.K. with me," I said, and after some discussion they lined up, the women participating reluctantly. They were all dressed in plain, third hand Western clothes, not colorful at all, just old. The women were uncovered and everyone assumed stern expressions for the camera.

I took out a roll of bills to pay the man $1, but he demanded twice as much after seeing how much money I had, so I handed it to him and then he invited us to stay for tea. That obviously made Reza uncomfortable since he was motioning that we needed to leave. But I accepted immediately, and our host showed us into his fly filled 8 man sized army surplus tent. While the women boiled water outside, all of the men sat in the cramped space which had an old rug on the ground, some pillows and small personal objects along the edge, and a portable radio.

The older man, who did all of the talking for the family, wanted to know my story. After I explained what I was doing in Iran, we asked about their lives. He said they were members of a tribal group I was unfamiliar with that lived near Shiraz in the summertime and then would move further south for the winter. They didn't tend sheep, the man said as we drank tea, but instead did day labor in town. There were 13 families in the group, the land they were on belonged to a friend of theirs, and they got water out of a nearby irrigation pipe. The man dictated an address for Reza to send the photos to, and it was carefully written down. When we rose to leave, he apologized profusely for not having anything else to offer us besides tea.

On the way back into the city, Reza talked about tourism in Iran. "The government, I think, say 2 million tourists expected next year". The actual number, I learned later, was one-third that figure. "Country must be ready for them. There once 100 guards at Persepolis and other sites in area. But now only 30. If we not careful, places will be destroyed and tourists don't come."

He also discussed the song on the cassette and how it didn't really mean what it said. While the singer might wail that everyone and everything was drunk, "He mean drunk in spirit, having special happiness," Reza said, "not drunk really". In response to my doubts, he indicated the famous Shirazi poet Hafiz didn't really mean it when he wrote that he loved wine, that it was a symbol for something else.

At Hafiz's tomb in Shiraz, Reza pointed out in the distance where the 14th century poet had resided. High on a hill under a solitary tree, a spot he supposedly never left according to Reza, the great man had lived alone.

"But in his poems he wrote about visiting the tavern frequently," I said. "And he was suppose to have had a wife and son. Plus he went to Yazd once."

"I don't know about that," was the noncommittal reply.

The traditional tea house near the tomb had pillows for seats and water pipes for smoking. The place was crowded and became more so when a French Elderhostel group of 62 entered. Two of the women sat with us, and I asked how they were. One of them replied wearily, "It is hot in these things," indicating the long coat that covered her body and the scarf that hid her hair.

Driving around the city later, Reza kept talking about the danger in some places. "The Shirazis are good people. But those who live outside city come in to steal." After a moment of silence he added, "The Isfahanis and Shirazis, but especially those from Isfahan, are afraid.

They show that in war with Iraq. They run away." It was the people of Kerman, however, that he talked about the most. "The Kermanis are not good. They tell lies. Plus they not friendly. Not good."

After awhile we visited the tea house at the tomb of Sadi, another famous poet from Shiraz. He had lived in the 13th century and had traveled extensively. As we sipped our hot drinks, Ali asked to speak to me. He was a brave 16-year old who already had a mustache coming along and wanted to practice his English.

While his mother looked on apprehensively for a moment, Ali told us his father was a petroleum engineer who drove a Peykon, the automobile manufactured in Iran. He wanted to learn English because it was the universal language, and he thought the United States was "very powerful, and very big". The U.S. loss in soccer to Iran, Ali said, was unimportant. His country, even though they won, didn't advance to the second round, which had been their goal. He wanted to be an architect after attending the University of Tehran and would do his two years of mandatory service once he completed his studies.

Requiring two years of service to the country from high school and college graduates was a practice already in place under the shah in the 1970s. At that time, everyone was required to do it, but now only men have to.

Shortly after the sun set, we came across a linear park next to a recently built wide boulevard. Hundreds of families were picnicking on the grass in the cool air and soft breeze of the early evening. Reclining men, women and grandmothers were taking drags from water pipes while the younger generation walked and talked. How any government trying to keep a lid on morality could compete with the flood of hormones in millions of adolescents, the advancement of technology in society, and a re-emerging middle class with some disposable income to spend was a question I had to ask myself as we joined the densely packed throng.

On this night, thousands of mostly young people moved in a human river along the sidewalk. Some of the girls had curled locks and makeup showing under the patterned veils or fashionably designed coats and scarves they wore. A mother was playing chaperon with one young couple while around us hand holding and other public signs of affection, supposedly reserved for married couples, was going on.

We walked by a small fenced rink for in-line skaters occupied by boys twirling around. At another rink, however, one courageous girl of about 12 was slowly, carefully learning the necessary movements as big guys zoomed around her. Under a street lamp along the sidewalk, a girl of ten was selling snacks while also reading a school book as the human tide flowed by her.

Reza wanted to eat western food, so at a very popular spot he had a pizza while I sampled an Iranian hamburger and french fries. His pizza, given the size of the crowd, was delivered really quickly, but it turned out to be undercooked. My hamburger wasn't bad, although buried beneath all the condiments I couldn't tell if it was beef or mutton.

Back on the crowded sidewalk, two college students asked Reza if they could talk to me. One was from Mashad, the other Azerbaijan, and they were both studying computer science using Windows '98. "I would like to see America, just once," one of them declared. When finished with their schooling, they said they would have to work for the Defense Ministry for 13 years to pay off their scholarships.

While they held hands, which many friendly Iranian men customarily do, we made our way through the mob. They couldn't understand how my wife could be in Germany drinking wine while I was in Iran. The Internet is banned in their country they told me, except for government use. One of them had seen a pirated version of "Titanic" copied off of a feed picked up by an illegal satellite dish. After some thought, they agreed that seeing American movies or television shows in Iran was uncommon.

These well-educated men knew of Madonna and Michael Jackson, *Huckleberry Finn* and *The Old Man and the Sea.* But they hadn't heard of rap music and didn't understand what the word politics meant. Upon reaching our parked car, they asked for my address and I gave them a business card. One man said he would write to me immediately, but I never heard from him.

Fire and Light

We were stopped at police checkpoints a few times on our way out of Shiraz. "They look for drugs," Reza said as we drove through a landscape which constantly changed. In one spot a shepherd watched over his flock wandering near a field of crops. Small farm plots dotted a long valley running beneath a high multi-colored range of mountains. Further on, scattered encampments of poor tribal tents lined the highway. In another place, scrubby plants dotted the desert land and the mountains were far off in the distance.

The two lane road toward Yazd was smoothly paved, and we drove along at 50 m.p.h. or more. One city we went through had two giant plaster parrots adorning the center of a large traffic circle. Stopping in the late morning heat for gas in the remote, small desert town of Abarkuh, a man walked up to us while we were standing at the pumps. With a laugh he proudly announced, "Abarkuh is just like Tehran".

The experiences of Rosita Forbes when she followed this same route seventy years ago on her five day journey from Shiraz to Yazd were much different. Riding much of the way in the cab of a tea and candle carrying truck, she described the perils of the trip. "Then we turned east across a plain, cut by irrigation channels and low mud walls. Over and through these we plunged, sometimes pushed by amiable natives in blue robes and comfortable turbans. For miles we jolted down the center of a dry river bed, negotiating rocks with tank-like energy. A new guide was necessary every few miles, for the 'road' was scarcely even a camel track, and I was amused to see that these came armed and bargained for payment in advance."

"At Aberguh, a straggling village on the edge of the salt desert, we fortified ourselves with tea and filled our empty petrol tins with water, for
there are no wells in the next seventy miles."

After filling up the tank in Abarkuh, or Aberguh according to Forbes'
spelling, Reza located a small restaurant with two large trucks parked
outside. We went in looking for lunch and discovered the place had no
rice because of a lack of business. When we asked for tea the owner had
to go to his home to fetch it. The fried mutton we were served, however,
was delicious.

The mud bricks of two old and abandoned caravanserai rest stops
were melting away in the sunlight as we drove through the single story
town. The horizon was dominated by an ancient tower which topped a
nearby hill. A girl on the street didn't know how old it was, but Reza
learned in Yazd it was called "Gombed Alee" or "Tower of Ali". He
thought it had once been the home of a holy man.

Driving on, we passed through a desert where nothing grew and the
land was just rocks and gravel. Later, however, it appeared as if small
stick-like shrubs, each with a few green leaves, had been planted by
hand in very neat rows. The triple digit heat of the afternoon, the effects
of lunch, and the dull sameness of the scenery combined to have us
both nodding after awhile.

In her book, Forbes gave the truck driver's view of their trip. "'This is
an evil road,' explained the driver as we lurched over the crackling red
earth, coated with salt. 'There is but one landmark between the ranges
and that is the ruin called Kaleh Khun' (the fort of red blood), 'because
robbers used to live there, but now the well is dry and it is deserted.'"

After rousting a cafe owner from his nap in a tiny desert village to get
us each a soda, Reza and I continued on. In the distance, a table-top
mountain was flooded in bright sunlight while the towering range in
back of it was dark from shadows cast by overhead clouds. The afternoon had cooled off considerably, and we were reviving as we sped into
the mountains.

The road twisted and turned through a red rock pass before emerging into a semi-lush valley of corn, tomatoes, and other crops. In back of the fields, huge rock faces appeared to have been chiseled into immense column-like formations which abruptly protruded from the earth.

Having spent a day in the desert without water after the truck broke down, Forbes was rescued by a passing car during her trip to Yazd. "The only living thing we saw for fifty miles was a wolf standing over a skeleton which he had picked clean," she wrote. "On we went into the mountains, where the track played leap-frog with all sorts and conditions of obstacles, ditches, mud banks, soft sand and rocks…we left the red desert with its mountains so inclined that they look like wave after wave of receding breakers, and came to Yezd."

After a seven hour drive, we pulled into Yazd. While we were checking in at our garden-style hotel, a tour bus full of traveling Italians appeared, looking for their rooms. Reza asked what I wanted to do and I mentioned visiting the local museum, but it was closed for the day. "It has nothing anyway," Reza insisted. "It was house of rich man. So just has furniture and other things he had. They kill him in revolution. Took his house and park across street. Also land this hotel on."

I had to wonder if the man had just been too rich. Being mentally clever enough to accumulate wealth was once an aspiration for many Iranians. The Persian tradition of serving as the middlemen in transactions, of negotiating the give-and-take of bargaining, meant that being clever was an attribute many Iranians envied. To become wealthy, however, a person had to be shrewd in their business dealings, which often created enemies. Being wealthy didn't always pay off, as the story of the rich man showed.

In the center of Yazd at dusk, the minarets of an ancient monument caught the fading light for a few minutes. Rays bounced off the blue tiled columns and the sun was eclipsed behind the tall towers.

A long row of stacked mud arches below the minarets made up a three story high wall of repetitive curved forms. The entire facade twinkled to life as electric lights came on in each recessed alcove. A prayer service was beginning in front of the monument, but only a small crowd had gathered. A larger one was obviously anticipated by the end of the evening since row upon row of room-sized rugs were being rolled out for the expected participants. The speaker was getting into form and his microphone broadcast voice drowned out all other sounds. When we departed the area later in the evening, he was preaching to hundreds of people, all the rugs covered by sitting faithful.

The sidewalks of the downtown area were crowded with shoppers, many of them Afghan refugees from the Russian invasion of their country in 1979. Almost 1.5 million Afghans moved to Iran because of the fighting, but they have not changed from their traditional customs since then. Wearing long shirts and pajama type baggy pants, the dark skinned immigrant men we saw had full beards and wore turbans.

Off of the bazaar, down a narrow pitch-black alley, framed in a doorway was a man sitting behind a desk in a small well lit office. Further along, two graceful arches over a passageway were dimly illuminated in the backlight provided by the entrance sign for a religious school.

As we walked around the central city, Reza continued to repeat his concerns about the people of Kerman. I had to wonder if that is why he wanted to drive all the way from there to Bam and back in one day. If we had done that, our time in Kerman would have been minimal.

Then he told me of a client he had some time ago. "He was Englishman who been this way many years before. When he in Zahedan then, he write name on mountain. This time he go back and find. In Yazd before, he meet friend in park. So now he want go back to park. We wait for hour. I ask him, why we wait? He say, maybe friend come. But friend don't come."

Returning to the hotel, we happened upon another driver from Tehran that Reza knew well. He was just pulling out, going to find dinner with his Canadian passenger. Reza asked if he had ever been to Zahedan, and the man replied, "No, only as far as Bam". The long desert crossing and all of its uncertainties was quickly approaching for both of us, one full of anticipation, the other with anxiety.

While reading a book in my room later about an Englishman's observations on modern-day America, I listened to the sounds of the swamp cooler over my head beating a constant rhythm. Looking around, I saw a large color TV set in one corner and a four-foot high lime green used refrigerator in another. A white kitty cat was painted on the side of the garbage pail, wall-to-wall green carpeting covered the floor, and a push button phone rested next to the bed. The promotional material for the hotel was all glossy exuberance, the drinking glasses were wrapped in plastic and the toilet had been sanitized. This room could have been in Yuma, Arizona, I thought, except for the squatter hole-in-the-floor toilet next to the sitter variety in the bathroom.

Outside my room in the morning, a well dressed groundskeeper swept the walk with a very long palm frond. Reza's friend asked him to pay a parking ticket he had received because he had to be on his way to Kerman shortly. Just after breakfast, the Italians boarded their bus and departed, heading for another tourist day.

The Friday mosque was almost deserted when we arrived, except for the sunlight and shadow which played off the arches and tile work of the enormous central alcove. A custodian was sweeping a domed-over walkway which alternated between shade and sun, white and black. Light cascaded down through a circular opening in the courtyard floor into an underground room used for summertime lectures.

After paying the parking ticket at a local bank, we walked through some of the tight twisting ancient alleys which are one of the things Yazd is famous for. The alleys, too narrow for cars to get through, wind their way around the center of the city, turning and bending in an endless system of corners and curves. The newer parts of town, of course, are all wide straight streets and huge traffic circles, built for the automobile.

But the old section of the city, with its high walls and arched-over walk-ways, is perfect for those on foot. The alleys are almost always in cool shadow, and the pedestrian need have no fear of being run over.

Down one alley and around a corner we stumbled across the local tourist office. An easy-to-spot-location had obviously not been a consideration in choosing the site. Inside we found a small show of modern calligraphy work displayed to mark "National Tourism Week".

After weaving our way through more of the maze-like system of alleys, we entered a public square where hundreds of chairs had been set up under tall shade trees. Black veiled women already occupied the back rows, and we were told that the Minister of Tourism from Tehran and other high ranking government officials would be speaking in a while.

Exhibits showing attractions from throughout the province had been arranged inside the adjacent "Alexander's Prison", which was rumored to date from the Great One's time. There was an exhibit on carpet weaving, and another explained the area's waterworks. A photo display depicted the local religious practice of dozens of men carrying a large paisley shaped wooden structure draped in black to mark the 680 A.D. martyrdom of Imam Housein, one of the Shiite sect of Islam's holiest men.

As we looked over the exhibits, a tourist office representative joined us. He asked what I thought of his country and what Americans think of Iran. "Most of my friends are afraid of it. They consider it very dangerous. Of course, most Americans don't know anything about the world."

With a snort of approval toward that last statement, the tourism official wondered how Iranians could be friendlier. "Our country, as you see, is very safe, safer than yours," he said with obvious frustration. I couldn't disagree with him.

The assembled chairs in the square were beginning to slowly fill as the appointed time for the speakers approached. Several tents nearby showed handicrafts, produce, and more tourist attractions from the province.

One of the tents also held a large display about the war with Iraq. In addition to the now common grisly photographs of the dead, there were poster-sized pictures of tanks and advancing foot soldiers which looked like they had been taken in World War II. A "sending-them-off-to-war-from-Tehran" photo had men in double decker buses going to the front, waved on by an enormous crowd of relatives. A series of collected editorial cartoons from around the world mocked the U.S., Carter, and Reagan. One showed the Statue of Liberty curtsying to a barrel of oil.

Dignitaries were just appearing and the speeches were about to begin when we departed to visit the Zoroastrian fire temple. It was outside the city center down an alley in a small modern building and the door was locked when we arrived. The caretaker quickly opened it and showed us into a rectangular shaped room, the walls of which were covered with the sayings of the master. Behind a window in one wall, the eternal flame representing purity of thought along with being associated with truth and justice burned softly, a small fire of logs and cinders.

Needing to get the oil changed in the car, Reza dropped me off at the local museum. The large two story modern white house built by the executed rich man sat in the middle of a formal flower garden. Other than the ticket taker and a young soldier at the entrance, I was the only one present.

The interior of the house was French bordello in style. The rooms had marbled floors, fancy ceiling scrolls in blue and white, and three rooms were covered by small domes. All the rooms, including the one with a curving bar surrounded by walls of green velvet and painted white wood strips, were quiet except for the sounds of my footsteps. The main room had mirrored alcoves at each corner and another room had a tiny pool in its center. The colors of the rooms varied, tinted glass windows allowed in various shades of light, and huge mirrors lined the main hallway.

Small displays in the house concerned mostly fire and light. Ancient candle sticks and samovars, some very old oil lamps, water pipes and "moon light" kerosene lamps were all contained in glass cases. One room was exclusively devoted to a long series of matchboxes. There were plain Diamond matchboxes and Swan Vestas; Chinese cheesecake adorned the cover of some while others showed travel scenes from Switzerland and Italy. "Sweet Maidenhood" brand matchboxes, Fiat 1500 type, and matches from Czechoslovakia were among the dozens shown.

Waiting for Reza to return, I sat in the rich man's confiscated park across the street from his house. Soon I was joined by two shoe shine boys, one of whom correctly pointed out that my Nikes were in need of repair. Fibbing, I told them I had no money, but they could see a thick roll of bills in my shirt pocket.

Using a silent communication system that was as swift as e-mail, there were eight poor boys dressed in ragged clothes standing in front of me within a minute. I decided I wanted their picture and asked that they form a line. After pushing and shoving to comply, they posed in various forms of seriousness.

To reward them, I took out the bag of small, colorful animal-shaped stickers I had brought with me to distribute to poor children. Instantaneously, there were 16 dirty brown hands in my face. I gave out a few of the stickers but quickly realized I needed a system to control the situation, so I told the boys to line up and tried to give them each one. But they were smarter than that and continued to crowd around, grabbing at me. Two men sitting on a nearby bench were smiling at my predicament. As I handed out a sticker, it immediately went into a pocket, the empty hand reached for another, and the whining plea of "Mister, please" continued.

The youngest boys were eventually satisfied, but the teen-agers persisted. One of them repeated over and over in a soft lament, "I have nothing. Give me something."

Reza pulled up on the street and as I moved toward the car the boys followed. Reza was yelling at them to get away from me while also chuckling at the situation. As we were ready to leave, he said I should give a particular boy one more sticker. With that, all of the hands crawled into the car like some sort of lurching multi-headed hydra. We finally pulled out and the boys were left laughing and comparing their trophies. As we drove away, I assumed their parents might not have disagreed with the sentence given to the rich man.

Over lunch Reza said that some of the boys may go to school part-time. Others, he thought, probably couldn't afford the clothes, notebooks and fountain pens required. Instead, their families may need them to work, so they would do what they could.

He also wondered what "Field of Dreams" meant on the baseball cap I always wore. I explained it was an American movie and listed the stars. "Who is woman?" he asked but I told him they didn't have important roles. "But when you young, you dream only of women," he replied.

On the way back to the hotel, we passed a young shrouded woman standing by herself at the side of the road, waving for a ride. Reza said, "I wonder where she go?" as he turned around to look. He almost stopped the car but decided against it. When he dropped me off near the lobby, he complained that a 3 hour nap wasn't long enough. "What there to do here?" he argued as I got out.

A pale faced woman in her 20s wearing a black veil and dark sun glasses walked through the hotel lobby as I was getting my room key. As she went by it occurred to me that it would be very easy to satirize this social situation. If Tommy Lee Jones and Will Smith could chase aliens for two hours in the movie **Men In Black**, why couldn't Persian ladies avoid being hunted every day by the alien race of Iranian men in **Women In Black**?

After napping, we visited the Zoroastrian "Towers of Silence". In 1971 they had been out in the country, far from the urban area of Yazd. Today the city has stretched itself out to include these two low, flat topped hills where until about 50 years ago the dead were placed to be picked over by birds. Some abandoned mud houses, crumbling away at the base of the hills, were smeared with graffiti. One saying read "Hevi Metal" while another stenciled sign advertised Samsonite luggage. Nearby, the wide straight streets and concrete utility poles of a new subdivision had recently been installed. All that was needed were the brick and steel homes to be constructed.

Reza announced over dinner, "We leave at 8:30 for Kerman".

"Eight," I insisted.

"But is only 391 kilometers."

"Eight is better."

"O.K. Whatever you want."

Coming Clean

In the morning we passed a steady stream of large container-carrying Mercedes Benz, Mack, Volvo, Iveco, and Scania trucks heading westbound. They lumbered like smoke-spewing dragons across the flat desolate landscape. The highway was heavily traveled until we came to a turnoff for the Persian Gulf city of Bandar Abbas. After that, cars made up most of the traffic going further east. In the 13th century it had taken Marco Polo eight days to travel from Yazd to Kerman, but we would be doing it in a few hours.

Barren desert had soon turned into blooming fields of pistachio bushes, and we sped by mile after mile of the small shrubs. It was harvesting season, and dump trucks piled high with unshelled pods still attached to green leafy stems were heading toward the city of Rafsanjun. On our way there, a gasoline truck going at top speed pulled up alongside a pickup loaded down with processed nuts. A man standing in the pickup's bed leaned over to give a small bag of pistachios to a money-containing hand which jutted out from the cab of the truck.

Wanting some nuts, since these were supposedly the best in the world, Reza drove all over Rafsanjun asking a series of people where good ones could be found. We went around and around the city center, following this direction and that, and Reza began to loose his temper. After finally finding a tiny shop full of large burlap sacks full of pistachios, he complained bitterly to the owner that the people of the town didn't know their own city. The nut dealer just smiled politely while completing the transaction.

Looking for a place to eat, we repeated the wandering exercise. Down one street and around a traffic circle, ask directions of people walking along, then retrace our route and ask directions again. Reza was cursing in symphonic-like bursts all the way, softly damning the town and its people.

We finally stumbled across a restaurant and over lunch he asked how much I had paid for my trip. I told him $1,800 and he agreed that was a good price. How much, I wondered, was he paid for driving me? After a long silent pause, Reza replied that he was a free-lance driver and could get clients from several tour companies. Quietly, he said he received $6 a day plus expenses.

Thinking for a moment, Reza inquired if the price I gave him for the trip included air fare. "Oh no. That was another $2,200." With a stunned look on his face he said, "It is very expensive. I want to cry for you. You pay too much." But how do you explain frequent flyer miles and tax deductions, airline pricing structures and cost comparisons with American tour company arranged trips to someone with no experience with such things? So I just kept my mouth shut.

Jumping into the car after lunch, Reza mumbled something to himself. Then he said, "When I pay bill, they make mistake. Only charge for one Pepsi. We had two. This whole town is confused."

Back on the highway, we were soon running low on gas and had to pull into a rural station. At first the attendant said he didn't have any, but then sold us just enough to get to Kerman. On the outskirts of that city, Reza stopped at another station where the line behind each pump was four to five cars deep. While we waited, Reza repeated softly to himself, "The Kermanis not good people".

The urban edge of Kerman, like the other Iranian cities we had seen, was dotted with partially completed buildings. Multi-story steel frames had been erected and maybe a few brick walls put up, but then construction had stopped, sometimes obviously for many years. I assumed the owner would have to be a little more clever in order to raise some additional capital to finish the work.

Immediately upon arriving at our hotel, the middle-aged proprietor offered us tea and asked us to sit down. The tea drinking custom, which was a little bit of the old Iran I remembered well, had apparently disappeared in many other places in the country, but not here. As we drank our steaming tea served in handleless glasses, the hotel owner said that he had known several Peace Corps volunteers. He listed their names, but I didn't recognize any of them. "They were good kids," he remarked.

When I told Reza I wanted to visit the city's traditional bathhouse, he looked at me strangely. "Most tourists don't do that. I think you go alone," he said sincerely, but later he called my room to tell me we had to be there by 4:30.

The bath was located in the bazaar, and sitting on the ground near the dark, domed entrance to the ancient shopping area was an attractive tribal woman cradling an infant. Next to her, another child slept peacefully. She asked Reza if he wanted his fortune read, and he replied gently, "No, I never had good chance in my life".

With only a little difficulty we found the 280 year old underground bathhouse. Reza definitely wasn't enthusiastic about entering and hesitated on the top step, but I walked down and pushed the door open and he followed. Besides the experience, there was another reason I wanted to take this Persian bath. At Christmas time in 1972 I had passed up the opportunity to visit the bathhouse, but now I was getting another chance, and I was going to take it.

In the large entry room, the air was steamy and plaster was crumbling off the arched walls. Small wooden cubicles were available for storage, and the manager told us we could either choose to keep our Jockies on or wrap a thin red striped towel around our naked waist.

The first step in the bathing process was to take a cold shower in a not-so-clean stall. As the running water dripped off my head, I thought that this was the Iran of my memory. No cockroaches were present, nor would I see one during the entire trip. But the dank muggy air, the grungy floor, and the arched ceiling of the shower room all added up to the exotic atmosphere of the way things once were.

After shaking ourselves off, we had to wait in the adjacent steam room because the masseur was busy with a customer. Three young men were sitting together on the floor in a corner, occasionally pailing themselves from a bucket of cold water. In the recess of one wall, a painting showed a scene from Ferdosi's epic poem. Rostom, the hero, was fighting his own son without knowing who he was. On another wall, two very faded naked bodies were displayed, their breasts so small it was impossible to decide what gender they were.

My turn for a massage finally arrived. A towel-wrapped and sweat-covered man in his 40s with very strong looking hands waved me over. After I lay on the cool, damp marble floor in front of him, he began by limbering me up. Stretching my arms out, then doing a sort of half-nelson move with pressure on both my shoulders, he was loosening my travel weary bones. Next, taking a cloth which had the texture of something between a Brillo pad and a dish towel, he washed my arms with firm strokes. Dead skin rolled off of me in large chunks and he repeated the procedure over my entire body.

When he had finished washing my back, he stood on it and slowly moved down my spine. The three young men had been conversing with me and just then asked where I was from. However, it was hard to concentrate on the Farsi to describe Tucson, Arizona as "a city in the desert 500 miles east of Los Angeles," with a 180 pound guy standing on me.

The next step was for him to place pressure on the inside of my knees while pulling my feet up toward my head. I resisted, and the masseur told Reza I should relax, but it hurt.

Following a thorough lathering up all over, several pails of cold water got tossed over my head. Having finished, there were thank you's all around, and then we took another quick cold shower. Toweled off, hair parted with a giant blue plastic comb, we emerged into the now shadow wrapped bazaar.

For centuries, the once-a-week bath was a way-of-life for many Persian men, but in a few years it will probably only be a memory, replaced entirely by modern plumbing. This time, however, I had blood in my urine a few days later for me to remember the experience by.

Near the old bathhouse, another ancient bath had been turned into a museum. Wax figures demonstrated how men from various professions—merchants, farmers, clerics, craftsmen—would occupy different parts of the sitting room. Wax men were also used to show the contortions of the massage and the relaxation later in a massive room where customers could nap and gossip. It was all displayed with antiseptic cleanliness and smiling comfort, not the reality of the cold marble floor and firm hands kneading the back.

In the deepening darkness of the early evening, the narrow corridors of the bazaar were crowded with shoppers buying fruit which was perfect with imperfections. Blemishes, scabs, and warts were on every piece, but each also probably came with real taste.

"Titanic" t-shirts and tote bags were for sale among the piles of dry goods in the bazaar, and young boys were trying to sell plastic sacks advertising "Bond Street" cigarettes. Most of the merchandise, however, appeared to be Iranian made. An oddly twisted male dwarf slowly pulled himself along the main floor corridor while at the same time pushing a tin cup in front of him. When Reza handed him a bill, it quickly disappeared inside his shirt.

The crowd was very thick as we worked our way out toward the street. Some members of the morality police were approaching and one tapped a man in front of us. The two top buttons of his shirt were undone and chest hair was showing. Twenty-five years ago, the Iranian men I knew removed all their body hair, but now some dark-haired men look like they are wearing wolverines under their shirts. Instead of buttoning up as requested, the man just pushed his way through the crowd. The young policeman stopped and stared in amazement, not certain what to do.

It would be so easy to ridicule the morality police. Imagine a training session held in a pitch black room with only the intense glare from a slide projector providing any light. The voice of an instructor comes out of the dark. "O.K. a veil which shows a little leg at the bottom, like this one on the screen, is that permissible or not? How about this next slide where some curled hair is seen under the top of the veil? Should we cuff the culprit?"

"Then there is the question of how long we give a woman to wrap herself up in public. Remember, when those veils are thrown loose to be straightened out, men can see her entire body. So what should it be? Three seconds too short? Then how about five? What about the colors of the veils? Should colorful ones be allowed? Look at some of them on the screen. Patterns, bright prints and even white ones instead of the traditional black. Is that really O.K.? Then there are questions about overcoats and scarves. They expose an awful lot of face as you can see in this picture. What do we think?"

Having left the bazaar, Reza and I drove back to the hotel and passed a stalled VW Beetle. Two women were trying to push start it, while attempting to keep their veils on. We also went by a body shop where a damaged car was being sanded. I thought these must be the worst, or the best, drivers and pedestrians in the world. The best for surviving, most of the time, in a land where road rules mean nothing. The worst for ignoring every conceivable safe driving and walking regulation.

Sitting in the hotel lobby was Reza's friend from Tehran. His passenger had gone off for supper with someone else so the three of us agreed to eat together. Reza left to wash his hands, and before he returned his friend told me that getting whiskey in Iran isn't difficult. "We just had to adapt to the new regime. So we make it out of watermelons now."

Then he asked, "Did Reza tell you he was prisoner of Iraq for 9 years?"

"No," I said stunned, having assumed all along that he had fled the country after the revolution. "Was he shot down?"

"Yes."

"In the U.S., we make senators of such people."

"You see what we do to them in Iran," he replied with mock humor.

While we drove around looking for a restaurant, in a singsong voice Reza's friend endlessly repeated that he would like to spend some time "tasting" Monica Lewinsky. He found her extremely attractive, he said, and wanted to invite her to visit Iran. He also couldn't understand how Bill Clinton could be in trouble for having a girlfriend. My half-hearted attempt at a religious-based explanation for the situation was answered by guffaws from both of them.

At 45, Reza's friend was a mustache wearing former military fighter pilot turned driver for foreigners who was graying, baggy eyed and putting on a large pouch. He insisted, however, that his sexual process was as great as ever. The same juvenile male behavior toward women that was so prevalent 25 years ago was obviously still present despite the new government. The Persian philosophy of many men that "enjoying life" meant eating too much, sleeping around with whomever you could, and listening to music all the time apparently hadn't changed.

In the morning, the talk of sex continued over breakfast. While Reza smiled sheepishly and kept quiet, his friend said with a huge grin on his face, "When God created man, he rushed. But with women, he took his time. All the men in world must like women!"

"Even those from Gasvin?" I joked, referring to an Iranian city which was rumored to have many homosexuals.

"Yes, even they hate the gays," he replied in all seriousness.

"So what happened with New City?" I asked of Tehran's infamous former red light district.

"It was torn down and now they turn the land into a beautiful park. But boys go there just to smell the ground and to dream about what once went on."

What do Iranian men do for girlfriends today, I inquired, assuming that a government of clerics may have changed the prominent role that prostitutes once played in the society. "No problem. The government likes women more than we do," he said with a laugh. "Of course," he added quickly, "there are two types of women. I am talking about those like Monica Lewinsky."

Changing subjects for a moment, he said, "I like the American people, but not the American government."

"But isn't the government people?" I asked.

"No, silly, governments are different. They are strange. People are good."

After breakfast, Reza spent 20 minutes looking for the car keys, which were eventually found under the sheets of his bed. "We are all getting old," I told his friend as we waited in the lobby.

He replied that he was very worried about Reza having to drive back from the coast alone by himself. "It is very long way. He must not fall asleep." When I showed him a small gift I had purchased he said, "This for your friend? I hope he like it. She? Oh, your girlfriend," he chuckled.

The horizon on the road out of Kerman to the east was dominated by mountain ranges and a few tall concrete grain silos. The garden town of Mahan sat at the base of one mountain, a stony surface from which the community gets its water.

An ingenious system of underground canals has been used for centuries to bring water from the mountains to many Iranian desert cities. A small but very important industry grew up to dig and maintain the canals, and these workers still serve an important function today.

The water the canals furnish meets the needs for drinking and bathing. It also irrigates the numerous public and private gardens found in most Iranian cities. Gardens in Iran are an important point of contrast to the ever-present desolation of the desert, and they offer a place to sit or stroll in cool shady surroundings.

The tomb of the Sufi dervish Shah Nematollah Vali was located in a garden setting in Mahan, and the massive buildings of the complex paid tribute to a man who devoted his life to Ali, son-in-law of the Prophet

Mohammed. Overlooking one courtyard full of trees and flowers was a small second story museum. On display were manuscripts, coats of armor and scented water carriers used by the desert wandering dervishes. A cloth which once covered Shah Nematollah Vali's casket had taken 16 women 8 years to embroider, Reza told me.

Several paintings of Ali adorned the walls of the museum. Most showed him in his usual pose as a fully bearded man in his 30s, built like a fierce looking linebacker and wearing a turban. His sympathetic eyes are almost always pointed heavenward. But one picture in the gallery had him as a somewhat older, less frightening and warlike figure.

In another building, the few dozen square foot room that the dervish Shah Nematollah Vali had lived in for 40 years during the 14th and 15th centuries was preserved, but it had been enlarged to allow visitors to enter the tiny space. The holy man's tomb was located in a large adjacent structure which contained several huge rooms. Pigeons were cooing in the high dome above one of them as Reza silently excused himself to go wash in the courtyard pool before praying.

The shrine's book shop was run by women, and a picture of Khomeini hung on the wall. This photograph showed a different side of the Ayatollah than usual, however. He sat with his son and two young grandsons, smiling like any grandfather. The intensity of his eyes had been softened for once.

At the top of the town were the hillside gardens of Tarikht, where a rushing stream of water cascaded down the center of a wide staircase. Tall pine and cypress trees lined the walk, and shooting fountains danced in the middle of the stepped, flowing waterfall. While sitting in the cool shade on an empty patio at the top of the hill, we looked out over dry desert and distant mountain ranges.

In the stillness of the garden, I thought that for many Americans, experiencing the reality of Iran could be like looking at a beautiful Persian mosaic. From afar it is majestic, but up close the individual tiles are somewhat rough and crudely painted.

A small cat carefully made its way across the patio, keeping an eye on us. Reza asked why the term "pussycat" was used in the west for sex. "In London and Paris, men go to pussycat areas for girls." I told him I didn't have an answer for that.

On the way back to Kerman, Reza wondered, "Will you write about Iran? Yes? What about?"

"My editor will decide, but he thinks I'll be killed anyway."

"You should call him and say hello," he concluded with a laugh.

For lunch we found a female managed basement restaurant with paintings of children and forest scenes covering its walls. The usually prominently displayed pictures of Khomeini and his successors were not immediately visible. The menu contained rice covered with a vegetable sauce topping, and the food was delicious. Most of the customers were eating their meals in silence, trying to follow the soap opera which was showing on a large television set.

In her 1931 book, Rosita Forbes wrote, "The domed roofs of Kirman look as if they have been blown out of a bowl of soap bubbles. The town is tucked away under one of the usual reddish-black ranges, barren beyond description. The hills have the quality of arrested breakers, like those near Yezd, for they hurl themselves out of the desert one after another, each peak leaning against the next, but none with any more solid foundation than an angry sea-in this case of sand."

Kerman's remote setting had its drawbacks when Forbes traveled through it. As one man told her, "This place is at the end of the world. Beyond those hills there's nothing but sand-a thousand miles of it before you come to India…A man must either get out of here quickly, get back to Isfahan or Tehran, where they understand the new ways, or he'll be forced back again into the old." Reflecting on that statement, Forbes said, "One of the main difficulties of the present Government is that the best educated men will not leave the big towns for exile in the provinces". That attitude, I quickly discovered when I moved to Zahedan in 1971, still persisted forty years after Forbes' visit.

Returning to the bazaar to visit another traditional tea house, we passed a historic building near the entrance to the shopping area. Stacks of arched-recessed alcoves lined the walls, and restoration work was underway on the brickwork of the ancient structure. During my visit for Christmas in 1972, I had stood on those then-crumbling arches to photograph the scene around me, but now they had mostly been restored to their past glory.

Inside the bazaar, a former public bath had been converted into a tea house where carpets and overstuffed pillows were available for reclining. Two university students wanted to practice their English, and we talked a little about Mr. Clinton's problems. "Why he doesn't keep a secret?" one asked of Clinton's sex life. After all, "he is the PRESIDENT" the man insisted. My reply was that in America, everybody talks about everything. Besides, I said, 250 reporters stalk Clinton every day, but I don't think they understood the meaning of my words.

In the hotel lobby later in the afternoon, Reza and I looked over a map of the country. His friend had left to drive back to Isfahan and then go on to Tehran. In the morning we would head in the opposite direction.

The map showed not only a paved highway all the way to Zahedan, but also a fork in the desert road which went directly south to the coast on the Gulf of Oman. That was certainly not how it once was. There was just one wash-board surfaced dirt path going east from Kerman 25 years ago. It was a rough trip which took 14 to 18 hours to complete by bus. Our drive, Reza thought, could be done in eight.

Back to Baluchistan

In the morning, Reza was wearing his usual driving clothes. He had on a threadbare, paint stained white shirt, once forest green pants which were badly faded, and puke lime-colored Adidas that had been purchased in the U.S. 19 years ago. The small plastic bags of melon and squash seeds he constantly chewed were next to his seat. The white Peugeot 405 GL had a wide orange stripe down its middle to signify that it was a taxi, and a poorly stenciled black taxi symbol covered the driver's side door.

After swamping myself with sun tan lotion, we set off. Since the air-conditioner was never turned on, rolled down windows provided the only relief from the 100 degree heat. My right arm jutted out of the car as the blazing sun rose in the sky.

Just outside of Kerman a series of four different utility lines, each on concrete poles of different sizes, paralleled the road. Traffic was moving fast through a desert which showed widely scattered green tufts of shrubs at some places but in others was only dirt and rock.

After two hours we arrived in Bam, a town I remembered only vaguely. In the 1970s the Zahedan to Kerman bus would make a quick stop in the date growing community, and the huge gardens of palm trees were all I ever saw of the place.

This time, however, we visited the ancient ruins for which the city is famous. Surrounded by a towering mud wall, the old Bam was a fortified community centered around a citadel built atop a hill. As we entered through the wide gate in the old town wall, three workmen were repairing damage to the historic entryway.

Inside the walls was a scene of crumbling buildings and melting mud which took incredibly grotesque shapes. Jagged edges, collapsed roofs and shrunken structures were what could be seen. Bam's former fort, sitting on a small knoll in the distance, now looks out over an abandoned town of hundreds of houses, shops and mosques slowly disappearing back into the earth.

As Reza and I walked up to the well preserved citadel, a tall, white-haired man wearing a New York Yankees baseball cap was coming down the hill. "How did the home run race turn out?" I inquired with serious interest as we passed.

"McGuire had 70, and Sosa 66, but he has a playoff game with the Giants to go." Thus, I found out one important fact from the only other American I would meet in Iran.

The top of the fort was a room which had views for each season. The "spring" window looked out over the town, "summer" toward the desert, and the "fall" scene was of date palms. In the nearby tea house, where we were the only customers, Reza chatted with the woman in charge. She told him she had a nine year old daughter, her husband was dead, and that she earned $40 a month. "Very difficult," was all he could say.

The gas station on the edge of town had a five car backup behind its only working pump, and east of the existing city a "new" Bam was being built. Focused around an automobile manufacturing plant and a luxury hotel, several large billboards proclaimed the area's attractions, but most of the buildings didn't appear to be completed yet, except for the hotel.

Only two utility lines ran further east, and after awhile even they disappeared. At that point, the desert was alone in its solitude. A few small villages, however, each with a tiny graveyard containing the remains of men killed in the Iraqi war, were scattered along the road.

At one point water and wind had created a lunar looking landscape of 20 foot high carved shapes and figures. Made of earth, these craggy surfaces jutted straight out of the ground like mud icebergs. Further along was one of the old lighthouses of the desert which long ago provided direction for wandering nighttime travelers. Once fires burned in the darkness at the top of these towers to show the way across the desolate, furnace-like land. Today, needed no longer, the desert lighthouse stood quietly in the bright sunshine next to the highway.

Both of these landmarks left an impression long ago on Rosita Forbes during her three day crossing from Kerman to Zahedan, or Duzdab as it was then called. After making the journey riding in a carpet carrying truck she wrote, "It was as if we came suddenly to a lunar desolation, but torrid instead of frozen...a vast pan, eight miles long and ten or twelve broad, had evidently once been part of a river bed, for it was full of huge mud stumps chiseled by the action of long vanished water into the forms of castles, pinnacles and towers. From a distance it is impossible to believe that these are not the ruins of some primeval city, for the stumps measure from three to twenty feet in height and are as varied in diameter, but the illusion is subsequently replaced by a feeling the extraordinary formations can be nothing but gargantuan molars ground down by the labor and passage of time."

Of the lighthouses reportedly built in the 18th century she said, "Towards noon, we arrived at the first of the two eighty-foot watchtowers, built according to local legend by Nadir Shah to guide his army on their march to India. These are thirty miles apart and in the days of the Mogul-Persian alliance, beacons flared from what were veritable lighthouses in the Sea of Sand."

Then she writes, "still, many centuries later, it would be difficult to travel without these landmarks, for, between Bam and Duzdap, there is only one village. Then for over two hundred miles there is no other habitation than the four or five mud huts occupied each by a couple of Baluchi road guards."

Today, emergency stopping stations pop up every 20 miles or so, a few covered bus shelters sit beside the highway, and there are frequent roadside pullouts. At these, truck drivers used the shade cast by their vehicles to take a nap or drink tea fixed on a portable burner. At one pullout a man silhouetted against the crystal blue sky was facing the afternoon sun, his dark shape bowing slowly in prayer.

We drove by one old building in ruins, all of its windows and doors removed. The mud walls of the structure looked forlorn as they slowly disappeared, a process which could take decades to complete. I thought that the building might have been the restaurant where Zahedan to Kerman buses would once stop. There had always been the same one item of rice and vegetable stew to order from the non-existent menu, but the hot tea that was served helped to wash dirt out of dry mouths. Today, just up the road from the ruin, a shiny looking new building offered a wayside attraction for passengers looking for a meal.

The bus trip in the 1970s had been over a rough dirt road which jostled passengers around for endless hours. They had to watch that when they bounced out of their seats, their heads didn't hit the overhead storage compartment. I thought the old road could be seen off to the side of the present paved highway, but Reza insisted it was another two lanes which would be improved some time in the future.

The sky was filled with cotton-candy clouds, and heat rose off the desert as we drove on. Trucks would appear as wavy, ghost-like lines in the distance and then slowly materialize through the haze. Traffic was sparse but steady and moved quickly on the two lane road.

Seventy years ago, Rosita Forbes and her carpet selling English driver didn't have a road to drive on. They had to cross the desert as they found it, using long strips of matting in order to get over the softest sand. "At Nadir's tower we removed the radiator cap and let half the air out of the tires," she wrote. "A little further on, while crawling through ridges of soft sand on first speed, the temperature rising toward 120 (degrees) Fahrenheit, and the engine shrieking its continual protest, we came upon a lorry which had been stranded for four days. Its driver, in rags, was prostrate under a tamerisk bush. We gave him water, flour and cigarettes, but he refused to leave his car."

In the afternoon heat, Reza began to nod his head periodically and was fidgeting again. Knowing he needed a break, he pulled off the road next to a large, fairly new restaurant. The business, however, was closed and the building abandoned, only one man living on the deserted grounds. We ate some apples and were told the next tea house was another 50 miles.

Mountains of red shapes and light green forms loomed ahead of us while a dry riverbed running next to the road weaved its way down through a narrow valley. Three tunnels cut in the mountain rock sped us on our way, and we were soon back to the flat desert.

Forbes wrote of this same passage, "we left the desert between breakers of red and gray rock and crept up a gully which, being a natural watershed, is subject to sudden spates. Here after heavy rains or rapidly melting snows, caravans are apt to be overwhelmed between the cliffs and all the beasts drowned…To the top of the pass we crept at two miles an hour, followed by a Baluchi with a mallet which he thrust under a hind wheel whenever the lorry hesitated."

We were waved over at a police checkpoint on the highway and a young soldier asked for a ride to the next village. There we found a small, dirty, fly infested tea house, and I felt I was home, back to the Baluchistan I once knew, except for the European television show which had everyone's intense attention.

Sometime later we topped a rise and could see Zahedan miles in the distance. It was from this same spot, exactly 27 years to the day, that I had first seen the city's night lights.

As we drove into town, however, I didn't recognize the place. There were cars and pavement, numerous businesses along unknown streets and many multi-storied buildings. Large, unfamiliar traffic circles and even new car show rooms were present. Zahedan sprawled out all over the desert, and I couldn't get my bearings.

Driving along, Reza said it looked like we were in Pakistan. The number of tribal Baluch people on the street certainly was very high, and many of them were probably refugees from the Russian invasion of Afghanistan in 1979. I noticed that even the men's pajama style shirts had changed from 25 years ago. The tails were much longer than they had once been.

While the Baluch are one of the primary tribal groups that live in Pakistan, they are a minor part of the Iranian population. Except, that is, in the country's eastern most province of Sistan and Baluchistan. Unlike 25 years ago, when the population of Zahedan was about evenly split between Persians and Baluch, today tribal members apparently greatly outnumber their Iranian rulers.

When we pulled up in front of our hotel and got out of the car, a man drove slowly by in a new model vehicle and said, "F___You!". Welcome back was all I could think.

My room was small, poorly furnished, and lacked air-conditioning. It didn't have a refrigerator or most of the other amenities which had been standard up to now. It did, however, have a flowery photograph hanging on the wall on which was written, "The finding of God is finding one's self".

Also lacking was a western toilet. Ceramic foot markers over a hole in the bathroom floor were the only option. For two years I had used this system, and now despite my out-of-practice, almost 49 year old knees, I assumed I could learn the squat method again. Plus I had brought toilet paper with me from Kerman, so I wouldn't have to be using my left hand to do the dirty work.

When Reza asked at the front desk why the hotel was so hot, he was told that Zahedan gets cold at night, and the central cooling had been turned off a month before. The clerk insisted that the city was cooler in the summer than Tehran. Whatever chamber-of-commerce promotional program pushed that idea was based on a fantasy. Many things might have changed since the 1970s, but the heat of the desert wasn't one of them. The man at the desk concluded by telling us to open our windows and enjoy the fresh air.

We had to take a taxi to the bazaar area because it was too long a walk, something which would have been totally unnecessary in the much smaller community of 25 years ago. We ate dinner just off the main street, and Reza seemed to be having difficulty adjusting to his new surroundings. The large number of tribal people, the distance from Tehran, and the dirtier environment had him depressed and worried.

Even though it was dark, as we strolled around after dinner I began to recognize some things. Beneath the new facades and between the enormous number of stores and businesses, I saw the old bus station office, now an ice cream shop. A blind beggar, feeling his way home, was emerging from the small L-shaped bazaar I had once shopped at regularly. Up the street, the military post continued to exist. So did the two-story building where the provincial engineering office had moved in early 1973, even though the space looked vacant now. Across the street, the girls high school still stood where it had been before.

Not having expected to go looking for my old house so soon, I couldn't help myself. It was only a five block walk and I wanted to see what had happened. I moved with excited anticipation toward the place I called home at one time, to a house I once shared with Sarkis and several other Iranian men.

Reza and I quickly passed an auto dealership which had $21,000 shiny white Peykons on display behind large windows. Just up the street was the dry riverbed which ran near the back of our house. Baluch families had once lived on its banks in shacks made of cardboard and palm fronds, but now the channel is a wide road, the streambed encased in a concrete pipe and paved over.

In the dark, down a side alley just off the main street, it looked like the old house was still there, but the garage appeared to have been converted into a new room. A tiny grocery at the end of the block certainly wasn't there before, so must have been added later. A new, two story, very ugly white house with many angles and corners was also in the alley. It definitely hadn't been there in the 1970s. Across the major thoroughfare, the small store full of dusty items where I once bought odds and ends was now a fancy looking sweet shop.

As we walked back toward the center of town, it looked like Zahedan still rolled up its sidewalks by 8 p.m. Reza asked in astonishment why I didn't have a car when I lived in Baluchistan. "I didn't need one," I said. "Besides, I couldn't afford it on my hundred dollar a month salary."

"Why you eat Iranian food?" he wanted to know. "All my U.S. Air Force friends in Tehran have best American food and beer flown in. That is what they eat and drink."

"Our cook was very good, and I like Iranian food. In my opinion, your friends' isolation was one example of why the U.S. didn't know the revolution was coming."

"But Mister David, I don't understand why you come here?"

"For peace, for happiness. But my Iranian friends thought I worked for the C.I.A.," I answered with a laugh.

The roosters were up before the *mullahs* the next morning. Long before sunrise, crows to the new day had begun. A few minutes later, the first call to prayer wailed out across the city. It moved from mosque to mosque, the plaintive cry bouncing around town, a soft song from a distant place, more intense as it got closer. When the procession of sound finally arrived at the small Sunni mosque across from the hotel, it was blasted out very loudly.

Some time later, shuffling feet could be heard on the street below my open window. Then a man pushing a cart went by calling, "Milk! Milk!". As he did, a few of the faithful made their way to the Sunni mosque. It was enclosed behind a tall plain wall, decorated only with Pakistani-style white curlicue figures over the front doorway.

The Sunni sect is Islam's largest branch, and those Muslims who follow its teachings are suppose to pray five times a day. Pakistanis and Baluchis are typically Sunnis. Persians, however, are mostly members of the Shiite sect, which prays three times a day. They also believe for religious leaders in a different line of descent from the prophet Mohammed than do Sunnis.

An old, gray bearded Baluchi man slowly working his beads was sitting in the hotel lobby when I entered. Showing him the picture from 1972 I had of snow in our home's courtyard, he smiled knowingly. "It has snowed once since then," he said with a grin.

During an early morning solitary walk, I came across a section of town near the hotel that looked like the old Zahedan. It had dirt streets and alleys, litter blowing around, and mud brick houses. In most of the city, however, glass, metal and concrete had replaced the old ways of building things, and asphalt now covered the roads.

When Rosita Forbes traveled this way almost 70 years ago, Zahedan was called Duzdab, or Duzdap according to her, and only existed because the British had ended their Indian rail line on the spot. She wrote of it, "Before the War, Duzdap, which means 'Thieves water', was only a well, at which caravans between Meshed and India were regularly raided, but England pushed the rail head from Quetta up here to guard the frontier, and a group of merchants followed. Today there is a cluster of mud bazaars flattened on the blazing plain, and a settled population of perhaps two thousand, Afghans, Baluchis, Sikhs, Turkoman, Persians, Berberis (who were originally Mongols), a few Russians, some Belgians to run the customs, and two Germans to organize the new National Bank...".

The small town in the middle of the desert didn't impress Forbes at all. She said of it, "Duzdap consists of two streets of mud dumplings flattened on the sand, but all around are reddish mountains spurting out of the plain with a suddenness that is disconcerting...Outside the town, which is still surprised at its own existence, the country must be one of the poorest in the world. Men live like their shrunken flocks among ranges, beautiful with the ambers, crimsons, and saffrons of utter aridity, and the few goats live on nothing at all."

When I first arrived in Zahedan in 1971, it had perhaps twenty or twenty-five thousand residents. Half were tribal Baluch people, the others Persian government workers and soldiers. There was a sprinkling of Sikhs to sell liquor to Muslim customers, and the poverty Forbes described was still present.

During my morning walk on this day, I sought some shade from the quickly rising heat and found a huge traffic circle built around a large water fountain. Under large pine trees, I sat and wondered just how big Zahedan had become. While I watched two Baluchi boys try to spin the front wheels of their bicycles as they jumped curbs, around me was a town that neither Forbes nor I could recognize.

Later, as we strolled over to the headquarters of the provincial government where I wanted to talk to the governor or someone else about the present Zahedan, Reza told me all of my questions wouldn't be answered. "It is because you are American," he said. Then he asked if I had brought my passport with me. When I told him they had demanded to keep it at the hotel front desk in order to meet police requirements, he became quickly indignant. Saying sternly that I probably wouldn't be let into the government building at all, he insisted, "They need to know who you are".

After calming down, he asked what I had done in Zahedan long ago. "I worked for the regional engineering office and did master plans for cities in the province and designed two low-income housing projects."

"But from what you say, you travel a lot."

"I did, but I worked sometimes."

"How you have time when you go to every part of Iran?"

"I managed. Besides, I like to travel."

Today, most of the provincial government's functions have been consolidated into one large, nondescript modern two-story office building. In the 1970s, various departments were scattered all around town in separate facilities.

The salt and pepper-haired guard at the entrance to the government complex asked for some identification and I said, not knowing the Persian for it, "Driver's license?". Reza quickly tried to translate, but the man replied in Farsi, "I graduated from an English course. The driver's license will be fine."

The governor wasn't the right one to answer my questions, the guard decided; the head of the engineering department was. He, however, was in a meeting with the governor and wouldn't return for two hours according to those in his office. "We'll be back," his male secretary was told as Reza and I left to wander the city.

Outside the government building, Reza asked a passing soldier how to find the bazaar. The young man responded by saying we should follow him. As we walked along, he inquired about our trip and told us that our last stop, the once-tiny fishing village of Charbahar on the Gulf of Oman, was a 10 hour drive.

A few blocks away was a fairly new covered bazaar which certainly hadn't existed 25 years ago. As I looked over gold jewelry, it was immediately apparent that nothing had written prices on it. The weight of the piece, not its artistic craftsmanship, determined the cost.

At shop after shop I stopped to ask about prices, and Reza grew more irritated as I went along. When I finally decided to buy a pair of earrings, he was relieved, but the store owner wouldn't bargain so I left empty handed.

Outside the shop, Reza loudly complained, "No one bargain in Iran. The shopkeeper tell you price, you pay. What is saving $1? It is nothing!" But I wasn't going to budge because of the principal of the thing. Bargaining was as Iranian as rice and fried mutton and I wouldn't buy under the new conditions, if that was what they really were.

Deeper in the bazaar, after some right and left hand turns, we came upon several long corridors filled with plastic kitchenware, men's clothes, and small shops stacked with bags of spices. Later, we stumbled onto the Baluchi women's clothing section. "You not interested in that,"

Reza said emphatically, indicating the row of stores which displayed the colorfully embroidered crimson vests and black pants these tribal women wear. But of course I was.

As a Baluchi man sat spinning blood red yarn, I slowly looked over the locally made merchandise. In this part of Iran, veils were traditionally used as accessories, not as coverings. On the street we had seen a few Arabic women from countries on the south side of the Persian Gulf. They were completely hidden, including their faces. The Baluch women, however, still show off their finery, and their faces, just like they did before the revolution.

In one of the bazaar's hallways we passed a well dressed Baluchi male dwarf, and Reza said, in English, "He should be in circus". Later we saw several beggars, including one terribly twisted tiny young man asking for alms.

Walking back to the hotel to get the car, we went by a street vendor selling cigarettes and matches. His friend came up from behind him and exclaimed emphatically, "Look, a foreigner". Twenty-five years ago these men may have been among the children who would harmlessly throw pebbles at me and yell "Unclean" as they ran away. It had been an innocent game for them then, and it was amusing for me. Today it is just "Foreigner" and some stares from middle-aged men.

The small pine and tamarisk trees which in the 1970s lined the road to the airport have grown into adults. There is a security gate at the entrance to the facility now, and the usually vacant campground which was once nearby has been converted into a multi-storied apartment housing complex.

Zahedan's airport had been enlarged, but the spartan waiting room of yesterday hadn't changed much. It did contain a glass case showing photographs of local war victims. Next to family photos of smiling faces were pictures of bloody and blank eyed corpses, no longer grinning. Reza stood staring into the case for a long time until I said I was ready to go.

On the way back into town, we turned off on the road to Pakistan. Passing a security checkpoint, we drove by high brick walls behind which garbage strewn industrial storage yards were hidden. "I think this is where the nightclub was that we came to every week," I said as we drove on. There were no signs of the building, however, and Reza reminded me that nightclubs were outlawed after the revolution, and most had been destroyed.

Returning to the security post, the guard asked what we were doing. Reza explained and then wondered, even though the soldier didn't look old enough, if he remembered the nightclub. "My beard may be graying," the man said sarcastically, "but I'm not that old."

In the center of a large traffic circle nearby, an enormous colored street map of Zahedan was displayed. Surprisingly, it looked very similar to the master plan I had laid out for the city long ago. The community was a much bigger place now, but its development seemed to have followed the general direction I had recommended.

With time to waste, we went looking for the train depot. The rail line from Pakistan still extends to Zahedan, but the long anticipated linkage with the Iranian tracks at Kerman hasn't yet happened. Stopping to take a look at the station, we found the high fence locked, and no locomotives visible.

As we headed back to the government office building, six camouflage painted military helicopters flew over, and Reza quickly identified them for me. Having arrived early for the interview with the chief engineer, we sat in a large waiting room which contained two desks occupied by male secretaries. There were also eight chairs for visitors, one live potted plant, and three of the plastic variety. No computer monitor was visible, even though one had been seen in another office.

Running a little late, Mr. Birjandi returned from his meeting with the governor and immediately entered his office through a thickly padded door. After awhile he telephoned out that he wanted to see in writing what I wished to discuss. So Reza scribbled down something about comparing city planning now and then, a subject which I assumed couldn't be too threatening. Within a few minutes we were shown into the chief engineer's office.

Sitting behind a large desk backed by filing cabinets full of folders, the bearded Mr. Birjandi was a heavy-set man in his mid-30s. Wearing a sport coat but no tie, since they are considered western and are thus "taboo", he had a photograph of Khomeini and other Iranian leaders prominently displayed on his desk.

Six black chairs for guests were arranged on either side of a low glass table and a plate of cookies lay on it. For a few seconds Mr. Birjandi studied the photograph of the master plan I had done for Zahedan as I informed him it was prepared for a future city of 100,000. "There are 420,000 people here now," he said without emotion, "but including immigrants there are almost 600,000". Even taking into account the Persian tendency to greatly exaggerate, that was some change from the town I lived in. "But, there are still only two movie theaters, just like when you were here," he laughed.

Reza asked if he recognized the location of the low-income housing project I laid out in Zahedan from the picture I had of it. "I think that it is in the city's entertainment district that we are developing now," he replied. "So I don't think the project was ever built." They both nodded politely but said nothing when I insisted it had been, since I had seen the walls going up in 1973.

Innocently, I asked where a desert city of this size obtains its water, but that question was ignored with sincere silence. About my inquiry if Mr. Birjandi knew any of the professional men I had worked with, including the one from his own hometown of Birjand, he said, "I was very young then". To my question as to how many engineers work for the office now, Reza abruptly interrupted and asked, "Why do you want to know that?". They finally both agreed on "Many".

Then I was the recipient of questions. What did I think about how Zahedan had turned out? "It is very big, but from what I have seen, it seems greatly improved." How had things changed? "There were many poor people then, and now there are fewer. Only four streets were paved twenty-five years ago, and now almost all of them are. Zahedan was a small place with maybe 100 cars in it, and now it has many."

I asked for a map of the city but was told I would have to get one from the mayor's office. While country maps were generally available in book stores and other places, city maps were hard to obtain. Reza had a large, detailed highway map of Iran but either couldn't get or didn't want street maps of the cities we had traveled to earlier. He knew his away around those communities as long as we stayed on the typical tourist routes, but once we got off of that often traveled path, he immediately became lost. It was then that he constantly stopped people to ask for directions.

After a man brought us tea, Mr. Birjandi showed me a plan for the future city and asked what I thought of it. "It seems to be good, but planning for the automobile is very difficult." Did I have any ideas for the Zahedan of the future? "In America, some cities have begun to go away from the car because building roads is so expensive. Buses and other methods of transportation are used to move people, but it is very difficult." When leaving, I gave the chief engineer my business card and said he should call me if he ever came to the U.S.

A small, out-of-the-way restaurant had been recommended to us for its excellent ground meat kebab. The suggestion was a good one, and it reminded me of the dingy establishment on Zahedan's main street where we often ate Friday lunch years ago. That place had no atmosphere, just men yelling to be fed quickly, but it served wonderful food.

This restaurant had 8 or 9 small metal tables, an all-male clientele, and a large poster of the Kaaba in Mecca on the wall. As we ate, I suggested that we leave at 6 a.m. for the coast. Reza replied softly, "The hotel don't serve breakfast at 6. But whatever you want."

After a sweaty nap we returned to my former home so I could get some pictures and a man of about 40 stopped to watch. He said he had lived in the alley for almost 20 years, and I showed him the photographs I had from before. Pointing out one from 1972 which had a taxi in it, I indicated that on this day another taxi occupied the exact same spot in the alley. I also showed him the snowfall picture, and his mouth dropped open in amazement.

When I explained who I was and what I was doing, he said with great sincerity that a flood had wiped out the entire area long ago. All of the homes had been rebuilt, and as he spoke the differences between the pictures I had and the reality in front of me became clearly obvious. The present structure I thought was our home had a brick exterior instead of a mud plaster finish. The width of the new house was less, the little store I noticed before had been built, and many other things about the block were altered. In the dark the previous night I had seen a house, but it wasn't our house.

Showing him a photograph of a teenager who often hung out at our house, I asked the man if he knew what had become of the boy. After much consideration, and talking about how old the youngster would be now, he said he thought it was Ali. "Today he lives in Kerman and is about 40 years old," the man said.

"His aunt Fatima was our cook," I added, and he nodded approvingly, but knew nothing of what had become of her.

As we slowly returned to the hotel, I was disappointed but not discouraged about what had happened to my former home. Time changes a lot of things and my past experience in Zahedan was one of them. We encountered a 4:30 traffic jam along the way, and it took us several lights to get through an intersection. When Reza parked the car, the black shadow of a cat running along the top of a wall could be seen on the beige bricks at the back of the lot.

Down an alley near the hotel, a large tan colored dog was barking frantically. A dozen small Baluchi children had circled a parked bus, taunting the animal which hid underneath it. The poor creature eventually emerged, and the children quickly retreated, but then the dog timidly returned to its safe spot.

During a dusktime walk by myself, high school aged boys were seen playing street soccer with a very small ball and tiny nets as goals. In the descending darkness, bright lights and tri-colored lit water illuminated a large traffic circle. A nearby park had a small amusement area with rides from the 1950s. Children could sit in swans, swing in rotating chairs or spin in teacups to be thrilled.

Six young, head shaved soldiers on their way to barracks joined me as I walked back toward the hotel. They wanted to know what I thought of their country and which was better, Tehran or Zahedan? They also asked what the exchange rate was for currency, and how much my trip had cost. When I told them truthfully, one said in disbelief, "That is not possible".

For dinner, Reza and I drove far out into the ink-black countryside, trying to find a garden restaurant which several people had suggested. Along the way we passed the city's entertainment area where long colored lights radiated from the center of a moving Ferris wheel. I may not have remembered exactly where the low-income housing project I designed was, but it certainly wasn't in this very new part of town.

We drove underneath a highway overpass which was under construction as part of a ring road being built around the community. From on top of a small rise nearby we could see the night lights of Zahedan spreading out for miles in every direction. The view was in no way similar to what I had seen when I first glimpsed the small city out a dusty bus window in 1971.

In the pitch dark we had to stop often to ask directions. Regularly spaced rows of lights off to our right looked promising, but there didn't appear to be a way to get to them. However, a road construction worker resting in a small tent told us to ignore the dirt pile put up to block traffic to the area. We followed his advice and eventually found a large formal garden, part of which was the restaurant.

There were 50 or more raised platforms on which carpets and pillows were spread out for customers. A large pool contained ducks that were flapping around, and a huge screen looked like movies must be shown on some nights. When a waiter came to take our order, he told us the restaurant was two years old.

A group of 60 black wrapped women arrived in buses and filled two entire rows of the dining platforms. Reza asked one of them what the occasion was, and she replied that they were from all over the country and were in town for a conference on women.

Kids ran around the outdoor dining area, playing tag and screaming just like they had done in the nightclub 25 years ago. As they shouted in glee trying to avoid being "it", a sanitary glove slowly floated through the air. Caught in the soft breeze of a cool, moon lit night, the glove descended in gentle waves near the restaurant's very long cooking preparation table.

While eating our meal we talked again about what time to get started in the morning. It was going to be a long trip and neither of us had ever been over the road before. Reza said, "Hotel serve breakfast at 7. We eat then. Leave by 7:30." I didn't want to argue so kept quiet.

Going South Again

After breakfast, it took Reza thirty minutes to get organized and check out of the hotel. Then he surprisingly announced we needed gas. Fortunately, we stumbled across a station on the way out of town. Unfortunately, only those who drove government-made Peykon automobiles could use it. While Reza went off to argue with the manager, two boys tried to sell me some socks. "Real cheap," one said, showing off several pairs enclosed in plastic wrappers. Reza returned fuming and mumbled that the man offered to let him have one gallon.

We were told that a station near downtown would sell gas to anyone. For twenty minutes we drove a few blocks, asked directions, went a few more blocks, and stopped someone else. The city's one-way street system was confusing, and without a map it was difficult to know where to go. Finally we found the station, waited in line for awhile, and got out of town just about nine.

We left behind a community with multi-story apartment buildings and huge construction cranes in constant operation, sprawling residential and commercial developments and even a university. It was a city I didn't know and probably wouldn't want to live in.

Rosita Forbes had headed north following her visit to Duzdab many years ago. Traveling in a truck full of pilgrims on their way to the holy city of Mashad she observed, "It is the tea habit which reduces average progress to eight or nine miles an hour. As the drivers never go to sleep if they can help it, driving red-eyed and half demented by exhaustion for anything up to seventy-two hours on end, they insist on stopping at every tea-khane(house) to relieve a thirst engendered by opium or cocaine."

We went south over a paved two-lane road and quickly overtook a pickup truck which had a large gun and some young soldiers riding in the back. They waved as we rushed passed. Heading in the direction of town was another pickup, this one with two small camels laying in the bed.

Enormous power towers followed the highway and some large black tents of Baluchi nomads were scattered across a desolate desert valley floor. Reza could drive at 50 m.p.h. or more because the road was in good condition except where the pavement ended in a few short construction zones. Then we had to slowly bounce along over a rocky dirt surface.

Via a somewhat different route, in early 1972 I had made this same trip in a Land Rover with Sarkis and three other men from the provincial engineering office. Then, only a graded track ran south from Zahedan to the desert oasis town of Iranshahr. After that, even the rough road evaporated in storm flooded riverbeds north of the coast. We were lucky to make 5 miles an hour for much of the way through the mountains driving along cliffside paths running with water. That journey, which was filled with heavy rainfall and many discomforts, had taken us two full days to reach the village of Charbahar on the Gulf of Oman. Now, despite our late start, Reza and I were trying to do it while the sun was still in the sky.

Near the small town of Khash a major military installation, including numerous three-story dormitories, had been built in the last 25 years. The city of Iranshahr, always known as one of the hottest places in Iran, had grown considerably. There was a fancy landscaped boulevard cutting through town and a new mosque which was painted in day-glo Disneyland-like colors.

The scrollwork on the ceiling of the hotel dining room in Iranshahr we found for lunch was also painted in similar bright garish tones. While eating, Reza looked exhausted, and I asked if he could go on. He replied completely without conviction, "We must keep going".

But before we did he had to pray, then find a few small items in the bazaar to purchase. He had to ask three people how to get out of town, and thankfully the last one waved at us to follow his sporty vehicle. He led us to the right road, and pointed out a nearby gas station. The attendant, however, said nonchalantly that they were closed.

Cursing to himself, Reza decided we could do without more fuel. The tank was still half full and the auxiliary supply of natural gas was a backup. At the security checkpoint on the edge of town though, the policeman recommended we fill up. "There is nothing between here and Charbahar except for some small jugs of gas," he told us with a smile.

So back through Iranshahr we drove to the only other gas station in town. Of course, it was on the other side of the city. As beads of perspiration covered his quickly crimson-turning face, Reza quietly but emphatically called damnation down on this place and its people. He stopped his litany of swear words only to ask for directions.

A six car deep line waiting for fuel greeted us, along with a young soldier holding a rifle to keep order. Like most stations we stopped at, this one had many of its pumps out of operation. Having to wait to buy gas, if it was available at all, could obviously result in frustrated customers, especially in a country with enormous crude oil supplies. Security precautions, apparently, were sometimes considered necessary.

Once Reza topped off the tank and we departed, almost one hour had been used in our search for fuel. The sun was moving toward the horizon as we drove out of Iranshahr again.

Ridge after ridge of ragged edged gray mountains loomed in the distance in front of us. Pools of water from a recent rain were alongside the pavement, and small ponds had formed in usually dry riverbeds. A tribal woman was walking along the highway, carrying a large metal pan full of dishes on her head. Eventually, the twisting road weaved into the mountains, chiseled rock faces of brown, red and green reflected in the afternoon light.

We stopped for a soda at a roadside camp where a Baluchi highway repair crew had set up their tents and cabins. The old wrinkly-faced tribal men, wearing long white beards, turbans and flowing robes, looked like they had gathered for some sort of "Santa Claus in pajamas" convention. Women in colorfully embroidered clothes held the small hands of barefoot toddlers while sticking their heads out of crudely made wooden shacks to look at us. This was the Iran I remembered best.

Passing through a small village, we had to drive around a very recent wreck. Two pickup trucks had collided head on, pushing their cabs back into the beds. Both vehicles looked like stomped on aluminum cans. The victims had been removed from the crumpled metal, but it didn't appear that anyone could have survived.

The frequent, very severe traffic accidents we saw throughout the country certainly left an impression. Erratic driving habits, high speeds, and the great increase in the number of vehicles from the 1970s was obviously taking a toll on human lives.

For almost 100 miles the highway rose and fell in the mountains. We went through small villages where goats wandered freely, donkeys rested their heads on each other, and thin cows looked up at passing vehicles. Dark skinned tribal men and boys strolled along the road's shoulder or chatted with one another while squatting near the pavement. At one place in the fading sunlight, a soccer match was being played on a dirt field carved out of a riverbed.

As we drove on, having heard the cassette several times already, Reza wanted to talk. He asked why we didn't have children, or even adopt them? "Having children is life," he said enthusiastically. "What you do with your time? Who take care of you when you old? Who bury you? Who wash your grave like I washed my father's?" I replied with vague uncertainties, trying not to question the differences in our lifestyles.

With late afternoon shadows lengthening, the mountain rock went from hard edged to soft tones of color. Donkeys were used for agriculture in small fields, but so were tractors. We passed one pickup loaded with caged chickens; all that could be seen were their fluffy white feathers sticking out between metal grates.

Frequent police checkpoints, at which Reza would always have to explain what a taxi from Tehran was doing in rural Baluchistan province, slowed us down. At one stop, the smiling officer wanted to see my passport and asked, "What do you think of America?".

Trying not to be antagonistic, I replied, "I don't know. What do you think of it?"

He said chuckling, "Mr. Clinton has problems".

Later, while maneuvering though more mountain passes, Reza complained bitterly about the last part of my itinerary. "I never make this trip again. They pay same here as in Tehran. So why I come here? Some other guys turn trip down. They know roads bad. I never come to Zahedan or Charbahar again. Should be two vehicles with two tourists for trip. That way, one breaks down, other can continue. I know Americans like adventure, but I never do this again."

As we drove through the mountains along an almost deserted road, I wondered if we could reach flat land before nightfall. Like a burning orange slicing through the deepening blue sky, the sun was approaching the horizon. As it did, an almost full moon simultaneously appeared high in the sky. We emerged onto the desert floor just before darkness settled in.

For the first time, the distant sea could be felt. We still had one hundred miles to go, but our skin became clammy, our hair stringy, and the night took on a different odor as the Gulf air consumed us.

Driving between 60 and 70 m.p.h., but at least with the head lights on, Reza was intent on getting to Charbahar as fast as possible. Lightning was flashing over the mountains to our backs, but the desert was under a star-filled sky lit by the moon. The car's lights revealed an occasional jewel-eyed, bushy tailed fox running across the road as we sped along.

Passing several bridge-crossed riverbeds, I looked for the one near the village of Negur which had been swollen with flood water in 1972. Then we had been forced to turn back to the coast because there was no way of getting over or through the fast flowing torrent. On this dry, peaceful night we just kept driving.

On the outskirts of Charbahar, a service station attendant told Reza he needed a permission slip from local government officials before he could buy gas. Mumbling to himself, Reza asked if I knew where to go. I pointed toward the water and said, "Head that way".

The city's main street stretched arrow straight for miles out from the bay around which the community had been founded. The wide shop-lined boulevard ended at the water's edge next to a pizza parlor and cargo ship-like hotel. Every room was an individual container, and each of the four decks was outlined with long strings of very bright fluorescent lights. It looked as if it belonged in Las Vegas.

The nearby government-run hotel we were staying at had been under construction when I first visited Charbahar in 1971. At that time it was surrounded by sand and the empty oil drums used by the dozen or so small fishing boats which bobbed in the bay. Now a lamp-lit, land-scaped waterfront park was between the hotel and the Gulf of Oman.

Once our road weary eyes had adjusted to the hotel's interior light, the place looked shabby and poorly maintained. The carpets were stained with many cigarette burns, the plaster walls were chipped and dirty, and broken fixtures hadn't been repaired. But at least the rooms had window air-conditioners that worked well.

First light the next morning revealed to a lone American visitor a fleet of 20 or so colorfully painted large fishing boats in the water across the street from the hotel. These boats, which were either tied to a long, enormous pier or anchored in the bay, were much bigger than those from 25 years ago. On the sandy beach, fishermen were working with nets next to several palm frond shanties which still occupied a small part of the waterfront. Garbage, humidity and the smells of life were everywhere as Charbahar was beginning another day.

Next to the Gulf, the small bathhouse where I had once showered under a stream of salt water was still standing but looked deserted. The historic government officials' house which had been built by the British during the last century was gone. A seaside mosque of Pakistani inspiration, a local landmark in 1971, continued to exist, but now was crowded between newer buildings.

Veil wearing pre-teen girls were making their way to school before 7:00, walking over short bridges which crossed the shallow sandy riverbed that had once cut the community in half. The two block long former bazaar area was mostly abandoned now, its single story concrete buildings permanently locked behind metal doors. A naked boy of two waddled along in front of the vacant shops, his brother and sister watching out for him.

The area near the bazaar had once been where most of Charbahar's poor Baluch families lived in palm frond shanties. Brick and steel homes have replaced them now, although many of these structures did not appear to be well maintained.

After locating a small, bleached-white mosque I had photographed on my first trip to the village, I looked to take another picture from the exact same spot. The domed mosque had stood alone back then, but now a crudely built brick wall and some scraggly vegetation obscured the view.

As I was leaving the mosque, a Baluchi man motioned me over to his nearby house. I showed him the earlier picture, and his college-aged son also came to take a look. The man called out for his wife to see the photograph and they stood looking at it, grinning at the passage of time.

A few minutes later, as I was walking back toward the hotel, the son tracked me down on his bicycle. With slow, deliberate words, he asked for an English lesson. Agreeing, I told him, "Come by the hotel at 6:00 tonight. No, make it 6:30, that way we will be certain to be back from Negur."

Hoping to find some clue about a 10 year old boy I had photographed on the beach in 1971, I asked two middle-aged fisherman if they knew him. Working on a boat which was almost on the same spot where I had taken the photograph of the boy, they looked at the picture of a smiling child sitting atop an oil drum and shook their heads "no".

By seven I was taking the first of several showers on this humid and sweat filled day. I had to admire my long-ago ability to remain in this climate for two weeks. I may have been only 22 years old then, but the weather was draining.

At breakfast Reza wearily asked what I wanted to do, and I said, "This morning, visit the bazaar and the new hotel. Then I want to go to Negur this afternoon. At 6:30 a boy is coming to practice his English."

"What boy?" he shot back with anger. "They must not be speaking with foreigners. It's not good. I will speak with him."

Trying to hold my temper in check, I pointed out that he hadn't objected in Shiraz or Kerman. "It was not good then also. And why you want go to Negur?"

"Because I spent a day there before, and I want to see it again. It was just a small Baluch village of huts and camels, and I want to see what has happened to it." With a sullen attitude, he ended the conversation by telling me he had already made arrangements to meet two of his friends who lived in town.

These men worked at the customs port and invited us into their air-conditioned office. As we entered, everyone in the room stood up, handshakes were exchanged all around, and then their interrupted casual conversation resumed. Soon orange sodas were served and the entire episode reminded me of the daily Iranian bureaucratic life I had once lived.

Reza explained that I wanted to see the bazaar, and his friends encouraged us to visit the new duty-free shops instead. When I asked what the population of Charbahar was, since it had been about 2,000 in the 1970s but now was obviously much larger, one man guessed 50,000 to 60,000 people.

Reza's friends arranged for a young office worker from Mashad to show us the free trade zone which was still under development. As we left the customs building, I tried handing an animal sticker to a small Baluch girl who was sitting in the shade outside. She recoiled in fear, screaming her fright. Her mother, however, accepted it with a laugh and a "thank you".

The free trade zone was a long series of 3 and 4 story shopping mall-type structures being built on top of a hill which overlooks the existing town. This "new" Charbahar will also include an office complex and 5-star hotel our guide told us. He said that a few thousand shops selling duty free goods should be open within two years.

Some stores were already doing business, displaying shoes and tea, electronic devices and TVs, refrigerators, washing machines, toys, clothes and many other things. These shops were small spaces of a few hundred square feet or less in size, but were jammed with merchandise. Most of the stores, however, were vacant, awaiting future occupants. The overall architecture was typical mall-like angles, glass walls and tile floors. As we walked along from building to building, I noted that no computers seemed to be for sale. "We have them," Reza insisted, but I didn't see any.

Reza was very interested in shopping and eventually bought a pair of tiny shoes for his youngest son, but there were several more things he wanted. He needed another pair of shoes, a backpack for his older boy to take to school, and some cologne for himself, so I sat and waited for him to look in shop after shop, comparing prices. While sitting quietly by myself, a storekeeper approached and wanted to talk. After telling him my story, I asked about his. "I have a shop on the main street in town, but am moving here shortly. After 6 years there, this is a bigger, better place."

Hundreds of mostly Baluch men were building the complex, which was far from completed. Around the site, dozens of women from Africa and the Gulf states squatted in what shade was available, waiting for their laborer husbands to finish the day's work. These women were dressed in thin, colorful fabrics, not obeying the modesty laws at all.

Twenty-five years ago, the future of the tiny fishing village of Charbahar had been undecided. Maybe, the government said, it would have an economy focused on water-based tourism. Or possibly a major military installation would be built. Or the fishing industry might be enhanced. Or perhaps a winter palace for the shah would be located in the area.

In today's developing future, however, people are expected to fly in from Tehran and shop, shop, shop. That approach has worked well at another isolated Iranian free trade zone, so why not here? Minneapolis may have its Mall of America, I thought, but on a hill overlooking the once isolated fishing community of Charbahar, the new Persian bazaar is under construction, and a local economy based on consumerism is being created.

As the three of us walked in the dust between buildings, a motorcycle slowly came up from behind and tried to pass. As it did, it hit a bump and clipped our guide, who fell to the ground with a thud. The driver stopped, and for a few seconds loud words were exchanged. But then all became friendly expressions of concern and pleasant hugs. When the motorcycle left, our host said, "He's a Baluch," in derisive explanation of the driver's motoring skills.

After leaving the free trade zone, Reza and I went looking for a highly recommended seafood restaurant on the current main street of town. Reza only had to ask two men before he found it. Many nearby shops appeared to have been permanently closed, and it didn't take too much imagination to think that this second generation of Charbahar would soon be history. Just as the former fishing village huddled around the bay had been eclipsed by a retail strip stretching out into the desert, soon the modern duty free bazaar on the hill will replace it.

While looking over the menu, Reza warned me that fish was danger-ous at this time of year because the weather was still hot. But I had it anyway, and the taste was delicious.

During our meal he asked, "Why you not tell me on way here you want to go to Negur?"

"Because it was dark when we passed it last night."

"But is 60 miles here to there and back."

"It is my trip," I said in muted anger at his lack of interest in what I wanted to do.

Before our naptime, he began to whine again about my proposed plans for the afternoon. "I must call company to get permission to go to Negur. It is out of route. Plus is problem with gas. Where I get it? It is 60 extra miles."

"Where will you get it tomorrow before going back to Zahedan?" I asked in frustrated exasperation.

"That is other problem. Maybe on way. I call company and find out what they say. We meet at 3:30 and see. O.K.?"

"We must go for the gas," Reza said when he appeared in the lobby ten minutes later than arranged. "If it is, we go to Negur. If not, there is problem." I decided to forget the whole idea and watch harbor activity instead. I didn't want to miss the promised English lesson as well as Negur in the likely situation that we would spend several hours search-ing for gas.

Shirtless, bronzed skinned fishermen were standing in the bay paint-ing the bows of boats while on the beach men strung nets to dry in the sun. As we sat and watched, Reza said there wasn't anything for a family to do here except shop for a few hours. That was certainly true for the present, I replied, but the future may see some changes.

Along the pier, a dozen or so large fishing vessels were tied up, their crews busy at work. The captain of one boat told us they could be out to sea for up to three weeks, but, he said, if the weather gets rough, they quickly return to port. "That is much different than when I was here before," I told Reza. "The boats then were very small, open ones which could only go out fishing for a day."

Later, while we ate ice cream in the lobby of the "cargo" hotel, the manager offered us newspapers from Tehran. Scanning the one in English, I saw a saber-rattling story about the problems with the Taliban government of Afghanistan and their murder of the Iranian diplomats. Over the next several weeks, however, the potential conflict between the two countries would subside without further violence.

Another article in the newspaper discussed tourism in the country. It stated that because of Iran's recently weak economy, an increase in the number of tourists was desired.

The extra money would certainly be helpful. As an Islamic state, Iran operates on a balanced budget because it doesn't believe in paying interest on debt. Its economy is largely dependent upon oil sales, and the falling price of crude oil has forced the ruling clerics to make some very tough decisions. If they want to continue to provide the services the exploding population has come to expect, more revenues will be required from things like tourism.

Back on the beach, as we sat watching another blazing ball of red descend into the sea to end the day, Reza asked me to fill out a tour company questionnaire about the trip. He also wondered what I would do when I returned to Tehran. "Probably go to the big white monument the shah built for the 2,500 year celebration of the Persian monarchy."

"Elevator there usually broken. Closed most of time," he told me.

"What time we meet for dinner?" he wanted to know as we returned to the hotel, apparently having forgotten about my evening visitor. "Seven will be fine," I answered, assuming a 30 minute English lesson would be satisfactory.

At 6:15 two freshly bathed Baluchi men in their cleanest tribal clothes appeared in the lobby. As soon as we sat down to begin our conversation in English, a hotel employee took a seat near us. If he could understand "How old are you?" or "How many brothers and sisters do you have?", it was not obvious.

The man I had met in the morning was 20 and from a family of seven. His friend was 21 and had eight siblings. Both were natives of Charbahar and were teachers with the Service Corps. In the shah's time, all high school and college graduates who didn't enter the military had to devote two years of volunteer duty in the fields of education, health care or development. Both young men and women would work in villages and towns throughout the country to teach or help out in other ways. The program continues, but as I had been told in Shiraz, only men have to participate now.

Both of these Baluch men wanted to become rich, especially the older one. They thought they could do so by owning shops in the free trade zone. They still lived with their parents but hoped to marry in 5 or 6 years and move out then. By that time they wanted to be driving luxury Japanese automobiles.

I wondered if they thought there were risks in the future of the free trade zone. "Risk" was a word they didn't understand and had to look up in a dictionary, but they still didn't catch the meaning of what I was saying.

"Perhaps people don't come, or they only come to Charbahar once and never return. Or maybe they come and don't buy. That is risk for the merchant. He buys many things but can not sell them." They shook their heads in acknowledgement but I wasn't certain they understood. As we talked, different men from the hotel took turns coming to sit near us, eavesdropping on our conversation.

Reza appeared at 6:30, sat down with a very weary look on his face, and spoke sharply to one of the men. I did my best to ignore him until, as he rose to leave, he asked what time I wanted dinner. "Seven," I blurted out in an angry tone while continuing my discussion with the men.

They said they wanted to learn English because it would help them in their future commercial endeavors. Books and cassettes could be used to practice, they indicated, but weren't as good as actually talking to someone. Only about once a month, however, did an English-speaking tourist whom they could converse with visit Charbahar.

I asked what the population of the community was, and one estimated 20,000, the other 40,000. "What do you think it is?" they wondered with a laugh. I told them I had no idea, but that it was about 2,000 when I was here long ago.

"It better now because of free trade zone?" they wanted to know.

"When I was here before, women carried water in jugs on their heads. Most people lived in shacks then. Houses are better now, and water is piped everywhere. So, yes, people are better off, and the free trade zone will probably help in the future."

At 6:45 Reza showed up again and asked the men their names and what work they did. As he jotted notes, my obviously nervous visitors made motions to leave. "We'll continue until 7:00," I said angrily, but that was only good for five more minutes. One of the men apprehensively looked at his watch every few seconds and finally said they had to go.

After a chilly and uncomfortable 20 minutes spent mindlessly watching the television in the hotel lobby, Reza and I went to drink a soda in silence at the pizza parlor on the beach. Then I excused myself, saying I wanted to read my book. "And I will write," he replied. Whether it was a report for the government, or the travel company, or personal notes, I didn't ask. My knowledge of Iranian secret security forces in the 1970s had left me uncertain this time about the difference between innocent concern on his part and possible police meddling.

Back in my room, I anxiously concluded that I didn't want to press my luck any further. My unappreciated solo walks and abnormal travel itinerary had taken their toll on Reza. I certainly didn't want him asking to see my notes on the trip if he became even more annoyed with me.

While not containing anything special, what I considered interesting about modern Iran would have been very hard to explain.

I also remembered something from the shah's time. A European woman had been arrested and accused of being a "communist" because she was caught taking pictures of things tourists usually weren't interested in. She was held for trial, and the possible sentence was severe.

I decided to keep my mouth shut about Reza's rude, intrusive behavior and the motives behind it. I had a plane to catch in the morning and didn't want anything to interfere with that.

A View Across The Gulf

By sunrise, my paranoia about being detained for police questioning had disappeared. I finished my notes, packed my bags, and got ready to leave the country.

In the hotel dining room, the waiter asked what I wanted. But every Iranian breakfast I had eaten had consisted of the same things: flat bread, cheese, butter, jam, a fried egg and tea. "Watermelon?" I wondered hopefully, but there was none.

Reza went off to the County Administrator's office to see about gas while I sat on a park bench watching the bay. In the water, fishermen were scraping the hull of a boat, preparing it for painting. Further out on a point of land, three large round oil tanks and a ship of cargo-container moving cranes covered a spot where once only sand had been.

About where I was sitting, surrounded now by new development and immense population growth, I had sat alone in 1971 and made up new words to Barry McGuire's "Eve of Destruction" to pass the time. Two weeks in Charbahar then, and another week in early 1972, had shown me everything about the place. I got to know the mayor well and learned a lot about myself, both in sickness and in crisis. Now I was waiting to leave a community, and a country that in many respects had completely changed.

One aspect of Iranian life that was still the same, however, was the fear of different opinions, of new ideas, of criticism. Control and subservience were what the shah and his government demanded, and they extracted it through a climate of fear. They created a fear of the secret police force SAVAK, a fear of being falsely imprisoned, a fear of the unknown.

Many in the present government want to follow that same philosophy of ruling through fear and intimidation. They, however, have to
consider today's rapid advancements in technology along with the generally greater availability of information in their attempts to keep power
while maintaining their view of Islamic moral standards. While in the
future some moderation of their fundamentalist viewpoints may be
economically necessary if Iran is to once again become a nation in good
standing in the world, the clash in the country between demands for
greater individual freedoms and upholding religious beliefs continues
for now.

For those Iranian political leaders who believe there should be moral
and spiritual limits on freedom, their solution is to ban much of what is
modern by labeling it western, and thus equating it with evil. Whether
that approach can succeed remains to be seen. Many of today's rulers
appear afraid of the rapidly evolving future, but that is simply life at the
end of our 20th century.

Rosita Forbes reflected on a similar Iranian internal conflict with
past history and an emerging future in her book. She wrote, "In Persia
there has been no gradual mental and social development. Tehran has
leaped a thousand years, and there is this entire period of time between
the graduates of the American College intent on chemistry and com-
merce and those members of their families who have remained
enclosed within the blind mud walls of some patriarchal village. The
conflict between the two points of view is often excessively bitter, for
there has been no gradual evolution between A.D. 930 and 1930."

While the country's current spiritual tug-of-war continues, the people of Iran remain hospitable toward visitors. Economic and population pressures have forced some changes from the way things were
formerly done. Bargaining isn't very important any longer. Social cour-
tesies are not as prevalent as they once were. Iranians from all walks of
life, however, remain very friendly to the traveler.

At the same time, most Americans are terrified of Iran and its people. Our government says that it "warns all U.S. citizens against travel to Iran, which remains dangerous because of the generally anti-American atmosphere and Iranian government hostility to the U.S. government". Washington, unlike Reza's friend who drives foreigners for a living, does not differentiate between people and their governments.

Many of the perceptions our two countries have of each other are totally wrong. It would be easy to superficially look at Iran as one, huge co-ed convent of black shrouded nuns where liquor is banned, but it isn't like that at all. Reza told me that Iranians are warned by their government about the U.S. being dangerous for them to visit. Our shared fear of getting to know one another has led to many wrong conclusions.

When I first went to Iran, no one I knew had any knowledge of the country. But events of the last 25 years, from the hostage taking to the "Great Satan" proclamations of Ayatollah Khomeini to the death threats against author Salman Rushdie have left their mark on us. We conveniently forget, however, that it was our navy that shot down an Iranian commercial jet in 1988, killing 290. We ignore our role in the Iran-Iraq war and the enormous personal tragedies it resulted in.

We also don't acknowledge Iran's long held desire to control its own destiny free from outside interference. It was the C.I.A. who kept the shah in power in the early 1950s, not the people of Iran. It was our government which encouraged the last king to buy billions of dollars worth of military equipment in the 1970s while he largely ignored the growing plight of the millions of poor people in the country.

Today, thousands of U.S. troops are stationed in the Persian Gulf area. They are there to protect our nation's middle eastern oil supplies. In the view of some Iranians though, they are also there to impose American values on the countries of the region. The outside interference in Iran's internal affairs, which Reza Shah feared when he talked to Rosita Forbes 70 years ago, still exists.

Before I took this trip, most of my friends made comments about how I would be killed. Those weren't jokes; they were being serious. But the reality of present-day Iran for me was completely different. Americans' views of the country may be one of a hostile, dangerous place. What I found instead was a nation of people that are still friendly and willing to go out of their way to help a stranger.

Back on the Charbahar beach, the heat and humidity of the morning were rising. In front of the hotel, two women were loading box after box of carefully packed goods into a small pickup truck. The duty-free merchandise would be taken to Tehran to be resold at a substantial profit.

A fair skinned, wavy-haired young fisherman with sand-covered bare feet sat down next to me. After a few silent minutes, he asked simply "Pakistani?"

"American."

"I am a Baluch," he said proudly.

Reza returned and announced as we loaded up the car that he had been able to secure permission to buy a tank full of gas in town. Plus, he said excitedly, he could get another along the way to Zahedan. He was returning there to buy pants and shirts for his kids and some perfume for his wife. His friends had told him the cheapest prices were in Zahedan, not Chahbahar. So he wouldn't take the Iranshahr-Kerman cutoff but instead drive one hundred miles out of his way to save some money.

As it cut across the desert near the Gulf of Oman, the road we took to the distant airport was being widened into a four lane boulevard. At one spot a mini-bus had broken down and was parked by the side of the pavement. While the driver worked to repair the vehicle, all of the passengers were sitting in the shade cast by a small willowy tree.

A small sign near them pointed out a narrow gravel and dirt path which wandered off toward the distant village of Nikshahr. It was over that route that I had first left Charbahar in 1971 in a sick, exhausted condition. I had to rely on a jug of water to retain liquids inside of me and to keep my fever in check. The bus ride had been a bouncing affair over mountain passes and through dry streambeds. There was no road really, just a trail. It had taken the bus almost twenty-four hours to reach Iranshahr with a late night stop somewhere in the desert for a little sleep. Today, by the new road, Reza could do the same trip in a few hours.

Outside the airport terminal, a large sign read "Industry-Services-Trade-Transit CHARBAHAR". Inside, even though ancient x-ray machines were available to inspect luggage, the old, personal way of frisking people was also used. A security guard demanded I open my bag and show him all of my clothes, including the dirty ones. A soldier asked me to remove the batteries from my camera so he could look at them. Then he wanted to know what I had taken pictures of, and I was glad I could understand him and say "mosque, people" in Persian.

The two business women from the hotel arrived in the pickup truck with all their containers of china, glassware and other things. They slowly handed over each box at the check-in counter but had far too many to take on the plane for free. In desperation they asked Reza to claim some of the goods as his, but he told them he wasn't taking the flight.

While we sat in the terminal, Reza reminded me that my friends thought I would be killed in Iran. "The man that picks you up at airport thinks Iran is dangerous? He will see when you return it is not." His final words to me were, "I hope you had good time and everything was O.K. If there were bad things, just forget them."

When the 707 without a first class section took off over the Gulf of Oman, the veiled female cabin attendants made the standard announcements in Persian and English. As we slowly banked to head west, I could look forward to finding a sign in the domestic terminal in Tehran which read, "In future, Islam will destroy satanic sovereignty of the west." However, the athletic shoe wearing passengers who were waiting to pick up boxes of consumer goods off the conveyor belt appeared to be ignoring that statement.

While the plane headed out over the great expanse of water, I thought back to that time 27 years before when I had first come to Iran. A time when I knew nothing of the country or its people. A time when it, and I, were much different.

1971

1971

Going There

As the PanAm jet descended toward Tehran, thousands of random street lights illuminated the huge checker board pattern of Iran's capital. The glow rose from mile after mile of flat land up into the foothills of a large dark mountain. While we banked to make our approach into the airport, looking at all of those lights below, I thought over the past few months.

When the letter, return address marked Peace Corps, Washington, D.C. arrived in March of 1971, I was expecting the offer of a job. I just didn't know where it would be.

During my junior year at the University of Wisconsin-Madison, an invitation from the School of Agriculture to find out about the Peace Corps had intrigued me. It led to my enrolling in a class where we were shown pictures of volunteers on farms in Brazil and then talked about what they were doing. The next semester, time was spent with other potential volunteers practicing Swahili for possible assignment to Kenya.

I knew if the chance came to leave the comfort of my hometown, I would take it. The nightly conversation at the local beer bar had grown stale, the prospects of a routine 8 to 5 work life was not one I looked forward to, and the appeal of foreign travel was strong. I was 21 and wanted to move on.

The letter from Washington invited me to join a group of volunteer urban planners that would meet in Philadelphia in the middle of June for a few days. From there the party would fly to Tehran, Iran for training in Farsi, the native language. If I was interested, they wanted to hear from me shortly.

If I was interested? While my soon-to-be-received degree in Landscape Architecture wasn't exactly the same thing, I had been thinking of becoming an urban planner for some time. Plus I was being offered a free trip half way around the world, a regular, if low-paying, job when I got there, and a life on my own. Of course I would take it.

But where Iran was exactly, or what life was like there, I didn't know. A quick look at the encyclopedia showed the country was east of Turkey and south of the Soviet Union. Something called a shah was the ruler, and much of the country was desert. Iran, it said, was the successor of the ancient kingdom of Persia, a major military power long ago.

Over the next few months I learned a little bit more about Iran. Vast oil reserves were the source of most of its income. The country's topography and climate varied from mountains and cold to desert and extreme heat. Its people were a mixture of Persians, who were Aryans and not Arabic, and numerous tribal groups.

I read the personal account of an American schoolteacher's year in the northern part of the country to find out what Iranians were like. It left the impression of different, but friendly people, where the men were in charge and the women subservient.

As a final refresher course on Middle East history, I went to see "Lawrence of Arabia" again. It had plenty of desert, tribal warriors and western saviors, so I figured that the Peace Corps in Iran must be about like that.

My friends took me out drinking the night before my departure, which was also my graduation day. The next morning, in a hung over blur, I sat in the sun listening to someone drone on and on about something or other. The black robe finery I was wearing was getting soaked in sweat. Among the oratory and ovations, the small group of graduating landscape architects talked about what they would be doing. I was surprised when the guy sitting next to me said that a fellow classmate of ours was also going to Iran with the Peace Corps. As we stumbled out of the football stadium, Gerry and I agreed to see each other again that evening in Philadelphia.

My mind was still in the bottle when I boarded the east-bound plane. The taxi driver in Philadelphia talked all the way from the airport to the Hotel Sylvania. When I handed him $10 for a $5 fare, he gave me five bills back instead of keeping it all, so I put the change in my wallet and walked into the hotel. He stood in the middle of the street, yelling to everyone, telling them of my stinginess.

An afternoon nap, a quick briefing by Peace Corps staff members, a couple of beers with the other dozen or so urban planning volunteers headed for Iran, and a quiet night brought some semblance of calm back to my mind. My roommates were both heading for west Africa to teach English, so while they ardently discussed which would be a better place to live, Ivory Coast or Upper Volta, I fell asleep.

The first thing we were told the next morning was that there were three goals for Peace Corps volunteers. One was for Americans to learn about other cultures. The next was for foreign nationals to find out about Americans. The final goal was to accomplish something on the job, but it didn't seem to be as important as the other two objectives to the program administrators who were talking.

Our group was then introduced to Barkley Moore, an icon of the Peace Corps movement and a legend for those involved with Iran. He was from the southern United States, a rural person in many respects, and seemed uneasy with his notoriety. Not sophisticated, and not particularly outgoing, he was just a short, heavy-set man in his late 20s.

He was renowned, however, for his accomplishments. In his six years in the Peace Corps he had founded libraries and schools and had started medical clinics and recreation programs. He had been a one-man good will tour for America during his time in Iran. Plus, at least in the Peace Corps, he was famous. He was on a pedestal, and we sat quietly while he told us of his experiences in a simple and humble fashion.

After the session broke up, Gerry and I agreed to meet in the lobby and go eat dinner. When we met, Barkley was sitting at the side of the room, looking lonely. We invited him to join us, and he excitedly agreed. During our meal he described in more detail what we could expect. He also told us what it was like to be young and a legend when all you really wanted to do was help other people. He was famous, and he was on his own.

My roommates were scheduled to leave by bus at 3 a.m. for French language training in Montreal. Before that, their group had planned a going away party. Everyone interested was invited to gather at an upstairs bar near the hotel.

That is what I had been told, but the entrance made it quickly obvious the place was a drag queen hangout. Photos of transvestites in their glittering gowns dotted the stairwell leading up to a large dance floor and dark bar. Since I wasn't interested in dancing with the patrons, I had a couple of quick beers and went to bed early.

Sometime well after midnight my roommates loudly stumbled into the room. The alarm went off at 2:30 and I helped them downstairs with their bags. As the weary-eyed group of young people silently filed on to a bus, the "ladies" from the nightclub were heading home, waving and yelling at us in the high pitched sounds of the unknown.

Our group's send off was much less memorable. Early in the morning we got on a bus for the trip back to the airport and flew to J.F.K. The pilot was singing us country western songs as the plane circled the city, Manhattan's skyscrapers shining in the sunlight below.

All day long we sat around, waiting for the PanAm night flight to Paris. After watching a baseball game on TV, chatting with some of the Peace Corps volunteer auto mechanics that were also headed to Iran on the same plane, and inspecting the multi-cultural parade passing through the terminal, eventually our flight was called.

As the plane rolled out onto the runway, I sat by myself, staring out the window. The sight of all those silvery aircraft with strange names written on them, flood lamps shining off the impregnated bulge of the 747s, was my last view of the U.S.

A few hours later the rising sun was reflected on the blazing blue of the ocean and the sudden dawn shook the sleep out of my mind. The French coast soon appeared, and we were to change planes in Paris for Rome and points further east. While waiting for the next flight, one of the to-be-volunteers came out of the toilet and loudly announced that an attendant was collecting coins just to get into the lavatory.

Flying over the Mediterranean after leaving Rome, the Peace Corps contingent was sitting together, talking about their plans. The 707 was smaller, the fatigue was mutual, and anticipation was growing so the newly forming family was getting acquainted.

Sitting near me, a tall, good looking young mechanic that was going to Isfahan for volunteer training pulled a batch of religious material out of his duffel bag. "See these flyers? I'll be using them to convert some Muslims. That's one reason I wanted this assignment, to be able to bring the word of the Lord Jesus Christ to the people of Iran. It may not be what the Peace Corps wants done, but it is very important to me."

"Christ saved me. My life in southern California was one of debauchery and drugs. When I wasn't having sex, I was smoking pot or dropping acid."

"But then Christ came into my life. Some friends invited me to join them at a prayer service. At first I resisted. I didn't want to be like them. But my life was a mess. When I finally attended, I had an awakening. I was saved. And I want to bring His word to as many Iranians as I can so they can be saved too."

The runway at Beirut was lined with tanks, but we were allowed to get off the plane and go into the terminal if we wanted. I chose to stay on board, seriously wondering about what kind of world this was. Gerry, however, got off to snap a picture of the airport. After doing so, he was quickly escorted back to the plane by two machine gun toting soldiers.

Since Iraq would not allow Tehran bound flights through its air space, we had to take a long circular route north across Turkey to get to Iran. It was almost midnight when the twinkling lights of the city appeared below. We had been awake for over 30 hours and on planes for most of them by the time we landed.

Our greeting was by Peace Corps staff people shuffling us into a waiting room, collecting our passports, and telling us to be patient. Outside in the dark, behind large windows, men in tattered coats held out their open palms and implored us for help. They pointed to sleeping children wrapped in the arms of their veil-covered wives. Behind the glass, making hand signals to indicate the childrens' hunger, they begged for money. As we walked out of the terminal and hurried onto a van for the trip to the Hotel Atlantic, they made a final face-to-face plea for help. All we could do was look at them sadly.

The silent van sped into town down the deserted streets of Tehran and by the marble exterior of the shah's newest monument to himself. It was a massive white, four-sided arch which was under construction to help celebrate the upcoming 2,500 year anniversary of the Iranian monarchy. Men were spread out across its immense smooth surface, working under the intense light cast by fluorescent fixtures, hurrying to get the thing finished in time for the October ceremony.

The language program director welcomed us in the lobby of the Hotel Atlantic and announced that breakfast would be served at 8 a.m. for those who wanted it. Other than that, the morning was free and lunch would be at 1 p.m. followed by a get-acquainted meeting. With that he bade us a good night's sleep, and we quietly rode the elevator to our rooms.

Gerry, a Southern Californian named George, and I were roomed together. In my tossing, fitful attempt at sleep, I thought I heard the sound of camels parading beneath our window. Later, George coughed a few times and announced suddenly that if he didn't feel better in a week, he was going to leave. In spurts we tried with difficulty to rest, but when one of us looked at a watch and saw that it was after 1, we had to hurry to make lunch.

Getting Acquainted

Over the next few days we timidly ventured out from the central-city hotel into our strange new surroundings. Tehran was a big city of almost three million people and the alphabet, some of the clothing, and certainly the food were all different from what we were accustomed to. One afternoon was spent on a van tour of the city, the driver facetiously telling us why Persians had to start the Shiite sect of Islam. "A Muslim", he said, "is not to fight another Muslim. So that was the only way we could continue our never ending war with the Sunnis of Iraq."

The van drove down streets crowded with speeding orange taxis and buses packed with people. The sidewalks were jammed with pedestrians and seated beggars implored those passing for help. Numerous poor people waved large, colorful tickets, trying to sell chances in the national lottery.

The center of Tehran where we were staying was a bustling office and commercial area. Tehran University, a few high-rise buildings, and the American Embassy were all in the vicinity. Some new six and seven story buildings were also under construction, each floor held up by closely spaced rickety-looking wooden supports.

Toward the north we were told, and several miles away, was where the shah and the wealthy lived and played. It was a long, expensive taxi ride up to that part of the city.

Most of the men we saw were short in stature and wore sport coats, even though it was very warm. In the central part of Tehran, people appeared to be middle-class, and many women were in dresses. Further south, however, the full veil, or *chador* in Persian, became almost universally worn.

Wrapped around their entire bodies, the *chador* hid women from view, except for the opening which allowed their faces to be seen.

One of the tour stops south of the city was at a carpet washing operation. In a large aquamarine pool, women and children rinsed hand woven rugs of all sizes. Above them, *chador*-covered women beat out dirt in a pre-washing phase. Stretching across the side of the rock face which formed the pool were various sized rugs of red, brown and white drying in the sun.

Out the van window, the southern sections of Tehran looked like an enormous village. Mud huts, communal water faucets and livestock wandering in the streets all gave it the appearance of something other than a large part of a major city. The pieces of Tehran just didn't seem to fit together.

The next day, Gerry and I were sent out to buy stamps as a language training assignment. We had to hail a taxi and tell the driver, in the few words of Farsi we had learned, where we wanted to go. On the steps of the Post Office was a long row of letter writers seated next to ancient typewriters, waiting for illiterate customers who needed to send something by mail.

That evening, most of the group walked a few blocks to Ray's, a basement restaurant that served cold beer and hot pizza. On the way back to the hotel, someone bought a watermelon from a street vendor. There was concern expressed about the potential for illness, all of us having been warned not to eat fruit or vegetables bought off the street. But we ate it anyway.

As we spit out seeds, George said that he had made a decision about staying in the country. "The only place I would work," he said seriously, "is in a hospital. It would be the one location in this dirty country that is clean enough for me. If they can't find a job for me in one, then I'm leaving." As he talked, the rest of us continued to eat the watermelon.

After a few more days in Tehran, we moved out to Karaj, a small town surrounded by farmland. It was only twenty miles away from the capital but in a completely different world. Our language training was to take place in a school building vacant for the summer and the five single men in the group would stay in a modern four bedroom house outside of town. A driver came every day to get us to class on time, Tehran was only a commuter taxi ride away, and the Iranian people seemed friendly. Our lives were very comfortable.

The ten week training session was intended to have five Iranian instructors teach us to speak and read Persian. We were also to learn about the history, customs and culture of the country as well as a little bit about what our jobs as urban planners would involve. At the end of the training period, we were told, we would be prepared to live in the country on our own.

My first letter home outlined our daily routine. "We drive to school each day and eat all our meals at the school. Our classes are 5 hours a day Farsi conversation and 3 hours Farsi writing. We're divided into three groups (I'm in too high a group and hopefully will be dropped down) of four each. This will last for three weeks at which time, we are told, we will be able to read and write Farsi."

At the end of those three weeks, George had left, fearing that his life was endangered by the primitive surroundings. Also gone from the group was a couple who had endured constant hassling by the local men because of her blond hair. Nine of us remained, and in the reshuffling I was assigned to the remedial language class, but at least I could say a few simple sentences in Persian.

To celebrate our new found speaking skills, the language program director organized a party at our house to which he invited local Iranian dignitaries. Before they arrived, we joked that each of us could engage the mayor of Karaj in lively conversation by saying, "I do not have an automobile" or asking him, "Do you have a telephone?". The evening was spent, predictably, with the Iranians in one corner of the living room and the Americans in the other.

The next day we boarded a minibus for the ride to the Caspian Sea and a weekend getaway. The narrow road north twisted and turned through mountains, the cliff edge only a few feet away. Whenever another vehicle was encountered, the drivers played a short game of chicken to see who would pass first. Scattered across the rock face a long way below us were the rotting remains of some vehicles which had not survived the hazardous course.

At lunchtime the bus stopped at a restaurant built into the cliffs. On wooden picnic tables under a bamboo roof, we ate chicken and rice and drank Pepsi or orange Nehi. By late afternoon we were wading in the waves of the Caspian with frolicking children and their *chador* covered mothers. The women looked like giant jellyfish as their veils ballooned over the surface of the water.

Upon our return from the seaside, Margaret, a nurse from California and the lone single female in the group, started hanging out with Hadi, one of our language instructors. He was a young, handsome man who lived with us and liked to party. Many Iranian men were short with dark features and wore mustaches. Hadi, however, was tall, fair skinned and clean shaven. He dressed well and was one of the boys of our bachelor pad.

The two of them tried to keep their relationship secretive for awhile, but the sounds of their lovemaking echoed throughout the house. Besides, none of the Americans was interested in Margaret; she was just too unusual for us. She had a mellow, laid-back California philosophy, used drugs very frequently, and took a talk-about-everything view of life which simply didn't mesh with ours.

The next several weeks were spent in the classroom learning more about the language and history of the country. Eventually we traveled for a week to Hamadan in the western mountains of Iran to join the Peace Corps volunteers who were training there to become English teachers. For a few days we also visited the auto mechanics studying in Isfahan.

Between all this travel we occasionally saw Harry, a Peace Corps psychologist. He was in Iran for the summer to observe and assist the recent arrivals in their new surroundings but his problems with the country far exceeded ours.

One day Harry met with the four single men of our group. "I don't know about you guys," he said intently, "but some of the things about this country really disgust me. The dirt, the heat, the toilets you have to squat over, I'm tired of them all."

"Plus, we can't talk to most women. The Persian men treat them like slaves sometimes and saints at other times. We can't get near most of them. I brought a large supply of condoms with me, and I haven't been able to use any of them."

"A lot of the time this place makes me sick. But this isn't about me, it's about you. It is important for you to talk about your true feelings and frustrations with the country. So let me hear from you."

"Do any of you feel about Iran the way I do? Do you dislike the country and regret coming here? Let me hear from you."

We looked at each other in disbelief and didn't know quite what to say. It was obvious that Harry, a middle-aged, over weight, balding New Yorker, was having many more difficulties with the country than we were. We sat uncomfortably for awhile, staring at each other in dumbfounded silence. Finally Jeff, the oldest of us, said, "Harry, I think that we've found Iran to be about what we expected. Sure its hot, dirty, and the women off limits, but we knew that before coming here. So I don't think any of us has a real problem with the place." But it was clear that Harry did.

A few weeks later Harry took our entire training group out for a night of drinking. Sitting on the patio of a restaurant, a small stream running beneath us, the stars above and a whorehouse just up the road, the vodka and beer flowed freely. We all got quite drunk, and Harry kept wanting to visit the ladies for hire. At the same time, he was very open about his dislike of the country and his desire to go home. We all felt sorry for him. At the end of the evening we climbed into a taxi and returned to our house in Karaj, Harry soon sleeping soundly in the back seat.

To prepare us for the health risks we could each face, everyone in the group received a series of shots. From some innocuous ones to the needle-in-the-rump gamma globulin vaccine, we were punctured on a fairly regular basis. Plus, we were sternly warned of the problems that could be caused by drinking untreated water, eating unwashed fruits and vegetables, or by following Iranian medical recommendations.

Nothing, however, prepared us for the rabies shot. The Peace Corps nurse repeatedly told us of the high number of rabid creatures in the country. If we were bit, she said, we should watch the animal for three days. If it survived, we'd be fine. If it died in that period, we were to cut off its head and ship it in ice to Tehran for testing. How we were to catch a wild animal she didn't explain.

She also told us that the rabies inoculation was a possible preventative, nothing more. She added that because it was a live serum, it would hurt. One afternoon we were all gathered in a classroom of the school and ushered individually across the hall to be vaccinated. Whoever went first returned and collapsed in a chair, grabbing their arm in pain. When my turn came, I rolled up my sleeve and bit my lip. The fire from the serum ran down my arm, and for a second my head went light. The pain was intense, but I stumbled back across the hallway and tried to keep a smile on my face.

For the next day the ache in my arm didn't disappear. I promised myself to stay away from dogs and other potential rabies carriers if that was what the shots were like for the disease.

To test the language we were learning, one day a few of us went shopping by ourselves in Tehran. While waiting for a shared taxi in Karaj to fill, I was singing, "We're doing our Christmas shopping at the Tehran bazaar this year" to the tune of a popular U.S. radio ad.

The bazaar was a maze of covered stalls selling everything, where give-and-take and bargaining were expected behavior. It was filled with dozens of merchants selling finely woven carpets from piles stacked to the ceiling. Other small shops had bags of rice, unknown spices, and chickens sitting quietly, waiting for someone to behead them.

As newcomers, however, we were more comfortable in the central city multi-story department store on Ferdosi Street. There, all the prices were clearly marked, and the merchandise was more familiar. Even if peanut butter was $5 a jar, at least they had it. A display case in a nearby shop held a variety of Swiss Army knives, all reasonably priced. I purchased one, not knowing when I might need it.

During our training sessions back in Karaj we frequently talked about Iranian history and the present form of government. A biography of the shah stressed his deep-seated resentment toward the overthrow of his father by the Russians and British during World War II. It had brought him personally to power but the shah's belief that military might could have prevented the coup still persisted.

The book also discussed the shah's almost mystical belief in his ability to survive. After having once been shot at close range and living, that could be appreciated. The book downplayed, however, the revolutionary events of 1953 which came close to ousting him. But it glorified the "White Revolution" of the early 1960s which through a series of policy changes was intended to make the country a more progressive place. In 1971, however, Iran was still ruled dictatorially by a constitutional monarch, at least that was what the shah was called.

While he wasn't seen in public very often, the shah's picture was certainly widely displayed. In every shop, office and business, there would be his face hanging on the wall. It was also on the money and on many television news programs. Plus, before every movie, while the Iranian national anthem played, a short patriotic film would be shown for which the audience would stand as jets flew over a waving flag and the shah was seen in his magnificence. Pictures of his wife and the young crown prince were also prominent. While Islam forbade the worship of idols, the likeness of the shah and his family were omnipresent.

Years later my college classmate Gerry told me that he had once run into problems because of the shah's picture. In his office in Tehran the royal photograph hung behind a filing cabinet on top of which Gerry would store books. Every day when he came to work he would find the books had been moved. He would replace them but the next day they would be gone again. Finally the office tea man informed him that the books were blocking the view of the shah's portrait, so he kept moving them.

One warm afternoon in Karaj, my two language training class partners decided to go out for a beer during the lunchtime break. They invited me along, but I declined, favoring a nap instead.

They hadn't returned to the house by the time the driver arrived to pick us up, so I was alone in the classroom for a few minutes with the instructor when the afternoon session began. Shortly, however, we heard two loud voices approaching down the alley toward the school. They were singing songs and yelling as they entered the building.

"We're never going to get this stupid language," one of them slurred as they both slumped into chairs. "Things have got to change or we'll never be able to say anything. So what do we do?" he screamed in frustration.

The language program director and head instructor both came rushing into the room, wondering what was going on. Discussing the situation with my classmates wasn't possible, they were too drunk for that. A smile, however, did come across the face of the chief instructor. He was an older, dignified Iranian teacher who was very proper in everything he did, but this show of passion had pleased him.

My classmates were sent home to sleep it off. Over the next few weeks they got more comfortable with the language. Plus, we were visited by some volunteers who had been in the country for six months, and it was obvious their speaking skills weren't much better than ours.

By the end of the training period, our language was even better, and we had become more accustomed to the Iranian way of doing things. Productivity was not very important, juvenile sex talk appeared to be the dominant topic of conversation among many men, and politeness was always important, except when dealing with women. Then, just about anything would be tolerated. Mothers and sisters might be held in high regard, at least within the family, but on the street all women seemed to be fair game for harassment.

To mark the completion of our 10 week training session, a party was held at a hotel in Tehran. Peace Corps officials, the four Iranian men who had taught us, and Essie, the urban planning program director, all attended. Also there was Fereshteh, the lone Iranian woman instructor for our group.

She was a recent college graduate who was western in her ways, didn't wear a *chador*, and did flirt with each of the single guys in the group. It was all good-natured fun because she could kid us in her language, and we didn't yet know how to respond.

After a few beers, I asked Fereshteh to dance. At the end of the song, I asked her if she would go out with me to Tehran's night club/bowling alley/recreation center some evening. It was in the northern part of the city and was known simply as "The Bowling Club".

Giggling "Yes", she added that she wanted to invite a girlfriend and Hadi along. She said she would set it up, and a few days later Hadi and I were riding a taxi in from Karaj for our "date", not discussing why he and Margaret had split up.

The women met us at the front door of the club and for the next couple of hours we walked around talking. The building had a movie theater, dance floor, and pin ball games and was the place to be for young, wealthy Tehranians. It was a great distance, both geographically and socially, from the poverty and conservative religious values of the southern part of the city.

At the end of our evening together, Hadi and I hailed a cab and left the two women standing on the curb in front of the club. They both lived in the northern part of the city, and it was a long ride for us back to Karaj.

By late August, Hadi had moved out of the house to return to his teaching job in Tehran. Gerry and I had been rooming together, and we both started getting bit by bedbugs. At first neither of us knew what they were, but the Peace Corps nurse told us that is how we got those small bites in neat rows all over our bodies. So we moved into two different rooms while dusting ourselves with DDT laced powder to try and cure the problem.

During our training period each of the urban planning volunteers had been given a short list of possible sites where they could chose to live. Everyone made a recruiting visit to one or more of these cities, and my choices were Shiraz, a lovely large city, Bandar Buscher, a military port community on the Persian Gulf, or Zahedan, the small, relatively new capital of Sistan and Baluchistan province on the eastern edge of the country.

Shiraz had an attractive city center, a fine bazaar, and beautiful domed mosques. It was nearby Persepolis, however, the 2,500 year old remains of an ancient palace of the Persian kings, that fascinated me the most. It was something totally out of my experience.

Built by Darius I and his son Xerxes, it had been burned by Alexander the Great in 331 B.C., possibly in retribution for Persian atrocities in Greece 150 years before. What still exist are giant stone columns which stand as guardians to the silence of the surrounding desert. The monumental entry staircase and majestic pictorial reliefs of life-sized lions and tribute carriers amazed me. It was inspiring.

Below the hill on which the ruins were located, workmen were busy finishing the modern tent city needed for the shah's celebration. In a few months, Persepolis would be crowded with dignitaries and journalists from around the world, but on the warm August day I visited, only a handful of people had come the 35 or so miles from Shiraz to see the site.

Bander Buscher was a modern city of slump block architecture built on the Gulf. It was hot, humid, and had no charm. After spending a long sweaty night in a hotel room there, I knew I didn't want to live in that climate.

As part of our language training, for a week we had each spent an hour a day at a local business in order to sharpen our speaking skills. I visited with the owner of a plumbing supply store, and we chatted about many things. When I told him I was considering moving to Zahedan but didn't know much about it, he said he had heard good things. "It is about the size of Tehran, I think, and has many advantages. Or, at least, that is what I hear".

Zahedan turned out to be a city of perhaps 25,000 people known only for its heat and isolation from the rest of the country. During my visit with Essie, the urban planning program director, we met with the provincial governor. He promised his support if I should choose to live in the community.

We also talked with the mayor, who pledged his assistance too. He gave Essie and me a quick tour of the town, pointing out some of the problems it had. Essie wrote of our visit with these men, "One thing I noticed was that, for all their interest in developing the city, the officials were not much interested in the future of the poor majority of the population, the Baluchis." The Baluch were the nomadic tribal people indigenous to the area who were moving into Zahedan from the desert, but they were not of much concern to their Persian rulers.

After visiting each of the three cities, and talking to the head of their respective provincial engineering offices, I selected Zahedan. In a letter to my parents I explained why. "I chose it for several reasons. 1)The job sounds and looks extremely interesting…2)The people seemed nice-hope they stay that way. 3)My other alternatives were undesirable but interesting." What I didn't tell them was that I didn't want to live in a large city, I disliked the humidity of the coast, and I wanted to get as far away as possible from the Iranian and American bureaucracies, both of which seemed to spend a lot of time doing nothing.

Thus, Zahedan was my choice. Before I could move, however, the staff at the Iranian Ministry of the Interior's city planning division, for whom our group of volunteers was working, insisted that I spend several weeks with them in Tehran. They wanted to familiarize me with Zahedan and the province of Sistan and Baluchistan of which it was the capital. This process should have taken only a few days. But because they thought Zahedan was a terrible place to send someone, the people in the Ministry did their best to delay my leaving for as long as they could.

I, though, hated the big city atmosphere of Tehran and wanted to get away. Besides, Zahedan was one of the farthest places in the country from the capital, and I thought that the only way someone could get in touch with me there was on my terms. By late September I was tired of the daily Tehranian routine of doing nothing but talking gossip and endless tea drinking, so one day I just announced it was time to go. After purchasing a bus ticket for Yazd to visit Jeff, my training companion who had recently moved there, I packed my two suitcases and was on my way.

Bus Ride to Zahedan

The luxury bus I was on made very fast time over the two lane paved highway which ran from Tehran to Isfahan. From there I would go east to Yazd, Kerman and then on to Zahedan. Older, more crowded buses, with poor air conditioning and worn tires but cheaper ticket prices, also made the trip south from the capital. Some large, slow moving trucks carrying sheep or commodities were on the road, but few cars were headed toward Isfahan.

The landscape between the two cities was mostly barren desert with an occasional earth-toned mud village of small domed houses and minor mosques. Along the way was Qom, one of the country's holy cities and a place we had been warned by the Peace Corps staff not to get off at. The potential for conflict with religious zealots who disliked non-Muslim foreigners was always possible, so it was easier to just stay on board.

The bus station in Qom was next to the bazaar, and out of the window I watched veiled women sorting through vegetables piled high on wooden pushcarts. Besides being the burial place of Fateme, sister of one of Shiite Islam's most holy men, the city was famous for a specialty candy made with pistachio nuts which was sold by children standing next to the bus. Brown robed *mullahs* and shopkeepers wearing white haj caps signifying they had made the sacred pilgrimage to Mecca were walking toward the central mosque for prayers as the bus pulled out of town.

It was an 8 hour trip from Tehran to Isfahan, and the bus stopped for only a short time before continuing on to Yazd. Our training group had spent some time in Isfahan, a beautiful city with the finest central square in the country. Historic mosques, their domes colored in blue tiles to match the sky, a fascinating covered bazaar, and a large open green space made the center of the city memorable. There would have to be time to return later since the bus was leaving on schedule.

Night had descended, and darkness wrapped the bus in its shadows as we headed east for several more hours through a desolate desert landscape lit only by the moon. No one spoke, and the quiet was comforting. The other passengers were business people on their way to Yazd or family members returning home after spending time in Tehran.

My Peace Corps training friend Jeff had given me detailed written directions to his house in Yazd. As I walked through the ancient central city's dimly lit, narrow, twisting alleys bounded on both sides by closely-spaced mud brick homes, I had to check his map often to make sure I got the right place. But he answered my knock, and I entered his five room house with a sign of relief. When we passed by the large courtyard, Jeff switched on a light. Thousands, no millions, of giant cockroaches went scrambling for cover. The walls seemed to be moving rapidly as tiny legs scurried for darkness.

I had heard stories of this house, how it had once been occupied by a Peace Corps volunteer and then deserted. After that, it was left to the roaches and other creatures of the desert. For some unknown reason, Jeff had decided to reclaim the place, but the task looked impossible. As I put my suitcases in a bedroom, he warned me, "Before you use the toilet, turn on the light, and then wait a minute. That will give them time to get out of the way."

In the morning we ate breakfast in a corner of the kitchen that had been declared a roach-free zone. A few of the huge creatures, their antennas slowing swaying, scrambled across the floor or peaked out of cupboards. Most of them, however, had disappeared for the day.

After Jeff went off to work, I strolled around the city, one of the country's most well preserved historic places. Yazd has a central city of great beauty which combines tightly packed mud brick domed dwellings with attractive and colorful religious monuments. One memorable mosque had blue minarets rising to the sky above an enormous arched entryway. Elaborate tile work formed calligraphed words along its sides. I could not read what they said, but the intricacy and beautiful rhythmic pattern of the art was unmistakable.

A teenage boy soon attached himself to me, wanting to practice his English. He had a motorbike and offered to drive me around if I would talk to him. That was a fair arrangement and would save me time. So while we rode out of town to see the burial tower of the Zoroastrians, where it was said corpses were once dumped for birds to pick over, he asked about the English words for intimate female body parts. At the city's grand Friday mosque, its dome decorated in tiles of blue and white, he wanted to know about the sexual promiscuity of western women. At sundown I was dropped off, and he promised to write me in Zahedan, that we should remain friends.

The next morning I toured on foot, afraid that I might run into my companion from the day before. On the surface, Iranian male behavior, at least for some of them, was infantile and tiring. All that many men could talk about upon first meeting was sex and how they needed more of it. After getting to know most of them, however, conversations would be about more interesting subjects and their generous natures and peace-loving dispositions would be revealed. That first hurdle, however, was sometimes difficult.

After sundown I left Jeff in his living room, wondering how he would conquer the roaches. The overnight bus from Yazd to Kerman, and then on to Zahedan, departed at 9 p.m. While drinking the complimentary soft drink and eating the hard candy offered by the driver's assistant before all long trips, I talked for a few minutes with the businessman sitting next to me who was returning home to Kerman.

"I am impressed that you can speak my language. It shows that you respect my country. It is appreciated."

"Hopefully before too long I'll know more. It has been kind of difficult."

"God willing, you'll learn. You know, you have come to Iran at just the right time. Next month our king of kings is holding a great celebration. It should be magnificent and very special. It will be on television. Do you have one?"

"I'm on my way to Zahedan. I don't know what I'll have there. But I didn't think about buying a TV."

"Zahedan? Why are you moving to Zahedan, Mister? It is a poor place with no attractions. You should stay with me in Kerman."

"But I think it will be O.K. It is quiet."

"I think many young foreigners travel through there. They cause my country great trouble. Most of them are drug dealers or prostitutes. We should deal with them harshly. Why don't they stay home, or respect my country like you do?"

"I'm not sure," I said as I reached to turn off the overhead lamp to try and sleep.

We arrived in Kerman at 4 a.m., but instead of leaving 30 minutes later as scheduled, those of us traveling further east were instructed to return at noon. Patience, we had been told throughout training, was a virtue needed to live in Iran and every day it was a lesson worth remembering.

After rubbing the sleep from my eyes, I drank a few glasses of steaming tea in a brightly lit bakery and ate some flat bread still hot from the oven. Then I went out in the early morning light to look for Jim and Cindy. They had been in the Karaj training group and had moved to Kerman only a few weeks before. I thought I would be able to pass the morning with them, if it was possible to find one foreign couple in a city of over 100,000 people.

Security was tighter than usual, and the military presence on the street very noticeable with the shah's celebration only a few weeks away. My seatmate on the bus had told me that Kerman was considered a possible location for trouble, if it should occur, so precautions were being taken. What I saw were young, head shaved soldiers in wrinkled uniforms carrying old rifles standing on street corners in the cool red rays of a late September dawn.

Remembering that Cindy had a job at an elementary school, I went looking for the nearest one. Getting there long before it would open, and not knowing whether it was the right place or not, I stood staring at the playground. As I did, a tiny, well dressed, white-haired, kindly looking elderly gentleman approached.

"Good morning, Mister. Are you an American? I thought so. Why are you up so early? Are you looking for someone? Perhaps I can help you?"

"My friends Jim and Cindy live in Kerman. She works at an elementary school. Maybe this is the one. But I'll have to wait for the school to open."

"Oh no. I know them well. They are my friends. Come with me, and I will take you to their house." He hailed a cab, and a few minutes later I was having breakfast with Jim and Cindy.

The rest of the morning was spent seeing where they worked, what they did, and finding out about everyday life in Iran outside of the physical comforts of Karaj and Tehran. We discussed the old man and what a happy coincidence it was that he had been out walking so early in the morning. Cindy said it was rumored he worked for SAVAK, the secret police agency known for its brutal tactics, but that was uncertain. I knew that I had been lucky to have him find me.

The bus for Zahedan finally departed at 1 p.m., and the paved road was quickly behind us. Also left behind were the luxury buses. An older vehicle with a well worn interior and lots of miles on it would be our transportation for the desert crossing.

A wash board surfaced dirt path was all that distinguished the road from the surrounding earth. The landscape of the *Dasht-i-Lut* or Great Sand Desert was barren of all life, simply rocks and dirt backed by tall gray mountains in the distance. A simmering heat rose off the land. We bounced around inside the bus, sweating profusely, and the going was slow. Dust filled the air, and soon a fine layer of it covered everything and everyone.

The middle-class Persian passengers from Tehran and Yazd had been replaced by long bearded Baluchi tribal men in turbans and colorful balloon type pants. As we rode through the desolation, the wailing, mournful traditional music of the country made sense to me. While current popular tunes were more upbeat and western, the instrumental and tribal music of Iran was a celebration of the desert. Its harshness, simplicity, and beauty all came through in rhythms that fit the place.

At sunset we stopped at a mud brick restaurant in a small oasis for a dinner of rice and greens, the only item on the non-existent menu. It felt good to get away from the vibrations of the bus, at least for a few minutes.

Glasses of hot tea covered a metal tray the restaurant owner carried from table to table. Grabbing a glass, the customer had to make sure not to burn his fingers since there were no handles. A sugar cube popped in the mouth to dissolve while drinking, the dust of the desert could be washed away for awhile.

Someone had told me that the country's rail line, as well as the highway system, ended at Kerman. That was one of the attractions of Zahedan for me. It offered isolation from Iranian government employees and Peace Corps bureaucrats that may want to come for a visit. They might fly in but with only four flights a week, I would be able to be prepared. I was going to be on my own and that was the way I wanted it.

Some government officials talked hopefully of the day when Zahedan would be linked by rail and road to the rest of the country, but I knew that was a long way off. For now, my solitude would be safe.

It was 1:30 a.m. before the bus crawled into Zahedan. For almost an hour we had been able to see its distant lights under a star filled sky but the going had been very slow. The driver announced that we should return to claim our luggage off the roof of the bus at 6 a.m. I stumbled out of the station, passed people laying in the late night heat on mats scattered along the downtown sidewalk, and went looking for a place to stay.

Fortunately a rooming house was still open and I asked to be awakened in four hours. After a fitful sleep of sorts, I had some tea and bread and tried to think clearly. A man approached and in broken English announced that his name was Jamal. He wanted to be my friend and said he knew the other American who had recently come to live in Zahedan. I promised Jamal in a few words of Persian that I would have lunch with him and wearily went off to claim my bags.

The central city bus station was swarming with people, bustling with life in the early morning light. They were yelling at porters to fetch this or that off the top of the vehicle, to be careful because things were fragile. Dark brown, wrinkled-skinned barefoot men in loincloths would climb an old but sturdy looking wooden ladder and point out something to the screaming crowd below. When they had a customer, the porter would lean the box or package on his back, a strap running around his forehead to balance it, and walk, bent over and face first, down the ladder. A few coins changed hands, and the process would be repeated.

After collecting my two suitcases and returning to the rooming house, I took a shower and then went off to the provincial engineering office at which I would be working. The director said I should go visit the governor, so I did. He was the most important official in Zahedan, and in my rough Farsi I told him I would do my best. His office was enormous and a large picture of the shah hung on the wall behind his oversized desk. Outside, beggars sitting in the dirt were pleading for help from whoever went by.

While eating a lunch of rice and strips of fried mutton, Jamal said, "Mister Robert moved here just last week from Isfahan. He tried to learn Farsi there. We are friends. Sometimes we drink beer together. He works at the vocational training school. You should take a taxi out to see him."

When I did, we quickly agreed that I would move in the next day to the four bedroom house he had rented but was living in alone. With that I returned to my room and sought some sleep. Life in Zahedan could begin in earnest tomorrow.

North to Zabol

Within a few days, the head of the provincial engineering office had quit to go study in Italy. That would be the first of almost one dozen changes in chief administrator of the agency that would occur over the next 18 months.

Numerous professional people in the office also came and went frequently. Almost everyone I worked with was looking to leave Zahedan as quickly as possible. They intensely disliked the place because of its small size, isolation from the rest of the nation, and lack of things to do. They wanted to get back to Tehran or the country's other large cities where they were from. What they saw as disadvantages about the community, though, made it attractive to me.

My first days in town were spent moving into Robert's house and getting acquainted at work. I had a wooden bed made, bought a thin foam rubber mat and a synthetic green and white blanket to go on top of it, and purchased a hat rack to hang my clothes on. Also acquired were a radio/cassette player and a woven mat to lay on the floor of my bedroom. With the moving-in money the Peace Corps had given us, Robert and I decided to buy a small refrigerator to go along with the two burner gas stove he had already purchased. The empty refrigerator box, together with the two suitcases I had brought with me, would serve as my closets.

Needing something to dine on, I found a large metal table in a shop outside the bazaar. Knowing that it was the Iranian custom to sit on the floor and eat meals off a large plastic sheet, I had the legs of the table cut off to about 18 inches in height. At least that way our food could be eaten sitting crossed legged on the floor, partially the way the natives did it.

I also obtained a post office box and bought myself a thick stack of aerograms. The thin blue, already stamped paper would be my communication to the outside world. There was a telephone exchange in town, but I didn't plan to use it in order to keep my isolation intact.

Letter writing had already proven to be very important. It gave me the opportunity to express what I was experiencing along with keeping in touch with those left behind in Wisconsin. In addition to my family, I bombarded my friends and even casual acquaintances with letters. When they didn't respond quickly, in a month or so given the travel distance, I would write and ask them what I had done wrong in another letter. After all, I had plenty of time, both at home and on the job, to write as much as I wanted, so why didn't they reply?

In the evenings the BBC overseas service came in clearly and supplied daily radio news from London. The English language paper from Tehran arrived only a few days after publication and contained the local twist on the news. Thus, I was able to keep up with sports scores from around the world and the happenings in the capital, if three or four days late.

After work Robert and I would meet to drink some beers and discuss our plans. He was in his early 20s and a veteran of Vietnam who was getting married in a few months to an Iranian teacher he had met during his language training in Isfahan. From northern Wisconsin, tall but thin and wearing a scraggly beard, Robert was usually very quiet. He did say often, however, that his job was a real challenge. He didn't have much experience teaching, and the students and instructors he was dealing with weren't familiar with modern mechanics. With a slight laugh, Robert concluded they would have to learn together.

Jamal sometimes joined us at one of Zahedan's liquor stores or restaurants that served alcohol. We would drink a few glycerine preserved beers, the additive providing shelf life in the heat but giving the consumer a quick headache. We often shared a plate of pistachios or cucumber slices in yogurt and told tales of the great things we were going to do.

In some of these restaurants, older men would suck on water pipes, bubbles rising in a glass jar as tobacco smoked on top. No women were allowed in these establishments, and the atmosphere was very casual.

Jamal told us that even the upcoming fasting month of Ramadan wouldn't shut the restaurants down. "Mister Robert, Mister David. Religion not so important here. The restaurants just cover the windows with wrapping paper and keep on doing business during the day."

"But what about fasting? Don't people do that?"

"Some poor people, and *mullahs* of course. But most people don't. Is very difficult. Is too inconvenient."

Robert and I had to chuckle at the hypocrisy as we drank our beers. "Kind of like fish on Friday," we agreed.

One day at work I was asked to join a group from the office going to lunch. We had been invited to the home of an employee of the Plan Organization, the governmental department that controlled the country's oil money. Ten of us sat around on his plastic sheet covered carpeted floor, filling our plates with rice and meat supplied by our host's maid. After lunch, she brought us tea, and we continued our conversations about life in Zahedan and America.

As we drank the tea, I noticed a short, *chador*-wearing woman enter the bedroom across the hallway. Our host got up and went in after her but emerged a few minutes later. When he returned, another man silently rose and went across the hall. This process was repeated for each man in the room.

Finally our host said, "Mister, now it is your turn to have her. She is waiting for you. She is very good."

"Thank you for the opportunity to be tenth in line," I said sarcastically. "I'll pass."

For the first month or so after I arrived, Robert and I ate many of our meals in restaurants. We quickly agreed, though, that hiring a maid to cook and clean for us would be preferable. The limited number of items available in restaurants, and with only a few places to choose from, meant we were eating the same thing two or three times a week. Plus, the money we would save could be spent on other more important things, like rugs or weddings.

Home cooked food was also a problem for us. I was occasionally trying to prepare American meals with Persian ingredients, but it wasn't working. Meatloaf with mutton somehow came out tasting differently. Beef usually wasn't available in the butcher shop, and when it was, it was very stringy. I also wasn't a very good cook, so our need for a maid was obvious.

To get me through the afternoons, I quickly fell into the habit of buying cookies from a bakery on the main street in town. Sitting around on my bedroom floor, having a glass of tea and several fresh cookies, the time after work and before the evening's radio programs would pass.

One day while eating my cookies, however, I tried drinking the Iranian concoction, *doogh*. It came in recycled Pepsi glass bottles and looked like 2 percent milk, but it was diluted yogurt with more than a taste of salt. It was disgusting. Friends had told me *doogh* was a great thirst quencher, but I tried it once and never again.

To show off the new resident foreigner, and to keep me occupied, after a week I was sent off on a bus trip to Zabol. Accompanying me was Hassan, a surveyor from the office. Our job was to review the mayor's proposal for a large and expensive traffic circle on the edge of the community.

Zabol, the second largest city in the province with a population of 10,000 or so, is located in a little corner of the country north of where Afghanistan, Pakistan, and Iran come together. It is near the site of ancient ruins, rumored to have been the home of one of the Wise Men. Zabol was the center of the Sistan portion of the province and was once an agricultural center, but drought and diversion of river water in Afghanistan had reduced the farming in the area considerably.

The bus ride from Zahedan should have taken only a few hours even though there was no paved road, just compact soil in a sea of dirt. The landscape was bare, nothing grew, nothing moved; it was simply brown emptiness. In the background, imposing mountain ranges rose to the sky, but the land was level smooth and barren near the bus.

Our first breakdown was to fix a flat tire, and everyone got off while the spare was installed. Later, another tire blew and once again we descended to wait in the warm October sunshine, but this time problems arose. One of the nuts holding the wheel on had been stripped, and it couldn't be moved. The driver and his assistant cursed their luck as the passengers made themselves comfortable by sitting in the shade cast by the vehicle.

Hassan and I tried to communicate about work and life in general, but my broken Farsi made it slow going. Around us women congregated in one corner of the shady area, holding their full-length veils in place by biting on a corner of the covering while tending to their children with both hands.

Bearded tribal men dressed in multi-pleated balloon pants and long shirts and young boys wearing the same type of clothing wandered off into the desert to relieve themselves. The driver decided the only way to remove the wheel was to hammer off the nut, so he traded turns with his assistant as they pounded away. After an hour or so of banging, the thick metal gave, the tire was replaced and we were on our way again.

It was dark when we arrived in Zabol and the glow of lamplights illuminated hundreds of people camped along the town's main road. We were staying with the mayor, and as we walked to his house a man approached and fell at Hassan's feet. "Master, give me a job," the man begged. "The drought has ruined me and my family is starving. I need work, please!" he implored. All Hassan could do was say that he would try.

The mayor showed us to a spartan room with two metal beds and a bare light bulb hanging from a fraying cord. Even though it had been a long day, Hassan and I talked about the poverty and starvation which was occurring in the area.

"There has been a drought here for years, Mister David. Plus, the government in Afghanistan dammed the river that once ran though the area. So there is very little water. Many people have left because they can't farm anymore. Those that remain are desperate."

"What will happen to them?"

"I don't know, Mister."

In order to survive, some people had turned to smuggling electronic goods and drugs in from Afghanistan. They would be executed if caught, but the immense border was mostly unguarded. With a high-powered Russian built motorcycle, a man could make a reasonable run from Zabol into Afghanistan and back in a few days. The profits were worth the risk to some, and smuggling was becoming a major industry of the town. For those who didn't want to break the law, government labor jobs were the only option.

Over breakfast, the mayor explained his plans for a new traffic circle. It would be out of town on the road to Zahedan and would be the largest in the city. It was estimated to cost $30,000, and how the vegetation it was to hold would be watered was a detail that apparently wasn't to be worried about.

Constructing traffic circles seemed to be the major goal of many politicians in Iran. From the tens of millions of dollars being spent by the shah for his new monument in the middle of a traffic circle in Tehran to the large dirt circles outside the smallest village, they were status symbols Iranian style. Not as expensive as sports stadiums or convention centers in the United States, but about as socially meaningful. When I tried to express my concern with building the circle before a master plan for Zabol had been prepared, the mayor would hear nothing of it. He wanted the circle as a sign of what he had accomplished, even though he had been in office only one month.

Later, while Hassan and I took a walk around town, I saw that Zabol was a one story city of mud brick buildings built around a small central square. It had several blocks of paved streets lined by the wide, open and usually dry concrete drains, called *jubes*. A few hardy but scrawny tamaracks served as street trees. There was an air of great despair about the place. Beggars outnumbered pedestrians, and the desert heat made the claustrophobic feeling intense.

Before sleeping that night, Hassan tried to explain why the mayor was so adamant about the traffic circle. "Mister David, in Iran traffic circles are very important. The community needs something to be proud of. They have nothing else. They are so desperate, it will be a good thing."

"How can it be so? People are starving Hassan. It will cost much money."

"Building it will create some jobs. That is good. Traffic circles are important to us."

"But it isn't even at the intersection of two roads. It makes no sense to me."

"Mister, it is the Iranian way."

I thought to myself that this was a case that I would have to take to the governor. Maybe I could convince him the traffic circle wasn't right, but I was wrong.

The bus ride back to Zahedan the next day was uneventful until we stopped in front of a tiny ramshackle home standing alone in the middle of the desert. This was our mid-afternoon prayer break, and as everyone slowly got off the bus, a girl of about six dressed in rags came out of the shack. She dragged her young naked brother beside her. As many of the men from the bus formed a line and prayed by bowing and knelling in unison, the little girl silently held out her hand, begging for survival. Next to her the young boy sat playing in the dirt, throwing it on himself, while a fly slowly made its way across his face. The fly crawled over the boy's eyes, and he didn't even blink or wave it away, he just continued to play in the dirt. In five minutes the prayers were done and the bus departed, leaving the girl with some coins in her hand.

A few nights later, the television set at Zahedan's lone nightclub showed scenes from Persepolis of the shah's celebration of the 2,500 year anniversary of the Persian monarchy. Royalty and dignitaries from around the world, including U.S. Vice-President Spiro Agnew and his wife, watched a parade of costumed figures from the country's impressive military past. Later, the guests dined on roast peacock flown in from Paris, drank Chateau Lafite Rothschild wine from 1945, and listened to music inside a great tent built near the steps of the ruins. The dry desert wind was whipping the sides of the tent in the background, but the television picture showed only smiling, laughing faces.

Some weeks later *Life* magazine gave the event extensive coverage in a major article with many photographs, but they didn't portray anything else that was happening in the rest of the country. The story did report however, "The lavish party was not without its critics…The shah shrugged off criticism. He had accomplished his aim: 'To reawaken the people of Iran to their past and reawaken the world to Iran.'"

The national media was glowing in its praise for the event, the shah, and the future for the kingdom. Of course, that was all that could be expected from a state-controlled press. One newspaper wrote, "The annals of 2,500 years of Iranian history have alternated between prosperity and misery, power and impotence. One of the ancient national legends relates the saga of the mythical bird, Phoenix. With the approach of old age, it would hurl itself into a fire, then rise from the ashes as a young, rejuvenated bird and start a new cycle of life. Perhaps no other legend can better symbolize Iran."

Those words proved to be more prophetic than the author could have realized. A few years later, when the shah was driven from his throne by a revolution based on the intense heat of the fundamentalist religious beliefs of millions of poor people, I remembered his celebration, that little boy, and the fly. The boy was probably dead by then. Somewhere in that vast expanse of emptiness, his tiny body would lie, wept over by his sister.

Flying South to Charbahar

In my notes on the trip to Zabol I wrote, "The thinking which calls for a (traffic) circle because the town is expanding must be reversed. If the city's officials can be shown the value in planning for the future constructively, Zabol can become a very nice city." Then I added, "Pray for rain".

But in my young naivete, I suggested that somehow a land use/street plan for the community could make things better. I wrote, "The future is full of possibilities for the city. It can become a nice place to live, or it can stagnate. To become the former, a good plan is needed; a plan which considers the people of the town."

How a land use plan was going to improve the lives of starving farming families should have been a question I asked myself. I was still searching, however, for a justification to the last of the three Peace Corps goals, accomplishing something on the job, so I ignored the issue.

Sarkis, one of the civil engineers in the office, helped me translate my report on Zabol into Persian. He knew enough English, and I enough Farsi, that we could slowly complete a paragraph or two at a time. When the report was finished, it along with those I would later write on the other cities in the province, would be sent off to the Ministry of the Interior in Tehran.

After work, I would sometimes wander the back streets of Zahedan. I wanted to be seen by people and let them know I was living in town. I also wanted to get a feel for the city, its residential areas as well as the major throughfares.

Zahedan was a single story community of mud brick structures with about 20,000 or 25,000 people. The census said the population was over

30,000, but those figures appeared to be unreliable and exaggerated. About half of the residents were tribal Baluch and the other half Persians who were there to administer, and control, the province of Sistan and Baluchistan.

I had been incorrectly told that Zahedan was founded in the 1930s by the shah's father to serve as the administrative headquarters for the province. The city was laid out in a grid pattern and had two main streets running perpendicular to each other. These streets were where the bazaar, a handful of restaurants, the two movie theaters, a few two and three story office buildings, and the military post were located. They were also two of the very few streets in the city, or in the entire province, that were paved.

Running to the airport, which was a few miles outside of town, was an asphalt road lined with recently planted trees. This street contained the largest and best landscaped traffic circle in Zahedan and was the grand entrance into the city. Since anyone of importance would fly in, not wanting to subject himself to the rough ride from Kerman, the airport road would be their first impression of Zahedan. This street was also the way to the secret police headquarters.

Homes in Zahedan were located on 12 foot wide alleys, or *kuchays* in Persian, which ran at right angles off of the main streets. There were a few dry washes cutting through town that interrupted the perfect grid street pattern. Next to the washes some poor Baluch families lived in cardboard boxes or palm frond huts. There was also a Baluch camp on the edge of the city where a large number of people lived.

An economic report on Zahedan prepared in 1970 outlined the important role the government played in the community. Almost one-third of the labor force was employed in government jobs, either as administrators or soldiers. That was three times the national average, the study said.

This report also suggested a lot of "ifs" for the city. If the train tracks extending into Pakistan were connected to the Iranian rail system at

Kerman, Zahedan would become an important port of entry. If mineral wealth was discovered in the province, Zahedan could become a storage center. If the city became a winter tourist destination, the report indicated it would need additional travel facilities. All of these "ifs" seemed a little far fetched as I took my evening strolls around a community where many people were barely surviving.

A week after I returned from Zabol, the new boss in the office told me I would be flying by mail plane to the fishing village of Charbahar. I was to stay there for two weeks and live with the mayor. Located on the Gulf of Oman, this small community was the reason the officials in Tehran were delighted when I decided to move to Baluchistan. There were great proposals for the future of the place, either as the site of a new winter palace for the shah, as a tourist destination for foreigners, or as a large military base. So the bureaucrats in Tehran wanted to know more about it. They didn't want to go there themselves, of course, but they wanted to know more about it, so I was sent. As an employee of the Ministry of the Interior, I was simply doing my job.

Just after dawn on a cool October morning, the small twin engine plane took off from Zahedan's "International" airport. Flying south would be a lot easier than the bus trip, I had been told. Three passengers sat silently as the pilot guided the aircraft up over the great expanse of desert below. Mountain ranges of gray and black rock were scattered here and there to the horizon, and a few light trails winding through the desert pointed out where the occasional vehicle would drive in this remote corner of Baluchistan.

After stopping at the city of Iranshahr to drop off some mail, and the other two passengers, we continued on to the coast. "Mister, are you an American?" the pilot asked when we were airborne again.

"Yes, I am."

"Why are you here? What are you doing in Iran?"

"I'm with the Peace Corps. I work for the engineering office. I'm sorry, but I don't know much Farsi."

"But what are you going to do."

"City planning for the Ministry of the Interior. Map drawing. I'll try to help."

"Did the Ministry send you to Zahedan."

"No, I chose it. Shiraz, Bander Buscher, and Zahedan were my choices. I picked Zahedan."

"That was crazy. Buscher I can understand. It is a hot, muggy, ugly place. But Shiraz is lovely. It was trees and water and poets and good restaurants and everything. Shiraz is much better than Zahedan. Zahedan has nothing but dirt and camels."

"I don't know how to explain it. I wanted to help."

Flying in over Charbahar, we could see that its shape followed the quiet blue bay the community partially surrounded. A few old buildings constructed by the British in the last century and the town's main street hugged the coastline. A little ways inland were some concrete block and brick buildings built recently as offices for the Persian bureaucrats that had been ordered to the place. A new 12 room government run hotel near the water was about to open, and a government employee housing project was on the edge of town. After bumping to a stop on the rough dirt strip that was Charbahar's airport, the pilot opened the door to the stifling heat and humidity of the day and wished me luck.

The mayor met me at the plane, and we drove to his office/home in an almost new Land Rover. It was approaching lunchtime, and he ordered his two young servants to bring us food as we walked up to the roof of his house. The sleeping porch there had a canopy over his bed, and the breeze from the ocean removed some of the sticky humidity from the air. It was still Ramadan, the month of fasting for Muslims, so the mayor quietly asked me not to let anyone know that he would be joining me for lunch.

Ramadan, according to a newspaper story I had seen, was supposed to be a month in which, "Moslems will spend each day, from sunrise to sunset, abstaining from food and drink. They must not swallow water or even allow themselves to inhale smoke from someone else's cigarette, if they can help it."

Two of the goals of Ramadan were to encourage increased alms-giving to the needy and to allow those fasting to have a better understanding of the plight of the poor. The assumption, apparently, was that money saved from not eating could be given away. The small hunger pains a person would experience during the month might also allow them to appreciate the daily condition of the less fortunate. From what I had seen, however, not many people tried to comply with the fasting rules.

The mayor was a Baluchi bachelor with a degree from a university in Germany. In his early 30s, he had only recently been assigned a government position and had been sent to Charbahar. He had some connections in Tehran but they obviously weren't substantial since he had received an undesirable posting. Mayors in Iran weren't elected, they were appointed by the government, and could be moved at will from place to place.

When he picked me up, the mayor was dressed in a suit but had quickly changed into tribal clothing once we were at his house. His baggy pants and flowing shirt looked to be a lot more comfortable in the sweaty climate. After a lunch of rice and fish, he offered me a bedroll to lie on, and a nap came easily in the heat.

Late in the afternoon, I strolled out to look at the town. Some camels wandered over the rolling, barren terrain and a few of the 2,000 or 3,000 inhabitants were visible. In the water, small open wooden fishing boats bobbed up and down, and as I walked along the beach a dark skinned boy dressed in rags and sitting atop an empty oil drum yelled "Hello" to me, so I took his picture.

A wide but shallow dry wash cut through the center of Charbahar, and palm trees dotted the town's sandy landscape. Also scattered around were the dome-like palm frond huts and small tents of the native Baluch people. They lived off fishing and the sheep and goats that they could afford to keep in this isolated outpost. There were only a few short stretches of paved street, most of the roads being just worn paths made by footsteps.

Ten or twelve stores were located on the main street, and all of the goods seemed to come from ports on the other side of the Persian Gulf. Even though my Farsi was not good, it would mainly be useless since most of the people spoke either Baluch or Arabic. I was to spend two weeks in Charbahar, but within an hour I had seen most of it.

My Iranian bosses in Tehran, however, had told me to do a land use survey of the place, talk to the mayor, and get an update on the five year old census. In general, I was to gather as much information as possible. So each day I would go out and walk around, drawing maps of where the two small and plain Arabic-looking mosques were situated and how the site of the government housing project related to other buildings. I also took pictures of the village. There just weren't that many structures to take pictures of. Most of the dwellings were huts and the Baluch people who lived in them probably moved on a very regular basis as they tried to feed their animals.

There had been talk about the future possibilities for the community when I had been at the Ministry of the Interior in Tehran. Staff members there said Charbahar was warm, had a beautiful beach, and was isolated. None of them had ever been to the village, of course, but they were certain it could be turned into a tourist destination.

A story in a Tehranian English language newspaper later in the year also discussed these possibilities. The author, while admitting she had never been to Charbahar, wrote, "at this time of year you can swim and water-ski in pleasantly warm seas". I had to laugh out loud when I read that, thinking back on the poverty of the place, the small wooden boats in the water, and the empty oil drums which lined the coast.

In 1970 the projection for the community, according to an economic report on the province, was that Charbahar would become a major fishing port. Nothing, however, was mentioned to me of those ideas a year later.

Before the shah fell, the future plans for Charbahar changed again. It was slated to become a military base with jets patrolling the Gulf of Oman. As I read about that proposal for the village in a magazine some years later, I thought again of the reality of the place.

Whatever the future plans, Charbahar in 1971 was so isolated that it was almost impossible to get to. A traveler could arrive by mail plane, fishing boat, or over an almost impassible road. But big plans, I was told, were being made to pave another road south from Zahedan all the way to the Gulf. A long bridge over a wide riverbed was already under construction north of Charbahar as part of this effort.

To pass my time, every morning I had long conversations with the mayor. He was generally bored being stuck out in this forgotten edge of the country, so we talked of Europe, the good life, and his plans for the future. He asked me to buy him some small personal items if I ever traveled to Europe, and I promised I would.

"It's not really such a bad place to be," the mayor told me one day. "Charbahar isn't like Europe, of course, but no place in Iran is. I don't expect to be stationed here long anyways. Someday I hope to get promoted to a job in Zahedan or somewhere larger."

"What this town needs now, though, is a good master plan. The new government operated hotel demonstrates that officials in Tehran are at least thinking about us. Some more streets will be paved shortly, so what we need now is a master plan. It will be the next step in attracting tourists. That way we can realize our dreams for Charbahar, at least on paper."

Each day, after an afternoon nap, I would go to the public bath near the beach to rinse the sweat off of me in a stream of salt water. Like most of the modern public baths in Iran, this one was inexpensive, clean, and had individual stalls for each of its customers. It just had salt water coming out of the faucet.

Drinking water for many of the people of Charbahar was supplied from a central well. Every morning and evening, veiled, barefoot tribal women would carry filled jugs of water on their heads from the well back to their huts.

At dusk each day I would sit on the beach, watching the golden sunsets. In my head I created new lyrics for popular American songs that I would sing to myself. Occasionally, one of the 20 or so vehicles in town would go bouncing by while I sang my songs. More often, though, a man would ride by on a small donkey, off in the direction of the market or hauling a load of wood to his hut.

Camels would also occasionally wander around. These dirty, mean-spirited but essential beasts were usually tied up to a post outside a Baluchi hut. They had a howling call and feet that mushed and spread out as they walked. They also drooled constantly and would bite if you got too close. But, as an Iranian map of the province proclaimed in somewhat broken English, "Despits motor transportation, camel has kept its importance in negotiating the hot deserts of Baluchistan".

All of the motor vehicles in Charbahar were either Land Rovers or pickup trucks. The main road from Zahedan, everyone told me, was very rough. Plus, only a few streets in Charbahar were paved, so vehicles that could take constant punishment, and were easy to fix, were required.

While we had to hide our noontime meal from public view, each night after dark the mayor would have a multi-course feast. This, along with a generous midnight snack, was the traditional way of meeting the rules of Ramadan. Once the sun went down, a fasting Muslim was allowed to eat anything they wanted, so many of those who participated in the religious ritual did not go hungry for long.

Over dinner, the mayor and I discussed politics and sports, Vietnam and Europe, life in general, and the future. The mayor was a man who was looking forward and knew what he wanted. He cared about his people and sought to serve them. We didn't talk about women much, but instead spoke about the world and what needed to be done to make it better.

After a week, the mayor announced he had been summoned to Tehran for some meetings. He told me that I would be left in the capable hands of his two young Baluch servants. These boys, both less than 12, were his cooks, cleaners, and helpers. Neither of them could read nor write, and they had no concept of what Zahedan was, much less the United States, but they would take care of me.

Having finished all of the data collection I was capable of, after the mayor left I spent my time lying in bed on his roof, listening to imported tape recorded music. Each day I would also tune his radio into the BBC overseas service and catch up on the news and the literary happenings occurring in London. Looking out across the Gulf as Big Ben chimed on the radio was my daily routine.

Electricity for the village was supplied by a generator 20 hours each day, but sometimes something would happen and it would shut down in the middle of the afternoon. The radio would then go silent, and I would close my eyes and try to think of the cool breezes blowing across the rooftop of the house.

Why I stayed the entire two weeks is beyond me now. Perhaps because that is what I had been told to do. Perhaps because I was enjoying the carefree existence of the place. Perhaps because I felt I couldn't leave until the mayor returned.

For a few days after the mayor left, things went by peacefully. It was quiet around the house, and there was little to do. One day I was walking down the main street of the village when I met two Italian tourists. These men had somehow made their way overland from Bandar Abbas, a port city hundreds of miles to the west. They extolled the richness of the sea life along the coast and asked if I cared to join them for a lobster dinner. "The locals don't eat lobster because of their religion," one of them said, "but we can order some from a fisherman at pennies per tail. So we'll get several this afternoon and come by your place tonight."

They arrived with a basket of lobsters, small but plentiful, and told the boys to boil them. Also for dinner were some rock oysters they had found along the coast. I chipped one of the blades on my new Swiss Army knife prying at an oyster but finally got it open.

To make the meal complete, the Italians had a lime, a little salt, and a bottle of whiskey. After a few drinks, we were singing songs in some sort of combination Italian-English and thinking we were very cosmopolitan. As we sat eating and drinking, the boys looked on in disbelief. They twisted their faces into contorted shapes as we stuffed ourselves. When offered some seafood, they turned away and said they could not eat the food; it was not healthy.

"So tell us, what do you do here?" the Italians asked.

"Work a little, drink some beer, and I'm trying to learn the language."

"It is certainly a beautiful place. You can't imagine what we saw coming here. Flocks of sheep and goats being herded by small boys. Camel caravans crossing the desert and villages where Europeans haven't been seen in years. They had no running water or electricity, but the people seemed to be happy. There were entire tribes of people moving from place to place. Some of them even had schoolteachers that moved along with the tribe. Everything was very beautiful, but very poor, of course."

"Our friends in Rome will never believe us when we get back there, but we have pictures. This is certainly a wonderful place. But it will be good to get back home, so we're leaving in a few days." They departed around midnight, staggering off into the dark, singing an Italian song.

My two weeks in Charbahar were also coming to an end. The mayor was expected to return shortly, and it was time for me to think about leaving. I went to visit the local official in charge of the mail plane and he welcomed me warmly. When I had spoken to him previously, he had given me the most delicious sliced pineapple I had ever had and told me there would be no problem in my taking the flight back to Zahedan. On this day, though, there was no pineapple, and he was sorry to inform me that things had changed. The plane would be full of dignitaries on the day I wanted to fly home. He apologized for the inconvenience, but said there was nothing he could do about it.

With only two flights a week, it was either wait for the next plane, and hope that there was space available, or take the two day bus ride back to Zahedan. I decided to depart on a set schedule and went to buy a bus ticket. There were only two buses out of town each week, but one was leaving in three days, so it would probably get me to Zahedan sooner than a chancy flight.

That night, as I lay on the roof of the mayor's house looking up at the stars with no thoughts going through my mind, I heard a scream from below. One of the boys came running up yelling at me for help. His Persian wasn't much better than mine, and in his panic I couldn't tell what he was saying, but it was obvious that he wanted me to follow him.

He led me to the kitchen where his companion sat sobbing over the sink, blood flowing freely from his towel-wrapped hand. A large knife was on the counter, and it was quickly apparent that the boy had cut off the index finger of his left hand while preparing dinner.

We wrapped another towel around the stump of his finger and I asked, as calmly as possible, where the doctors lived in town. The government workers housing project was just across the road, but I didn't know if that is where they stayed or not. We went out into the cool night air, and in the moonlight I followed the boys.

The doctors' house was toward town, next to the dry wash. Lights were visible inside, and I tried knocking a few times on their fence gate, but no one answered. I could see movement in the house, but a large sandy yard was between the gate and it. They probably couldn't hear us, so I just opened the gate and walked in. Wearing a bathrobe, one of the doctors appeared on the porch with a surprised look on his face and asked what I wanted. When I showed him the injured boy, he calmly said, "Take him to the emergency clinic in town. He'll be fine."

We went walking off again, the boy still sobbing to himself and me wondering about the health care of this country. But at the clinic they attended to the boy immediately and within a few minutes had him stitched up. It proved, after all the towels had been removed and the blood washed from his hand, that he had cut off only the tip of his finger. The boy would have a stub at the first joint to remember this night by.

By the time we returned to the mayor's house, both the injured boy and I had calmed down a little from the excitement. While we sat in the kitchen, waiting for more of the stress of the evening to wear off, both boys were laughing at me. My barging into the doctors' house was not something an Iranian would typically do. Displaying superficial politeness was very important to them, and just walking into someone's home, even in an emergency, was not considered proper behavior. I told the boys to blame it on my American upbringing. I was from the wild west, after all, or that is what many of them thought.

The next day things were back to normal around the house, but by the afternoon BBC "Radio Reader" program, my intestines were starting to hurt. Sounds were coming from inside me that were angry. Diarrhea was a common problem for almost everyone I knew and I had tasted my share of it. But I could tell this was something worse. Fortunately, the Peace Corps medical staff had provided us with little yellow pills. "Take six at a time until the symptoms stop," the label read. I put the bottle next to the bed and waited for the worst.

What happened then was scary. First my system emptied itself of all the food I had eaten in the last few days. Then a black, slimy liquid started coming out of me that looked evil. Squatting over the hole-in-the-floor toilet, my legs had lost their strength and were just barely able to keep me upright. I was popping pills every few hours and wondering what I was going to do. The bus was to leave for Zahedan in less than two days, the mayor was due back in the morning, and the narcotic in the medicine was beginning to affect my brain. Strange thoughts filled me that night. Dying at a young age in a desolate place, buried in a desert climate, was what I imagined.

The boys asked what they should do and insisted that I visit a doctor. All I wanted, though, was enough liquid to offset what I was losing. Dehydration was my worst fear, and so I kept drinking lots of water. I was afraid to go to the clinic because of the horror stories we had been told during training about Iranian medical practices, so I just lay in bed and moaned.

By 2 A.M. the pain in my stomach had started to recede and the pills had stopped me up. My mind, however, was swimming in and out of reality. I was cursing the local official for depriving me of a plane ride and instead forcing me to take a broken down bus across unknown desert territory back to Zahedan. Thoughts of murderous vengeance against him occurred to me, and then I faded off to sleep.

The morning found that I had taken over thirty of the pills and that I was weak but alive. Eating was out of the question; I was too afraid that I would open up my intestines again. With a shaky hand, I wrote in the journal I was keeping of the trip, "Advice:Don't get sick in a Persian home and don't take too many diarrhea pills". The mayor returned at lunchtime and expressed sympathy with my condition, but there really wasn't anything he could do if I wouldn't visit a doctor.

By late afternoon I was well enough to slowly walk down to a main street shop and buy a gallon jug in which to carry water for the bus trip. My lips were parched, my legs weak, and my head was blazing with fever, but I knew I had to keep drinking water. Either that or I was in serious trouble.

While we had been warned during training about the potential dangers with tap water in many parts of Iran, I had been drinking it everywhere I went. I hadn't had any major difficulties until now, but once I had a problem, there really wasn't much choice but to keep on drinking it.

The next morning, after stuffing worn and unwashed clothes into my suitcase and filling the jug with water, I made my farewells. It had been a mostly pleasant two weeks, but I was leaving exhausted, sick, and scared. The mayor drove me to the bus and wished me well.

"Mister David, take care of yourself. Is there anything you need? Is there anything I can do for you?"

"Bus driver, listen here. I am the mayor of Charbahar. This is my American friend. He isn't feeling well, so you take care of him. Do you understand?"

"Mister David, we'll probably meet again someday. I'll see you in Zahedan, or you'll return here. We'll talk some more about Europe and America. Be sure to take care of yourself. It's a rough trip, but you'll make it."

Standing by the bus were the two Italians, waiting to head north. They were in a jovial mood because it was time for them to return to Italy. A long bumpy bus ride to Zahedan and then by plane to Rome would get them home. They were excited.

The bus departed on schedule at noon. It was an older vehicle that must have once toured the main highways of Iran. Now it was used in a remote corner of the country where pavement and service stations were just fantasies. Before leaving, packages and a few goats had been loaded on top along with several spare tires and some containers of gasoline. We would be on our own until we reached Iranshahr, so the bus had to be prepared. Clinging to my water jug, I found an empty seat and got ready for the ride. It was to take 30 hours, and I set my mind, and insides, to the task.

The way north started by heading west along the sandy coast. We drove on the beach, the ocean spraying off to one side, a high mountain range of dark mass on the other. After an hour, the bus turned into the mountains and made its way slowly, very slowly, over a track cut through the rock. This wasn't a road; it was a donkey trail. A newspaper account of the path said, "It passes along river beds and crosses the streams so often…that it would become monotonous but for the fact that it's rather like being on a perpetual roller coaster. The dust, too, at times, is choking."

The going was at a few miles per hour as we dove down into dry streambeds and rose up along tall cliffsides. The driver was turning the wheel frantically, and there was no room for error. In back of him the passengers were bouncing all over the bus, but we were making progress, even if at a glacial pace.

A Baluchi man was sitting next to me, and we would bounce out of our seats in unison as the bus hit a rock or dipped down into a deep hole. I was slowly drinking my water, trying to keep my fever in check and my mind concentrated on making it back to Zahedan.

Just at sunset we emerged from the mountains. It had been several hours of torture, but the worst part of the trip was behind us. We stopped at a tiny oasis named Nikshahr which seemed to consist of a few date palm and banana trees and a small shack that sold soda pop and snacks. After draining out of the bus, we stood stretching our limbs and tried to make sure we were still all together.

The driver and his assistant checked over the vehicle and softly cursed to themselves simultaneously. They had found a leak in one of the brake lines which needed to be fixed before we could go on. Their repair kit consisted of a few hand tools and not much else, but like almost all Iranian bus drivers and auto mechanics, these two proved to be wizards with what was available. Within 30 minutes the leak was repaired, and we were on our way again.

As we sat watching the men work on the bus in the light cast by an oil lamp, the Italians asked me how I was getting on. "Surviving," is all I could say.

We were suppose to make Iranshahr before stopping for the night, but it was obvious that wasn't possible. While the dusty track flattened out and the going was faster after the mountains, the distance was too great. In the dark silence of the bus I was wondering how I would fill up the jug when it ran empty. Under the shiny moonlight outside, the desert was deep black with only the dark silhouette of mountain peaks breaking the view to eternity.

The moon was bright enough that the driver left the headlights off. Driving in the desert at night without lights was a common Iranian practice, even if there was traffic. "It saves power from the battery," I was told. It just seemed stupidly risky to me.

About midnight, in the vast emptiness of the desert, we reached a single house that had a lamp burning in the window. The driver stopped and announced he was going inside to spend the night, and anyone who wanted to sleep on the floor could join him. After my seat companion left, I decided the bus would be more comfortable. I curled up across two seats, arranging and rearranging my legs, trying to find a position that would work. Sleep came sporadically. The night was cold, so I pulled out some clothes from my suitcase to put on. Sometime in the middle of the night I shook the jug. There was still a little water in it.

The next morning we stopped in Iranshahr, and I filled up the jug. This was one of the country's hottest places with summer temperatures reaching 130 degrees. Life then, for those who had to stay, was lived in the basements of buildings, and activity ceased from 10 to 4 each day. The Baluchi tribal people would take their flocks to Pakistan for the season, and many of the Persian government workers could flee to Tehran, so it would only be a tough few that would stick out the heat.

On this cool early November morning, however, the desert sun felt good on my aching body. My fever had fallen, and the driver promised us good time. The dirt path north was mostly flat and fast. At one point we came to a small cluster of palms and stopped. From a shack among the trees a young, blind woman appeared. Everyone on the bus deposited a coin in her open hand before we left. The man sitting next to me explained that she lived with her mother in this remote place, and the offerings of strangers were what they had to rely on. Giving to the poor was a common Iranian custom, but in this case, it was the only way these two people could survive.

While the going was much smoother and faster than in the mountains, it was still a great distance to Zahedan. The driver estimated we would arrive by 10 P.M., so I rationed my water supply carefully. The desert was again the stark nothingness that was called Baluchistan. It was brown emptiness broken only by the occasional oasis or mud hut village of tribal people living on the edge of starvation.

At a rest stop, the Italians asked me where to stay in Zahedan and I offered them an empty room in our house. They preferred a bed after spending the previous night on the bus, so I directed them to the best, and almost only, hotel in town. As we approached Zahedan, its lights visible from miles away, I congratulated myself on surviving the trip. The water was just about gone, but I had made it.

My insides had not given me trouble in two days. As I started walking home from the bus station, however, I could tell that was about to change. My pace quickened, and then I began moving as fast as I could. The young guards outside the military post on the main street watched me hurry by, illuminated under the light of a single street lamp.

The suitcase and water jug were swinging in my hands as I jogged the few remaining blocks. The front door, of course, was locked. As calmly as possible I opened it, dropped my belongings in the hallway, and ran to the hole-in-the-floor we called a toilet. My intestines gave way, and I cursed my luck, but at least I was home.

I popped more pills into my mouth, drank some water, and got beneath the blanket of my own bed. The wooden frame and thin foam rubber mattress felt good. Sleep came despite my worry about what was happening inside me again.

In the morning I found that Robert had secured the services of a maid while I was gone. I also learned that no appointment was necessary to see a doctor at the government run clinic. The Peace Corps had printed some information on the medical practices and medicines of the country which I took along with me, just in case.

The doctor I saw had been educated in England, so I had no trouble describing what was happening. He told me to rest, eat only yogurt and soup for a few days, and take a prescription he wrote out. Unfortunately, it was on top of the Peace Corps' banned list of medicines. He quietly cursed to himself about Western ways and offered an alternative. Within a few days I was back at work, promising myself I would never take that many diarrhea pills again, or leave without a return ticket.

A few nights later Robert and Jamal took me out for a belated birthday dinner. I opened presents sent from Wisconsin and was grateful that I was seeing my 22nd year.

Settling in

Our new maid was a very thin, coffee-skinned Baluch woman. In her late 20s with tightly rolled deep black hair, she only knew how to cook a few dishes, her specialty being meat stew. While her cooking skills were limited, she could prepare rice well. Mountains of rice is what all Iranians seemed to eat each day. It was served with every main meal and if it was sprinkled with a saffron topping, that was even more special. In the western-style grocery store where I occasionally shopped were several sacks of different types and qualities of the grain. I couldn't tell them apart, but our maid could, and she would be doing the shopping for us.

While most people bought food in the bazaar, the small grocery store offered an alternative. It had neatly arranged items on shelves, marked prices on almost everything, and cash registers at the checkout stand. None of these, of course, existed in the traditional Persian marketplace. The store also had only a few customers on the occasions I shopped there.

At work I had an office to myself and sat behind an enormous and ancient wooden desk. Most of my time, however, was spent in another room with the engineers, surveyors, and draftsmen. Everyone except the secretaries, the only two women in the office, would gather together each morning at 8 or so for a glass of tea and gossip. Since there wasn't a lot of work to do, or at least we weren't encouraged to do much since there was no money to build anything, we sometimes talked for hours. Occasionally I would work on a master plan for a community or my report on Charbahar with Sarkis. Much of each day, though, I spent

171

explaining life in America, asking about the ways of Iranians, and doing crossword puzzles found in the English language newspaper.

The conversations with my co-workers gave me the opportunity to learn something about them. Many were sending large portions of their paychecks to their families in order to help with the cost of schooling for siblings and the day-to-day expenses of their parents. They all thought the U.S. involvement in Vietnam was crazy, that my country had no business being there. Despite the lack of work, most of the men wanted to accomplish something because they saw the need was so great.

One of the most frequent topics of discussion among us was the difference between our two systems of manners. For Iranians, blowing your nose in public or pointing a thumb at someone were considered crude and unacceptable. Also taboo were handling anything with your left hand and being outwardly hostile toward someone of the same social class.

Their social customs were called *tarroff*, and a more stylized, over extended and established method of public manners has probably never been invented. It included playing a game of status whenever a group went though a doorway or was served tea. From the highest to the lowest ranking person, the chance would be offered to go first or take the first glass. Everyone knew, though, that the opportunity would come back to the highest status person.

Tarroff included bowing slightly to superiors when you shook their hands, telling someone you were their slave as an expression of respect, and offering your possessions to a guest that might have politely admired something you had. An Iranian was also never to turn their back on another, since that would be insulting them. If it happened accidentally, the offended party would say, "A flower has no back" to indicate no personal offense had been taken.

Our friend Jamal regularly mocked these customs by quietly adding tag lines to the standard *tarroff* sentences. In passing someone he knew on the street but didn't like, he would stop to greet him, bow lowly, and say he was his slave. As we walked away, he would mutter, "You son of a bitch".

I applauded his ridicule of the system, and over beers we would have a contest to see who could come up with the best *tarroff* insults. In public, however, we continued to follow the rules of the game.

As the sun went down each afternoon, I usually walked around town, trying to have my face seen and getting to know the place. Occasionally little boys would yell "Unclean" and throw small pebbles at me, then run away laughing. I always tried to throw something bigger back at them, while shouting that they were "Uneducated", just to send the message I wasn't frightened.

On some of these strolls I would pass large room-sized rugs spread out upside down on a paved street, waiting for cars to drive over them. People told me this was a method used to clean the carpets, but I never did understand the logic behind it.

My evenings were spent listening to the BBC, reading, and playing some of the cassettes I had purchased in Tehran or my family had sent from Wisconsin. Frequently I would also walk to the bazaar to look at rugs or talk to a shopkeeper. At first I asked Jamal to come along because I knew the merchants would try to cheat me if I wanted to buy anything. As an American who didn't speak the language that well, I was fair game for them, but eventually I became more comfortable with going alone.

Bargaining is an Iranian tradition of long standing. As I learned the language by using it daily, I started to engage in the challenge of trying to find out how low I could get a merchant to go on the price of something.

There were a few lessons in bargaining that had to be followed. First, if you bargained, you had to buy. It wasn't polite to haggle over something that you didn't really want. Second, the philosophy that you cut the price in half as a starting point was for uninformed tourists. Finally, any imperfection in what was being purchased, any angle that could be used to gain an advantage, anything that would work to get a lower price, was acceptable.

The true bargaining session depended upon how the customer was sized up by the shopkeeper, the quality of the merchandise, and the mental agility of each side. Sometimes the give and take could consume up to 15 minutes or more, but I found it fun. Plus the line I used about being in the country to help the people and finding that all I received in return was high prices came in handy.

Zahedan's bazaar was a short, partially covered L-shaped structure. Most of the small shops sold either food items, clothing or goods imported from Pakistan. Inside the dark, arched-roofed interior were sheep skin coats and camel hide lamps, poorly made tribal rugs and Japanese electronic equipment, tailors and shoe sellers. Outside was where the produce merchants gathered daily. At the entrance to the bazaar was a meat market with several sheep heads stacked on the sidewalk, their eyes staring blankly while hundreds of flies circled them looking to land. Sheep head was a Persian delicacy which required an acquired taste that I didn't have, so I never asked for it.

Also outside the bazaar was where many of Zahedan's beggars would congregate every day to ask for alms. There were the infirm, blind people, and widows or abandoned mothers who refused to turn to prostitution in order to survive. One man who had lost both legs pushed himself around on a little board supported by roller skate wheels, his hands wrapped in black bandages to protect his knuckles.

Alms giving is a chief tenet of Islam, and these beggars, although very poor, were at least not starving. The generosity of my co-workers toward them was impressive. They would make it a point to leave a few coins almost every time we visited the bazaar.

By late November the desert air was turning cold. While our mud brick home had no heating, which eventually meant we had to buy kerosene space heaters, the office did have oil-burning stoves. They put out a very limited amount of warmth, however, so everyone had to pack in tightly around them. On especially cold, clear days we would sometimes stand next to the sunny wall in the courtyard, using the reflection of the rays to warm our bodies. Combating the frigid temperatures reduced even further the little work that was being accomplished at the office.

Jim and Cindy had invited me to return to Kerman for a traditional Thanksgiving celebration, and I gladly accepted. The bus ride west was another dusty, bouncy affair, and I wondered if I would ever want to fly instead.

Jeff was joining us in what would be a familiar rendition of the holiday. He craved Iranian sweets but had the unfortunate luck of living in a place where rosewater was added to most recipes. Its sticky, syrupy flavor dominated the taste of everything that contained it and meant that Jeff didn't buy any cookies or cakes in Yazd.

To help him get by, I brought along a five pound box of Zahedan's best baking. It was a selection of soft cookies, small tea cakes, and other local specialties. By the time we parted two days later, most of what was left in the box was crumbs.

Jeff was holding a Christmas party in Yazd for those that could make it, and I told him I would be there. But in early December another new boss for the office arrived and almost immediately decided to take a two week trip to see the southern part of the province. He wanted the American to go with him so I had to write Jeff that my plans had changed and I would have to cancel.

The trip did not last as long as planned because the new boss cut it short to get back to Zahedan. We had taken two vehicles, so a few of us finished some surveying work and returned two days later, but I still had time to be in Yazd for Christmas. The thought of a 24 hour bus trip, however, much of it over dirty, bumpy roads, was not enticing, especially after having just bounced around in the back of a Land Rover for 10 days. I let my cancellation stand.

Upon my return from the trip south I found that Jamal had moved in with us. He covered his bedroom walls with photos of Iranian and American movie stars, and his few possessions were laid out neatly on a small metal folding table. He worked at both the Water Department as well as occasionally at Robert's school, so we didn't know how often we would see him.

Almost immediately after moving in, Jamal started complaining about the maid's lack of cooking skills. She was limited in what she could prepare, but Robert and I felt sorry for her because she was very poor. Jamal, however, thought she might be stealing from us so we were careful about how much shopping money we gave her.

He also explained to us the importance of having a diet balanced between "hot" and "cold" foods. Some foods, like dates, were considered to be very "hot". Others, like yogurt, were "cold". Eating some of each, Jamal insisted, could keep a person healthy, but consuming too much of only one type could cause serious problems.

Jamal also ridiculed my dining room table. "Mister David," he said, "meals should be eaten sitting in chairs."

"But Jamal, I thought Iranians liked to sit on the floor. Everyone seems to do it."

"That is for uneducated people, not for us. Just like we use silverware instead of our hands to eat, we should sit at a table like human beings, not with the bugs crawling around on the floor." Since I had saved the sawed off table legs, Jamal quickly had them welded back on.

While it didn't make any difference to me how we ate our meals, by this time I had become very comfortable with sitting cross-legged on the floor. I could sit that way for hours while visiting someone, drinking tea and talking about the world outside of Sistan and Baluchistan province. At night I would sprawl out on the straw mat on the floor of my room, listening to the BBC or taped music. With a covered floor, who needed furniture?

The big rage in Iran at the time, however, was to own high priced, over stuffed, French-inspired, ugly furniture. The Iranians had even borrowed the French word for it, and having a room full of "meuble" was a middle-class aspiration. But as one English language newspaper pointed out, "it is not really furniture at all, since it does not provide comfort and does not fulfill the function of furniture". Instead, it was materialism as show piece, a very un-Iranian like trait.

Other than buying carpets, many middle-class Iranians did not seem to be caught up in the consumer game. Their homes were modest, they usually didn't own automobiles, or if they did, they were compact models, and they didn't have a lot of clothes and other possessions. They spent their money, instead, on helping their extended family.

The Christmas holiday for Robert and I wasn't going to be much. I had mailed off hand drawn cards to the United States weeks before, and my family had sent me a box load of goodies. But being away from the cold and the snow and the friends of Wisconsin for the first time on a Christmas made it a little sad. It was just another day, really.

We gave the maid the day off and I decided to try cooking meatloaf again. While walking to the bazaar to buy some potatoes, a long-haired, dirty clothed young man stopped me. He asked, in the best American English possible, if I knew when the bus to Kerman left town. It wasn't until late afternoon, so I invited him to join us for Christmas lunch.

Over a poorly prepared meal which was a welcome change to the stew and rice that Robert and I ate most days, our guest described his travels. He had visited India and had just entered Pakistan when he was stuck in Karachi for days by the Pakistani/ Indian war. "I saw planes diving over the city's port, dropping bombs followed by immense explosions," he said, "and naturally I wanted to get out as soon as possible. The place was a mess, and the Pakistani people are very depressed because of their defeat."

He had taken a bus headed west and, fighting a bout of diarrhea, finally arrived in Zahedan. "It was terrible. I couldn't get my insides to stop up. Of course, there is no bathroom on these buses, the driver wasn't going to stop for me, and I couldn't just get off. So I crawled to the back of the bus and emptied my suitcase of anything I could use. Plastic bags, the thing my toilet stuff was in, anything. The bus was rolling on, and I just had to keep going."

As Robert and I laughed loudly at the excruciating images of a desperate traveler, he continued his story. "Finally I got down to a sailor's cap I had. After I filled it up and threw it out the window, I didn't know what I was going to do. Fortunately, the diarrhea stopped. I still don't know what I would have done."

That night, the BBC played carols. Later, I lay on my floor listening to a cassette which my brother had sent me. It was a tape of top 10 tunes, family conversation, and additional tidbits from home. It, and the many other cassettes he and my family would send over the next 16 months, helped me to pass my time in Zahedan.

After hearing the Beatles sing about leaving Tucson, Arizona, I put on the wailful tunes of Bob Dylan's "John Wesley Harding" and thought of other places. My first Christmas away from home was lonely, but at least it was over with.

A few days later, Robert flew off to Tehran to get married. He expected to return with his bride and move into a new house, but when he came back he was alone, the bureaucracy standing in their way of being together. His wife was a teacher, and the Iranian government decided that she couldn't switch jobs in the middle of the school year. They would have to live apart, at least until summertime.

1972

1972

Jamal and Fatima

Over the next several months, Jamal introduced us to the Iranian bachelor way of life. He would bring poor prostitutes to his room twice a week, at first telling us a tale about how they were illiterate and he was going to write letters for them.

The women would spend an hour or so and then go back to their families. The two most frequent visitors were poor Baluch women who had been abandoned by their husbands. Both had children to support, and prostitution was the only way they knew how to do it. They had no education, no money, and no other prospects in a male controlled society.

Jamal's suspicions of the maid grew so intense, and she missed so many days of work, that we eventually fired her. The next day Ali, a teenage boy who lived down the alley and who liked to hang out at our house, said his aunt Fatima was looking for a job. We hired her quickly, and she proved to be a much better cook.

After work, Jamal sometimes drank beer and smoked hash in the living room with Robert and I, and his exploits and dreams both grew to immense proportions as the evening wore on. He also had another side to him which we soon discovered. He was a movie fan who saw his life in terms of the great stars in their best roles. He claimed he was "Zorba the Greek", ridiculing the authorities and living a carefree life. In reality, though, he was a minor bureaucrat with the water agency and while he made fun of many things privately, in public he was always condescending and softspoken. He didn't make much money, but every month would send some of what he had to his mother in Shiraz.

Short, even by Iranian standards, Jamal liked to pump up his chest and wear heeled shoes to appear taller. He was clean shaven and couldn't explain why Iranians, both women and men, used a cream to remove all the hair from their bodies. At the same time, though, most of the men seemed to prefer mustaches.

Over time, more Iranian men moved into the house. They were professionals from my office or Jamal's and most of them looked at Zahedan as a temporary stopover on their way back to Tehran or wherever they came from. They hated the place, its isolation and lack of things to do, and wanted to get out as soon as possible.

But while they were there, we would get drunk often and tell stories of what we would all be doing in a few years. On some nights, we would go to one of the two movie theaters in town and howl at the Indian features of non-physical romance and extraordinary acrobatic daring which were frequently shown. When Jamal's lady friends appeared, they would visit each Persian man's room in succession, and then be on their way.

This emergence into Iranian culture also taught me the language well. At our frequent drinking parties, during the weekly trip to the one nightclub in town, and on the job, I had to speak Persian or not speak at all. No one else besides Robert spoke English fluently, so proficiency in Farsi became important.

When it was announced many months in advance that Richard Nixon would be visiting Iran in May of 1972, Jamal wanted to invite him to come to Zahedan. To contrast the difference between our two countries, since a letter asking the shah to visit would probably get the writer a jail sentence, I sent off an invitation. The State Department wrote back with their regrets, but Jamal was impressed by the response anyway.

Our life was very comfortable. Fatima, the new maid, was a Baluch woman who was an excellent cook and housekeeper. She had a cleft palate that had never been corrected, so she would keep her *chador* over her mouth whenever one of us spoke to her, but communication between us was very limited anyway. She was shy, and as Jamal liked to remind us, our servant, so conversations outside of what we wanted to eat for lunch or what needed to be done around the house were rare.

Fatima was a small woman in her mid-20s who was married to an elderly, white-haired man. They had a young daughter that would accompany her mother to the house every day. Even though the girl was only three, she also often wore a *chador*. Both mother and daughter would usually keep their veils on at all times we were in the house. Fatima was a devout Muslim and followed its beliefs. Her family was poor but not destitute, and they lived somewhere out on the edge of the city in a Baluch camp.

We paid Fatima the equivalent of $4.20 a week, not much, but probably more than any other maid in Zahedan made. Persian men were, in general, very stingy with their money when it came to paying for household help.

For her salary, Fatima worked from 6:30 a.m. to 3:00 p.m., six days a week. In addition to the money we paid her, she took home all the leftovers from our meals, so she would typically cook much more than we could eat.

When we were at work, she would begin preparing rice for lunch. This was a process that took hours and had to be done very carefully in order to get the best possible result. To accompany the rice she would cook lamb, fish, or chicken. Her specialties, however, were stews made with cabbages, carrots, potatoes and other vegetables. She also prepared a stew with meat covered in a pomegranate sauce which was my favorite.

Fatima would also clean the house, go shopping for groceries in the bazaar, and do the laundry. She washed our clothes by beating them with a rock and scrubbing them with soap under a running faucet. There was no flowing stream in Zahedan, but her clothes cleaning method was just as if there had been. Once the laundry had been washed, it would be hung on a metal clothesline which was strung along the wall of the courtyard.

While we were home, Fatima almost always stayed in the kitchen with her daughter. Our only communication with her was by way of a trap door to the dining room through which our food would be passed. All we saw of her on most days was her flowing *chador* appearing in the morning or leaving the house as we stretched out to take an afternoon nap.

Our home was a four bedroom mud brick dwelling built around an interior courtyard. A small reflecting pool in the center of the patio was always dry because water was just too precious. A few hardy poppy plants grew up around the pool, their bright red flowers bringing some color to the place. We had a hot water heater which was a real luxury in Zahedan, a garage that remained empty, and a kitchen with a gas burning stove and small refrigerator. We were upper class citizens in Zahedan and lived like it.

The rent money being paid by our roommates combined with our individual $110 a month salaries quickly gave Robert and I each fairly large savings accounts. Every two months the Peace Corps also sent a check for the total rent due on the house, but somehow we always seemed to forget to tell them about the Iranians living with us. Robert was saving for the time when his wife could join him. I wanted to buy rugs and travel as much as possible.

There was no pressure at work for me to do anything. Plus I was away from the Peace Corps and Iranian government bureaucrats of Tehran and not involved with the budgetary and personnel games they constantly seemed to be playing, so time went by quickly.

There were some cultural adjustments that Robert and I did have to make. Our toilet was a hole-in-the-floor that had to be squatted over. Instead of toilet paper, for washing up a vase of water was available next to the hole while a sink outside the toilet was used to keep the hands clean. This sanitary arrangement was the reason behind the use of the right hand for all public exchanges since the left hand was the "dirty" one.

I was told the workday in summertime, when it arrived, would be divided by an afternoon nap, which made sense given the heat of the desert. Telephones were very expensive and unreliable, so we did without one. We had no television, so conversations with roommates, male get-togethers, and the radio were the primary methods of passing the evening. But life was easy.

When the heat returned to the desert in late April, we moved our beds out into the courtyard. The temperature dropped rapidly at night, and underneath a sky full of stars, blankets were often necessary. At sunrise, the main mosque in town would broadcast the first call to prayer of the day over a loudspeaker, awakening everyone. The wailing, plaintive tune was somehow soothing in the early morning light.

The mosque was on one of Zahedan's main streets and was a modern, undistinguished looking building. Its most memorable feature was a tower which was topped by the speakers over which the call to prayer was played. At the peak of the tower the word Allah was spelled out in neon tinted green, the most important color in Islam.

I understood that in large cities the call to prayer was sung by blind men. This was an important feature since from their position in the minarets high above a mosque, they could look down into people's courtyards, and thus into their private lives. In Zahedan a tape recorded message had to suffice.

After a breakfast of hot flat bread, butter, jam, and tea, I would walk the few blocks to the engineering office swinging my empty black briefcase. Jamal would take a taxi to the Water Department, and Robert would ride his bicycle to work. He had fiddled with it, so he sat very high above the wheels. As he rode along, children would wave and call out "Mr. Camel" when he went by.

Social life in Zahedan consisted of the occasional movie, getting a sandwich after work, or meeting at a bar or someone's house to drink. Every Thursday evening we would go out to the one nightclub in town to eat dinner, have a few drinks, and listen to a four piece band try to imitate western music. Friday lunch, since that was the religious holiday for the week as well as Fatima's day off, was eaten at either the restaurant that served rice and fried lamb or the other one that had rice with ground lamb.

Friday afternoon lunch was an event. Both of Zahedan's main restaurants would be packed with men of every description, all eating the same thing. The din from their conversations filled each place with words. The fancier restaurant had numerous metal card tables and folding chairs which were quickly occupied. It also had an upstairs dining area reserved for women and children. Shoeshine boys, dressed in rags and looking hungry, would walk around the restaurant trying to make a few pennies.

The typical restaurant in Iran usually had only a very limited number of things on its menu. There was rice with mutton kebabs, broiled chicken, vegetable stew, and maybe one other dish available. These were items not often eaten at home, and the difference between Fatima's cooking and restaurant fare was immense, hers being much better. Most Persian restaurants offered food as sustenance, not a stylish event.

The nightclub was a mile outside the city and had the largest menu of food items in town. It also served beer and was the place to be on a Thursday evening for the affluent of Zahedan's society. Most weeks we would go out and get drunk, talk of our exploits for the week in voices that grew louder as the evening went on, take a taxi home, and stumble into bed. The next week we would return with the dozens of other groups that were regulars at the place, and everyone would go through the same performance again.

There were also a few sandwich shops and liquor stores that we patronized for their beer. One served delicious cucumber and yogurt salad, along with fried lamb testicles. Another was owned by a Sikh gentleman who was a friend of Jamal. As we sat drinking in the office above his liquor store one evening, he told me, "In Iran, you can talk about anything but the shah, religion, and female family members. Remember that, and you'll be all right." I found it to be very sound advice.

Rain

Early in the new year, an unexpected directive came from the Ministry of the Interior in Tehran announcing that several road construction projects would be funded in the next few months. A team from the engineering office needed to travel throughout Baluchistan to begin preparing for this work by surveying the proposed streets and gathering additional information.

A group of five from the office, Hassan the surveyor, Sarkis the engineer, Reza the draftsman, Ali the driver, and Dave the American, were in a Land Rover which set out on a cool, overcast January afternoon for a tour of the southern part of the province. We were told rain had been falling in some areas which was very unusual since it had not rained in years in much of Baluchistan. The change, we agreed as we left Zahedan, could be interesting.

The first night we stayed in the schoolhouse at Saravan, a small town on the road to the coast. Blanket covered foam rubber mats on the floor were our beds.

The local government administrator heard I was in the surveying group and invited me to join him and his friends for supper. It turned out to be a regular gathering of Iranian men except that a foreigner was present as a conversation piece. Over beers and a dinner of sandwiches and canned foods, I tried to hold my own in the talk concerning the United States, sports, and life in Baluchistan.

Being a novelty attraction was something I had become accustomed to. Learning more about Persian men, as they got to know a little about me, was a fair tradeoff. It also covered two of the three principles of the Peace Corps, the other being the elusive one of trying to get something accomplished on the job. Everyone knew, of course, that the last objective was the least important to the American bureaucrats that ran the program.

Saravan consisted of large date palm orchards, a short main street of shops, and a residential area where a few thousand people lived in mud brick buildings and Baluch huts. It had some paved roads with more being worked on. The town seemed prosperous and was a nice little place.

The next day, after completing our surveying work in Saravan, we traveled on to Iranshahr. The mayor put us up in his guestroom, and as a light rain began to fall, he served us supper. Sitting around a plastic sheet spread on the floor, an oil lamp providing light, we passed plates of cold cuts and canned fruits and vegetables.

"This weather is very strange," the mayor said as we ate. "People tell me it hasn't rained here in nine years. So this is very rare. I don't know how much is expected, but it is welcome."

"Nine years?" I inquired.

"Yes, Mister. This is a very dry desert, so we will see how much falls."

It was still raining in the morning, and huge pools of water had formed in the desert. The brown sameness of the land had been transformed into a shiny mirror of liquid. The drive south was slow since the dirt road was turning into mud, but we kept going.

We had gotten an early start because it promised to be a long drive to Charbahar. I briefly visited with the third Peace Corps volunteer in the province, Jim, a young Wisconsin dairy farmer teaching agricultural practices at a training school 20 miles outside of Iranshahr. Then we moved on toward Nikshahr, the tiny village where the bus had broken down on my trip north from the Gulf a few months before.

As we bounced along the muddy track, no other vehicles in sight, Sarkis showed me how to eat a pomegranate without creating a seedy, sticky mess. Selecting one from a bag we had brought with us, he squeezed the dark red fruit for a minute. "You must do it firmly, but gently," he said. "You need to make it soft and pliable."

Taking out his pocketknife, he poked a small hole in the pomegranate, put it to his mouth, and pushed on it hard. The juice came streaming out, a refreshing break while traveling through the wet, muggy desert.

At Nikshahr we quickly ate a lunch of yogurt and canned beans, and Hassan surveyed the route for a new water line. It had stopped raining by the time he finished, but we hurried anyway to pack the Land Rover and get going again. The trip through the mountains to Charbahar was hazardous enough, but with water running in the usually dry streambeds and the possibility of having to drive in the dark it would be doubly dangerous.

The land had become soaked with water, and hints of green were starting to show on long dormant vegetation. The sand in the stream bottoms was soft, and we had to drive very slowly through them. The four wheel drive of the Land Rover allowed us to keep going through some of the wider water logged channels. At one point a truck was stuck in a riverbed, its driver pondering how to free his vehicle from the wet sand. We stopped to help, but the vehicle wasn't budging.

By late afternoon a light rain was falling again, and our drive was mostly in silence. Ali and Reza traded turns at the wheel as we all wondered how far we could get while it was still light. The path through the mountains had become a test to see if we could avoid the pitfalls of the course and reach the coast before nightfall.

We couldn't. Rain was still falling at dusk when Hassan asked if we should stop. "I think we need to stay in a streambed tonight. It is too dangerous to keep going. Reza, you can't see anything, and if you drive off one of these cliffs, we're done for."

"God willing, that won't happen Hassan," Reza sternly replied. "I'll go slowly, and a bed tonight will feel much better than sleeping in the Land Rover. We'll be fine. You'll see."

"I don't know. It is a long way, and it is very dark." But at a few miles an hour we went on, the headlights illuminating a running wash here, a path along a cliff edge there.

The rain finally stopped, and under a cloudy sky and dim moon we at last reached the coast. The mile or so of hard packed sand between the mountains and the ocean was all covered in water, shimmering in our headlights. Which direction we had to go was easy, just keep the breaking waves on our right and the dark mountain peaks on our left. But other than that it was driving along a beach covered in two inches of water, hoping to find our way.

The quiet of the Land Rover was broken when Ali yelled that he saw a light ahead. We went toward it and came across a small shack with two security guards sound asleep. After waking them for reassurance, we returned to the beach. Soon the few lights of Charbahar were visible, and we knocked on the mayor's door at midnight, looking for a place to stay.

A light morning mist covered the Gulf, and the ground was damp beneath our feet as we surveyed the route for two future streets. Food in the village was in short supply because trucks couldn't get through the mountains. Fish was available but everything else was scarce. We had already eaten a lot of beans and other canned foods, and the prospect of more of the same was not enticing. The mayor offered us whatever he had and we were relieved to be among friends. The Middle Eastern custom of helping travelers had been put to the test and passed.

By noon it was raining heavily, and the forecast was for another week of storms. If that happened, the five of us would be spending a lot more time than planned in Charbahar. We had been one of the last vehicles to make it through the mountains, and with more rain, the route home simply wouldn't be passable until it dried out.

That afternoon we sat around the room the mayor had set aside for us, drinking beer, playing cards, and listening to the BBC. By the next morning rain was still falling, and Hassan was growing impatient with the weather. He decided we should try another way home, a new road that went east toward Pakistan before turning north.

After waiting another day for the rain to stop, which it didn't, we set off anyway. The new road was a smooth gravel path, and Ali was driving fast because we all wanted to know if we could leave the coast. The one uncertainty was a bridge being built over a usually dry riverbed about 30 miles north of Charbahar. The mayor didn't know how near completion the work was, so we were going to find out.

Approaching the river, through a damp windshield we saw dozens of workmen busy building a major structure over a wide span. They were still far from linking the two sides while below them a violent river was rushing toward the Gulf. There was no way we could get across that watery chasm.

Weeks later Jim-the-farmer told me a story about that turbulent, ephemeral river. Two Land Rovers full of scientists had approached it from the north the day before we were there. At that time the river was more of a rushing stream, less of a raging torrent. Wanting desperately to get across, but not knowing if it was possible, they unloaded one of the vehicles and sent it off. The driver slowly inched his way through the swirling water and reached the other side.

With that success, the others loaded up the second Land Rover and set off. But they had extra bodies, and more equipment, and the added weight soon got them stuck. With water quickly rising, they abandoned ship and swam to shore. There they watched the Land Rover slowly move south, being washed inexorably toward the Gulf.

After realizing we couldn't cross the raging river, we retreated to the nearby village of Negur and asked for hospitality from the local government administrator. His was one of only two concrete block structures in the place, all the other dwellings being the palm frond huts or black tents of tribal people.

Negur was a Baluch village ruled over by an appointed official and looked down on by a military post built on a nearby hill. If it had any fame, it was because of the desert dwelling crocodiles that inhabited a riverbed east of town. The primary diet of Negur's Baluch residents was dates and bread. Like most members of the tribe living in rural areas, that is about all they could afford, or obtain. They earned what little money they had by tending their flocks of sheep and goats, and some of them carried goods throughout greater Baluchistan on camelback.

While the tribal people were terribly poor, at least some of their villages did receive help from the government. As part of his 1963 "White Revolution", the shah had instituted a series of social reforms. One of them required every high school and university graduate to serve a term in one of the country's service "Corps", either education, health, or development.

These young people would be assigned to villages like Negur to do what they could. It was an impressive idea to have the well-off youth of the country helping the poor. A November 1972 newspaper article on the upcoming 10th anniversary of the "White Revolution" said of the Literacy Corps, "Although the idea of an organized campaign against illiteracy is relatively novel in Iran, it has already paid excellent dividends. The number of children and adults in the 6-35 year age-group that have become literate has gone up by more than 12 percent and is currently around 40 percent. It is expected that the percentage will increase to around 75 within the next five years."

Hassan had brought along a master plan for the village prepared in Tehran, and he decided to chalk out the roads shown on it. The rain had stopped, and, ignoring my protests that this place needed lots of things but not asphalt streets, the others went to work while I stayed inside the local administrator's home.

From my bedroll on the floor I watched them silently survey between Baluch huts and drop chalk in the straightest lines they could. Soon the rain started to fall again, and the chalk began to disappear. A camel was lying in the path of one of the future "streets", and Hassan had to get the owner to move it before they could proceed. Within a few minutes the rain was coming down heavily, and the men retreated to the room and joined me for an afternoon nap.

The rain was still falling when we arose. Over a late lunch of rice and mutton patties, Hassan and I argued about the importance of laying out future streets in this impoverished village.

"It's crazy," I said emphatically. "These people need many things like a school, a medical clinic, and jobs. Asphalt streets aren't important. What are they going to use them for, to walk their camels on? The only vehicles here are owned by the mayor and the military. The Baluch don't need streets."

My voice rose as I continued my strident lecture. "It seems like the United States is a paradise many Persians are striving to copy. My country, despite its paved streets, is no paradise."

"Mister David," Hassan fired back in a loud voice. "We are professionals and should do the job we were sent here for. As I've told you before, things are different in Iran than in your country. Paved streets are important to us. Tell me, how many streets in America aren't paved."

"Not many."

"So why shouldn't we want the same thing here? Asphalt is a sign of progress for us. It might not help these people, but at least it will show them that the government is doing something for them."

Sarkis, the civil engineer, interceded to calm us down. In a hesitant manner he said that maybe the American Mister had a point. Maybe the money could be spent in a better way. Sarkis had gone to college in Turkey and had an outlook on the world different from some of the others in the office. He concluded with a chuckle, though, that it didn't really make much difference what any of us thought, the rain was taking care of the street issue. As he said that, a downpour was washing away most of the chalk from the ground.

By the next morning the chalk lines were all gone, and we were reduced to reluctantly returning to Charbahar. Our money supply was running low, and Hassan wanted to wire for more, but the lines were down, so for the next three days we could do nothing but wait. Wait for the rain to stop and the track home to dry out enough so we could head north.

We played cards, drank beer, and talked about life. Hassan was growing irritable because he wasn't accustomed to doing nothing or being away from his wife and children for so long. He searched for news of someone venturing through the mountains, but nothing was moving; it was just too wet.

Finally things changed. On our third day back in Charbahar, the sun emerged, and by late afternoon the word spread that a vehicle had made it through the mountains. Hassan went off to confirm the story and returned to say excitedly that it was true. He decided that we should leave in the morning and told us to get ready for a rough trip.

At sunrise we were off. The water had receded from the beach, and we made good time along the coast. Once we turned into the mountains, though, we slowed to a crawl. Water was still flowing in the streambeds, and we took turns walking in front of the vehicle to guide it to solid ground. At one point we had to build a bridge of rocks, branches, and other debris to get the Land Rover across a small stream. Ali slowly drove over this trash heap of a road, and we continued on.

After six hours we emerged from the mountains at Nikshahr. To make up lost time, and to relieve the frustrations of the last week, Ali drove fast over the gravel road to the north. At one point we hit a bump, hard, but just kept on going. Darkness caught us at Gas-re-gan, a small village rumored to be a town full of syphilis sufferers, and we spent the night in a room at the schoolhouse.

In the morning the radiator was empty, a small hole punched through it by the bump in the road. Hassan was in a hurry, so we set off, depending upon the water lying on the desert floor to refill the radiator. There really wasn't any other choice, since there was no way to repair it. At first we could travel 15 minutes before having to stop, then 10, then 5. A trip which should have taken us only a few hours was taking all day. The weather had turned cold, and by dusk a light snow was falling as we slowly moved toward Iranshahr, one of the hottest places in the country.

Eventually the radiator gave out completely. Ali had to spend the night with the vehicle while the rest of us flagged a bus down and rode into town. The mayor kindly made arrangements for a room at the local orphanage. The school was having a talent show that evening, so the four of us, wearing clothes which hadn't been washed in awhile, got to watch singers and comedy skits.

The next day the Land Rover was towed to a garage, the radiator fixed, and we did some quick surveying. We would be going home in the morning, and everyone was impatient to get on the road. Much of the work we had been sent to do had gone undone, but at least we were heading in the right direction.

The morning dawned clear and cold. The vehicle was not operating properly, so we had to stop at the small town of Khash to have it worked on again. It was after dark when we drove into Zahedan, and they dropped me off at my front door. Even though in my room I only had a bed and clothes rack plus closets made from an old refrigerator box and two suitcases, the place looked like home. It was a relief to be back.

Spring Break to The East

Upon returning to the engineering office the next day, we found dandelions blooming in the cracks of the courtyard pavement. Set against the starkness of the plain whitewashed mud walls and the desolate beige desert surroundings, their yellow flowers added a refreshing touch of color.

"In my country, these are considered weeds," I told Hassan. "We destroy them as quickly as they appear. They ruin the lush emerald carpet effect we try to develop with grass." He softly replied that they were a precious flower that should be nurtured. I couldn't disagree, seeing them in this place.

Reports later in the year indicated that Baluchistan was greener than it had been in almost half a century. All of that water had to be welcome to the desert vegetation, and they had taken advantage of it.

When I had visited with Peace Corps volunteer Jim at the agricultural school south of Iranshahr, we had agreed to travel together to Pakistan and Afghanistan over the Iranian New Year. While officially only a three day holiday centered around March 21st, everyone told us that all government workers took two weeks off. We decided to take some additional vacation time and go and see the exotic sights to the east.

Before Jim arrived in Zahedan, I invited everyone from the office to celebrate St. Patrick's day at our house. Of course my co-workers had no idea what the occasion was, but the description I gave of green dyed beer intrigued them. I tried to explain the American tradition of honoring an Irish holy man by getting drunk, but somehow they couldn't grasp the concept.

Also attending would be Essie, the Peace Corps urban planning pro-gram director, who was in town on a site visit. Gerry, my college friend now living in Tehran where he was helping to design a large park in the southern part of that city, had come with him. They had driven out, stopping in Yazd and Kerman along the way, and arrived dusty and hot. They brought a case of Budweiser from the American Embassy, and the beer went immediately into the refrigerator, so it would be cold on the 17th.

I had decided to prepare spaghetti since it was the only meal I knew how to fix for the sixteen or so people expected. Fatima offered to cook a good dinner for us, but I declined. This was something I wanted to do myself.

My mother sent some appropriate decorations of paper shamrocks, leprechauns, and the saint himself. Our dining room looked very fes-tive, and American. The space, I concluded, would be tight but suffi-cient. As the evening approached, I just didn't know quite what to expect.

On the designated evening, everyone from the office came, including the middle aged widowed secretary. As they sat around the table nerv-ously exchanging small talk, I was rushing in and out of the kitchen, and beer was flowing freely for those who drank it. When the spaghetti was served, most people didn't take much. As one of them explained after another beer, "Mister David, in Iran we don't eat spaghetti very often, and I don't like it". The night was a success, however, and for the next year the subject of the green party was a frequent topic of conversation in the office.

After everyone departed, I was simply going to throw the leftover spaghetti away, but Jamal insisted we give it to the poor Baluch people instead. He took the large pot it was in and walked to some of the nearby shacks which lined the riverbank. Within a few minutes he returned, the pot empty.

Jim arrived the next evening, and over supper we discussed our travel plans. I expressed my frustrations at not having completed the paperwork needed to leave the country. An Iranian re-entry visa was required, not to get out of the country, but to get back in.

To obtain the re-entry visa I had to have my boss or the governor sign a form. I had tried the typical bureaucratic channels to get a signature but had been unsuccessful. The office boss was not helpful, telling me in all seriousness that if I didn't return, he would be held responsible, so he wouldn't sign.

"They keep stalling me, and I just feel like leaving," I stridently told Jim. "Then let's see what the border guards do when I return."

"Don't do that," Essie warned anxiously, "because you might not be able to get back in." But with a few beers in me, it certainly sounded like the right thing to do.

In the morning, Jim and I went off to see the governor. His male secretary told us it would only be a few minutes, but after waiting two hours, I decided that was enough. I just got up from my seat and walked into his office, his secretary imploring me to be patient just a little longer.

The governor was sitting at his huge desk, a look of bewilderment crossing his face when he saw me. Behind him, a stoic shah looked down on us from a life-sized photograph. Somewhat startled, the governor asked what I was doing. His secretary, who had rushed into the room after me, explained it to him. The governor quickly signed the form, and Jim and I went to have a beer to celebrate.

The next day we took a taxi the 25 or so miles out to the border and walked across without a problem. On the Pakistani side were only a few huts and some large trucks waiting to get into Iran. The nearest settlement in Pakistan was about 80 miles away, and we had to sit around all day before a large truck heading east appeared. With the driver's permission, we hopped in the back and bumped along over the dirt road.

Arriving in the village at sunset, we located a room with two rope spring beds, minus mattresses, and went to get something to eat.

After dinner we walked around the small town and found a steam engine at the train station, puffing away in the moonlight. Some freight cars were behind the locomotive, and the engineer was busy in the cab. We called up to ask where he was headed and how soon he was leaving. He said, "Quetta, in a few minutes," and that if we wanted a ride, we could sleep in the crew quarters. But, he insisted, we had to return in a few minutes.

Hurrying off, we collected our bags and walked as fast as we could back to the station. The train might be slow but it had to be more comfortable than taking a bus which would have people hanging from the doors, riding on the roof, and oozing out the windows. Buses in Pakistan weren't like those in Iran where everyone was assured of a seat. Instead, they resembled those tiny cars at the circus where person after person would amazingly exit, so we wanted a ride on the train.

As we approached the station, the whistle of the locomotive blew, and a cloud of billowy white steam came from the stack. The train slowly moved forward, and as it did, we started running, and yelling. It was just like in a movie except this was for real. But as fast as we ran, the train moved faster. We were left standing at the station, laughing to ourselves.

We returned to the rope spring beds and spent a fitful night, trying to get some sleep as the hemp tore into our backs. In the morning we found a large Mercedes Benz truck headed toward Quetta and arranged to sit above the cab with several other travelers. We were pressed together in an open compartment with low wood walls that showed us the countryside and let the sun and wind at us. A bus was leaving the border at the same time but the truck was less crowded, offered fresh air, and would get us to our destination much faster. While the Baluchi men sitting next to us pulled turbans around their faces, we had red bandanas wrapped cowboy-style over our mouths to try to keep the dirt out.

The truck sped through the desert over a smooth dirt road. We only stopped for a fast lunch of rice and meat at an open-air palm frond covered restaurant. Chickens ran through the dining room as orange Nehis were passed around to wash the dirt out of our mouths. We were soon back on the road and within a few hours had passed the train. It was stopped in the middle of the desert, waiting for an unseen something. By nightfall, the truck had pulled into the good sized city of Quetta. We quickly found a room and then went looking for a public bath.

The hotel desk clerk offered us a hot water shower for an extra $1, but we knew the public bath would be cheaper and provide all the warm water we wanted. At least that was the way it was in Iran. But when the bath house attendant led us to our individual booths, we found no shower, just a large pan of water with an enormous sponge floating in it. We both chuckled heartily at our predicament, but did manage to get the thick layer of dirt off our filthy bodies.

The next day we discovered that Quetta's shopping area consisted of open air stalls selling produce, nuts, and clothing. While most Iranian bazaars had an exotic feeling of dark narrow passageways crowded with people and shafts of light descending from openings in domed roofs, this line of shops and carts had more of the ambience of a farmers market.

The mosques were also much different. They were whitewashed and the entrances were decorated with ornate styles of plaster curlicues and squiggles. Without domes, these mosques were plainer and much less interesting than those in Iran.

Only a few cars, some buses, and an occasional donkey-pulled cart were on the streets. The trucks we saw all had large, elaborate scenes of planes, mountains, and other monumental objects painted on their wooden sides. Golf carts used as taxis sped around, but in general not many people were visible.

While sitting in Quetta's central park, we were approached by a disreputable looking older man in tattered clothes and two-day old beard. He offered to exchange money for us at a very favorable rate, but we declined since we had been told at the border only to change money at official banks. After our refusal, he wondered if we wanted to see some handicrafts. I agreed, and we arranged to meet later at our hotel room to look over what he had.

"I have some rugs and other things as you can see," he said, unrolling a few small carpets from the duffel bag he carried. "This one is worn, but old and valuable. It is very nice, isn't it?"

"But it is torn and shabby," I replied, "and not worth very much. I'll give you ten dollars for it." The man stood silent for a moment, sneering at me. He had a criminal air about him and appeared sinister. Over his shoulder, I could see standing in the open doorway the hotel's young Pathan desk clerk, dressed in flowing robes and wearing his tribal cap. He was looking at us with concern, an expression of unease riding across his face. Near me, Jim was pacing in nervousness.

"Ten dollars? You must be kidding. It is worth much more than that. What do you have besides dollars? Maybe we can trade."

Looking in my suitcase, I pulled out a transistor radio. "How about this? A radio for a rug? That's about even." We shook hands, and he left. After he did, the desk clerk berated me for inviting an evil man into his hotel, and Jim chastised me for dealing with a thief. I thought I had made a pretty good bargain.

After two days in Quetta, we flew to Karachi. The ticket was affordable, and the alternative of an overnight bus trip through a furnace-like desert with dozens of other people crammed into the vehicle was not appealing.

As the prop plane circled the Karachi airport, the damage from the recent war was obvious. Blackened oil tanks near the port indicated that enemy planes had hit their marks. The Indian army had crushed the Pakistani forces and could have overrun the country. According to news reports, however, American diplomacy had prevented that from happening.

Our government's assistance was why the Pakistanis were so pleased to accommodate two young traveling Americans. "Your country saved mine by its intervention to stop the Indian aggression," one of them told us, "and we shall forever be grateful."

The airport was nearly empty, and we had no idea where to stay. We found a cab and told the driver to take us to a nice, centrally located hotel. We forgot to mention cheap in our description, so when he pulled up in front of a multi-story establishment in the center of the city, we thought we had made a serious mistake. In quite proper English, however, the driver said, "The rooms are about $10 a night for two, and it has a bar, swimming pool and restaurant. Very nice place. You'll enjoy it."

Before we could get into the hotel lobby, though, a group of six unwashed boys dressed in ripped, dirty clothes surrounded us on the street, begging to exchange money. The doorman ran them off, and we were shown to a large, air-conditioned room. The actual price, including a buffet breakfast, was $8.00.

Central Karachi was a mixture of tall new buildings, a large park, and a strategically placed Gothic-style Episcopal cathedral. The green lawn and typical British setting of the church contrasted sharply with the mass of Islam swarming around it.

On a bus tour of the city the following day, we stopped at a outdoor laundry where thousands of white sheets were hung out to dry along the Hab River bank. In the water, dozens of people twisted and pounded and soaked clothing by hand. Nearby, fully covered women, their bodies shrouded by veils and with faces hidden behind screens, walked down the street cradling babies in their arms. A protest march was winding through downtown, placards and signs demanding something we couldn't make out. In the suburbs we visited a new, white domed mosque of immense size but no real attraction.

The next day we went to a government run shop that sold Pakistani handicrafts from around the country. They were so different from what was available in Baluchistan, being made of inlaid wood and shiny brass, that we both wanted to buy a lot to ship back to the U.S.

Since we were both short of cash, and the shop didn't accept travelers checks, we found a cab and asked the driver to take us to a place where we could exchange money. The sun was setting and street lights popping on as we drove to a tightly packed residential part of the city. Down narrow alleys, children running and screaming in front of us, the driver slowly went this way and that. Apartment buildings were four or five stories high on either side of the street, and people were hanging out open windows, yelling to their neighbors in the twilight.

When the taxi finally stopped, Jim and I were a little nervous about our fates. But the smiling driver turned to us and said, "I'll be back in a minute. This is my house, and I've got the currency you need. I'll pay you the going blackmarket rate."

"You see," he added, "I have family in the U.S., and I need to help them. Our money is no good there, so I must save dollars to send. Plus, if I ever want to take my wife and children from Pakistan, I must have dollars to do so. That is why everyone wants dollars. They are all thinking of leaving the country. Wait here, I'll be right back."

Within a few minutes, the driver returned with a thick wad of bills in his hand. Shortly after that, we were buying presents for those in Wisconsin, the humanitarian gesture toward the taxi driver and the much better black market exchange rate soothing our consciences about the illegal act. We did wonder, however, what the sales clerks thought about our quickly found cash.

The next morning we went by train up the Indus River plain to Hyderabad, an ancient capital of the Baluch tribe. Long before there was a Pakistan, the Baluch had ruled the area. Now they were just one of several tribal peoples that made up a nation of sky-scrapper dominated large cities and desperately poor rural areas.

Hyderabad had a hectic, colorful open air market with rural people from all over the region bustling about. The suits and sport coats of

Karachi had been replaced by the balloon pleated pants of the desert. Overlooking the city from atop a hill was an enormous but abandoned mud-brick castle, a lonely testament to the power that the Baluch once held in the area.

Further north along the Indus River was Mohenjo Daro, one of the oldest cities on earth. To get there required taking a bus through the lush spring green countryside. We saw water buffalo pulling plows in lime colored rice paddies and people, lots of them even in the remotest of places, walking along the side of the road. The colorful landscape was a sharp contrast to the brown sameness of Baluchistan in Iran, the crowds of Pakistan versus the vast emptiness of the desert.

At a railroad crossing in a tiny village we transferred back onto the train. By the time it arrived at the Mohenjo Daro depot, the sun was setting and the station master informed us there were no accommodations in the area. For the night he offered us our choice of wooden benches in the small waiting room of the station. We stuffed some dirty clothes into pants for pillows, stretched out, and tried to get comfortable. Even though it was still March, the heat and humidity of the night combined with the unbending wood beneath our backs did not make sleep easy.

By 6 a.m., the sun was up and the horse drawn carriage the station master had summoned was waiting to take us to the ruins. The ride went through the mist of morning rising off the river, casting a light gray sepia tone over all the shades of the early part of the day. We passed through a waking village, mocha-colored women in old faded clothes emerging from small huts to wash off, tethered horses snorting at the dawn, barefoot children already beginning to run around in the dirt. In the early light and rising mist, the poverty and desperateness of the place looked almost picturesque. A photograph, however, would not have revealed the disease, the hunger, or the death rate.

Arriving before the office to Mohenjo Daro opened, the curator invited us to share his morning tea and bread. Breakfast helped to get the bench sores out of our backs as we talked.

"So tell me, what are two young Americans doing here? Why did you come to the ruins."

"We both live in Iran and wanted to visit Pakistan. It is much different from the desert of Baluchistan that we are familiar with. Plus, the history of your country intrigues us."

"You live in Iran? But you are Americans. Why would you live in Iran? And what is life like there?"

"We're with the Peace Corps, just trying to help out. Life in Baluchistan is a lot different than here. You have British customs and food, like warm beer and cold toast. We eat rice and toppings. Here you have lots of rain and green fields. In Iran we have heat and desert."

"Thank you both for coming. It means a lot to me. My countrymen and I are especially grateful to you as Americans. Your government stopped the Indian assault, and we will never forget it. But enough talk, let me show you Mohenjo Daro."

A long series of brick foundations, passageways, and the remains of walls of rooms which had once been home to thousands stretched out across the flat floodplain of the Indus. Our guide explained the commercial importance of this strategic site as we looked over the surrounding fertile land, the emerald shoots of rice plants tinting the soil.

One impressive feature of the 4,500 year old community was its public toilet system. With open stalls lined in a row along a major walkway, business conversations could continue despite the call of nature. The city's sewer system was much like those found in most modern Iranian cities, and it was probably considerably better than that of the village we had ridden through earlier.

When we left, the spiritual presence of the crowds of people that once lived at Mohenjo Daro could be felt in the warm spring air. The ghosts which were in our minds from a mostly sleepless night seemed appropriate to the atmosphere. As we returned toward the station, the small village was full of activity, men in the fields, women working on the ground, bent over or squatting to clean rice as they prepared lunch.

Catching an overnight train to Lahore, Jim and I shared a four person sleeper with a traveling businessman. As a break to the padded seats and slowly turning ceiling fan of the compartment, we stood for awhile between swaying cars, the rumbling motion of the train and the cool breeze of the evening air washing over us. The conductor soon appeared to have a smoke. He spoke in wondrous terms of the great role America had played in saving his country from an all-out attack by the Indians. The gratitude of the Pakistani people, he said, would be eternal.

Stopping in the evening at a station to allow the train to add cars, we decided to dine in shifts. Our roommate warned us of thieves and said that if we left our luggage unattended, it could be stolen. So I went first to eat, walking down a platform engulfed in humanity and filled with heat and steam from the surrounding trains.

The station restaurant was tiny, with only a few small round metal tables encircled by tall stools. A menu written in an unfamiliar language was on a blackboard with letters which were undecipherable to me. Some brown skinned men were bent over plates, quickly shoveling meals into their mouths. Pots of strange looking food were simmering on a cast iron stove, and the coffee-skinned cook nodded at me as I entered.

I found a free space and asked the waiter for an unknown something from the menu. He brought me a plate of curried rice and meat and it burned my mouth sharply. But with plenty of water available from a bottle on the table, and a soft drink or two, it was bearable.

After arriving in Lahore in the morning, we checked into a hotel and then hired a guide to show us the city. He took us to one of the world's largest mosques, its interior courtyard bigger than a football field. Unfortunately, its size was not matched by any splendor. It was just a big, plain building. Another stop on the tour was at a former palace where the entrance stairway was constructed so that elephants could parade up to the royal chambers.

By the time we returned to our hotel, Jim was feeling poorly. We attributed it to the water-buffalo milk he had used in his breakfast tea which I had avoided. While he sat in the bathroom retching, I read his copy of Solzhenitsyn's *One Day in the Life of Ivan Denisovich*. It was a long night, listening to his sickness.

By noon the next day, however, Jim was feeling better, and we booked sleeping berths on the night train to Rawalpindi. There was only one other man in a compartment with bunks for eight. The evening was hot and humid, but the ceiling fans and open windows kept us comfortable. In the morning, though, a fine layer of dust covered our sheet wrapped bodies and everything else in the car.

Dawn revealed a landscape mixture of fertile fields and dry tan dirt. Shortly after sunrise a young boy entered our car and asked what we wanted for breakfast. The Pakistani man riding with us explained that the boy would take our requests, and they would be wired ahead to the next stop. There we would be served a hot meal, made to order.

After taking our selections, the boy left. Because there was no platform between the cars, he opened the door, climbed a ladder to the roof, jumped to the next car, and scrambled down to the door of that carriage. The train continued on at 25 m.p.h. or so as he made his leap.

The Rawalpindi station was crowded with people heading out of town and others welcoming travelers. We selected an old English inn from a deck of hotel postcards that young boys were holding up, urging the arriving passengers to give one of them a try. Our suite had separate bedrooms, a sitting room, a nice garden, and the price was very reasonable.

Toward evening the maid knocked on our door and asked if we wanted to see any local carpets or handicrafts. When we said we did, she returned with an old man carrying a large bag. In it were a few small rugs, a hand woven shawl, and some other items. He said he was a refugee from the recent war and was having to sell off his possessions to survive. That wasn't likely since all of the things he had were new. But if I could use sympathy to bargain in Iran, why couldn't he try the same approach to sell things in Pakistan? He quoted us very reasonable prices, and we bought most of what he had.

For dinner we went across the street to the former British Army officers club. It still served the finest in Pakistani imitations of English food. We retired to the bar after eating and were soon joined by an Irishman quickly descending into drunkenness.

He was a U.N. employee working in the area and slurred, "I hate this place. I hate the people, I hate the food, and I hate the climate. There is nothing I like about it."

Taking a long swig of whiskey, he continued. "The people here would just as soon slit your throat as offer any assistance. They are lazy and don't learn, don't even want to learn. Government corruption is rampant, and it is difficult to get anything accomplished. Plus the food they eat here is disgusting. Have you seen the sheep heads? I can't stand it."

"So why do you stay?"

"The pay is good, and I get to go home every six months or so, but I'm thinking of getting out. I can't stand it here." The venom toward his surroundings continued to flow, so we were soon departing.

The next day we visited Islamabad, the new capital of the country. It had modern administration buildings, wide streets, western-style housing developments still under construction, and totally lacked charm or character. The city's antiseptic appearance had been intentionally designed by world-famous architects. They wanted to create a government center focused on the automobile to replace the pedestrian-scale and hectic environment of Rawalpindi. The result was a soul-less community of no attraction.

I thought the most interesting sight we saw in the new capital was of muddy shoeprints on a toilet seat where someone had squatted on it. That showed that you could take the squatter away from the people, but you couldn't get the people away from the squat.

As Jim and I headed west toward Peshawar the next day by bus, the landscape became more familiar. Mountain ranges loomed in the distance behind a foreground of desert. Most of the passengers were Baluch and other tribal men returning home, businessmen and big city residents having been left behind in Islamabad.

Peshawar proved to be an uninspiring place. The bazaar was small and undistinguished except for a man who carried an old rifle through the crowd. We had been told that gun sales at a nearby village were the most interesting thing to see in the area so we rode out to take a look. The bus we took was crowded with tribal men preening themselves while looking into small compact mirrors. The sight of these big, burly, hairy men gently cleaning their bushy black beards in a very feminine fashion made me grin.

Every shop on the short main street of the village seemed to be loaded with firearms of all types. Handguns, rifles, and even a small weapon in the shape of a fountain pen were for sale. If someone was interested in testing one, the salesman would step out into the street and fire off a round into the sky, not something either of us was accustomed to seeing. We were told that the Pakistani army didn't even try to control the village, the history and reputation of these men as fighters keeping them away.

The only bus from Peshawar through the Kyber Pass and on to Kabul left very early the next morning, and neither of us was interested in getting up at that hour. Plenty of buses at all times of the day ran out to the border, so we asked if there was transportation from there to the capital of Afghanistan. The hotel desk clerk told us cheerfully, "Oh yes, sirs. Too many buses to Kabul. Too many buses."

Before we could leave the country, however, Jim and I needed to obtain exit visas from the Pakistani government. When we went to get the required stamp, an official asked us to have a seat, offered tea, and took our passports. After examining them for a minute, he frowned and said there was a problem as we looked at each other in bewilderment.

"You see," he said in a sing-song lilt, "you were suppose to have obtained an entry visa when you came into Pakistan, but you entered at a place that didn't know the new rules. So, you see, you are technically in the country illegally. Not a good situation. Not good at all. Before I can give you an exit visa, you must have an entry visa. You will have to go back to where you came in and get one."

Jim and I simultaneously let out a loud howl of protest. We couldn't, we wouldn't, do that. It was hundreds of miles away, and we would not retrace our trip. As we screamed our objections, a smile emerged from behind the official's beard. "Just kidding," he said with a smile. "With the war and all of the changes being made, it is difficult to keep the paperwork straight." As he stamped our passports, he thanked us for visiting his country.

The next day we took a taxi out through the pass. Soldiers wearing fancy uniforms and elaborate headgear stood watch over the rock walls towering above them. The border crossing was a small green spot in the mountains with a guard post on either side of a wooden gate blocking the unpaved road. Young world travelers from Europe and the U.S. were sprawled out a lawn, lying in the sunshine, looking like they expected to be there awhile.

We needed to get one more form stamped by the Pakistani military before we could leave the country. It was a currency regulation requirement, and inside the border post the officer in charge asked to see the exchange receipts we had been given at banks. That caught us by surprise because after Karachi we had exchanged all of our money on the black market, never expecting this request.

Looking at each other nervously, and trying not to stumble too much with what he said, Jim offered the officer the few bank receipts he had. "We didn't know we were suppose to keep them so we threw most of them away," he timidly explained as he turned over the evidence.

The officer looked through our scant papers, sighed, and said, "You've changed money on the black market, haven't you? You need to know that it's bad for the country as well as being illegal. So next time, follow the rules, O.K.?" With that he stamped the necessary form and we walked out into the bright sunlight.

There were no buses waiting to take us further west, so we asked the young foreigners lying on the grass when the next one to Kabul would depart. The world travelers looked up at us and laughed. There were no buses to Kabul except the early morning bus from Peshawar, they insisted. After venting our anger at the "Too many buses" desk clerk, we stood beside the dirt road and stuck out our thumbs.

In a remote place like this, traffic was very sparse, but we knew that the top of a truck was always a possibility. Within a few minutes, however, a van pulled up, and the driver asked in perfect Persian where we were going. "Kabul," we said, and he told us to hop in. Meanwhile, the world travelers continued to lounge on the lawn, apparently content to spend their day that way.

Farsi was spoken by many people in Afghanistan, so we would be able to communicate, which was fortunate since most of the people we encountered didn't speak any English. Besides, while Jim and I had both been slow learners of Persian, by this time each of us was quite proficient with the language. Showing off our speaking skills was something we enjoyed doing.

The back of the van was fully carpeted: floor, walls and ceiling. A well dressed man was lying there on overstuffed pillows, looking relaxed. He asked what we were doing in this part of the world and how we liked it as his driver maneuvered us across the border.

We wondered what he did for a living and he said something that neither of us understood, so he explained it slowly in words we knew. "You sell things, like guns and ammunition. But you don't work for the government, and you don't have their permission to sell these things. So what you do is illegal. In English that's called smuggling, and you're a smuggler," was what we concluded with nervous laughter.

Stopping along the way for a tea break, our host talked about the poverty of the town we were in. Starvation was occurring, he said, and many people had died. He claimed women were selling their infant children to foreigners in order to save them. Looking around at the skeleton-like figures huddled silently in the shade, that wasn't hard to believe.

At dusk we were dropped off in front of a cheap hotel in central Kabul, our ride having been both informative and free. The room we were given was dirty and depressing, but we didn't expect to stay long.

Kabul proved to be a shock. The extreme poverty of most of the people combined with scenes of drug-crazed young foreigners living and begging on the street contrasted sharply with the incredible surrounding scenery of massive snow capped mountains. The city was a large, ugly place of no interest, and one day there was enough for us.

We visited the American Embassy to find out where the Peace Corps office was located. While waiting to talk to an official, we saw a flyer on the bulletin board which read: "Notice to Travelers-Selling or Using Drugs in Iran is Illegal. Penalties are Severe, including the Possibility of Execution."

To compare notes, Jim wanted to talk with an American volunteer teaching at an agricultural training school in Afghanistan. The nearest one, according to people in the Peace Corps office, was a five hour trip north of the city. So by the early afternoon we had found a shared taxi stand from which a car headed for a specific destination would leave once it was full. After waiting for a few more passengers to arrive, we were soon off.

As we drove through the flat farmland outside the capital, the taxi driver was surprised we knew his language. He thanked us for caring enough about the people of his country to learn to speak to them. Then he blasted the world travelers who visited Afghanistan. "Those that come here and get hooked on drugs are a disgrace and should be taken out and shot," he exclaimed vehemently. "Why anyone would go from a rich country like theirs to a poor country like ours to waste their life is beyond me."

Driving up into the foothills of the Hindu Kush range, the mountain tops were disappearing in the gathering clouds above us. Farms had become terraced, small plots of vegetation dug out of the granite colored mountainsides. The farms formed a green checkerboard pattern against the rock face. Later we entered a rugged valley, a wild river running below the road, the turbulent water boiling over huge boulders with great velocity. Occasionally a battered and broken vehicle could be seen lying on the rocks hundreds of feet below us. The fate of the passengers wasn't a mystery.

As we rose in elevation, the temperature was dropping and the once blue sky was turning gray. A few small patches of snow appeared on the rocks next to the road, and then some flakes started falling. As we went up, toward the highest mountain tunnel in the world according to our driver, more snow had accumulated. The heater of the Mercedes Benz was working well, but visibility was falling fast as we climbed.

At the entrance to the tunnel the snow was flying fiercely, and a small group of vehicles had congregated. No traffic was moving, and the driver went into the storm to find out what was going on. After he returned through the blinding white, snow swirled into the car when he opened the door. He explained that a large truck had turned over inside the tunnel, jackknifed across the road. No one could get through in either direction. The accident was expected to be cleared up in awhile, so we would wait.

As we sat in the quickly cooling car, snow began to pile up around us. Daylight was fading and it began to be difficult to see some of the other vehicles which had packed in around the tunnel entrance.

"This is all the Soviets' fault," the driver moaned. "My government wanted a tunnel built through the mountains, and the Americans and Russians proposed to do it. They both said they wanted to be our friends."

"The Americans suggested building the tunnel further down the mountain. It would have been longer and more expensive, but wouldn't have had as many snow problems."

"The Russians said, 'Don't worry about the snow. We'll dig the tunnel higher up, and it will be shorter and cheaper.'"

"So my government took the cheap way, and snow closes the road quite often. Travel from Kabul is frequently uncertain, but today, of course, is special because of the overturned truck."

After three hours of waiting, the windows of the taxi were thick with frost, and a deep carpet of snowy powder covered the ground. Our words were producing clouds of breath, and it was getting on toward night. A decision would have to be made soon about what we were going to do. The driver said he wanted to stick it out, but that didn't seem very reasonable to me.

But then a honk was heard coming from the gaping dark mouth of the tunnel. Emerging headlights soon appeared at the entrance as a truck had gotten through. The men working inside had somehow managed to push the huge overturned vehicle to one side, so traffic could narrowly get by. We slowly moved passed the fallen semi-trailer and were soon speeding down the mountain.

Even though we were hours behind schedule, the driver stopped at a roadside restaurant for dinner. It was a rickety wooden building with only oil lamps for light. A small smoke filled room was full of bearded tribal men in their pajama-like costumes and clean-shaven businessmen in suits. They were all sitting on the floor, passing around some communal bowls of rice and lentils. Mutton was the only other item available, and a slab was delivered to us, and our hands quickly tore the meat apart.

It was almost midnight when we reached the driver's destination. The village Jim and I were going to was still some miles away, so he arranged for us to sleep on the floor of the local schoolhouse. Wondering how we would get to where we were going, the driver told us we could find another taxi in the morning. It had been a long day, he said, and he was going home.

The Peace Corps volunteer we visited was from Wisconsin Dells and lived in a real hovel. It had no running water, just a small stream nearby. His landlord served as his maid since the men of the village didn't want the American to see their women. There was no electricity, just kerosene lamps for light. He seemed pleased, however, with his situation.

He told us a Peace Corps tale which was quickly becoming legendary in the country. A young volunteer had moved to a rural community near Kabul. When he arrived, the elders had greeted him warmly. He was the first foreigner to live in the village and they welcomed him, but that night a knock on his door led to a warning from several armed men. He should be gone by morning. The women of the village were not completely covered when they went out. The men did not want the outsider seeing them. The American fled back to Kabul before daybreak.

Our return trip to Kabul was much less interesting than the outward bound journey. A fellow passenger, however, was a Peace Corps volunteer who rode a horse from mountain schoolhouse to mountain schoolhouse. Once back in the capital, with our funds running low and our vacation time almost over, we decided our trip was near an end and we should start heading home.

The next morning we were on a bus which would drive through the cold desert for two days to get to the Afghan border town of Herat. When it stopped for the night in the city of Kandahar, we checked into a rundown hotel near the bus station. The place was cheap, dirty, and was where the world travelers stayed. On the filthy plastered walls of our room, a Western woman had left handwritten notes, telling in anatomically explicit terms what the sexual preferences of Afghani men were.

A few days later in Herat, Jim wanted to buy a sheepskin coat for his eventual return to central Wisconsin. He carried on a long bargaining session with the teenager who was watching the shop where we stopped.

After the negotiations were successfully completed, the boy asked if we wished to join him for a movie in the evening.

It was an Indian film, a Hercules-type adventure. The hero would kill dozens of men, but later they were seen attacking him again. Down on the main floor, which was for men only, the tribal crowd was really getting into the action. In the balcony where we sat, the teenager elbowed me in excitement while he stared intently at the fully covered women who were sitting a few seats away from us. There was nothing visible of them except the bedsheet-like garments which completely covered their heads and bodies, but our companion was thrilled.

In the morning we rode out in a van to the Iranian border with an older Englishman, two Germans, and a long-haired young Frenchman. The dirt road traveled through desolate scenery which reminded me of Baluchistan. As we went along, they asked us about our life in Iran, and we talked of their travels to Nepal and India on the great circular drug route.

At the border station, each of us was separately taken into a small room and asked a few questions by an Iranian guard. In ten minutes we were back in the van, heading toward Mashad. The Frenchman quietly congratulated himself as he pulled a small packet of hashish out of his crotch. "They didn't catch me," he exclaimed excitedly as I told him people got shot in Iran for that sort of thing.

Arriving in Mashad just before dark, and not knowing where our friends lived in a city of several hundred thousand, Jim and I took a room in a cheap hotel. For breakfast the next day we both ordered fried eggs and were surprised to have them served in a metal bowl floating on top of two inches of hot oil. As we used our flat bread to scrape the eggs off the oil, the other patrons looked at us strangely. Guess they thought greasy was the way we wanted them.

We spent a few days in Mashad with our Peace Corps compatriots once we located them in the governmental office where they worked. In the bazaar, after withdrawing some money from my savings account, I purchased a room-sized rug for under $100. It was the non-dyed, natural-color style preferred by many Europeans but disliked intensely by Iranians because they were so plain compared to typical Persian carpets.

Walking around Mashad, Jim and I had to avoid the spit and stones thrown by some teenage boys who were the self-appointed guardians of the sacred city. Mashad is the burial place of Imam Reza, one of the Shiite sect of Islam's most holy men. The city took its religious role very seriously. It was the only urban area in Iran that I knew of where Coke was the preferred soft drink. Everywhere else, Pepsi was the major product. Pepsi, however, was bottled by a company supposedly owned by a member of the Bahai faith, an officially unrecognized religion whose members were considered to be heretics. To show their displeasure, the people of Mashad drank Coke.

Our trip over, Jim flew off to Tehran on business, and I returned by plane to Zahedan. I had a suitcase full of purchased possessions, a large rug tightly rolled inside a small wooden box, a few dozen photographs, and almost no money in my wallet.

A week later, Jim knocked on my door on his way south into Baluchistan. "I'm leaving the country," he angrily shouted as I let him in. "Some of these people are idiots, and I've had it with them. I'm getting out of here."

Offering him a beer, I asked what had happened. "When I got to Tehran, the officials at the Ministry of Agriculture said they had arranged a transfer for me from my training school. They thought I would be pleased, but of course I was dumbfounded, and all I could ask is, 'Why?'"

"They said they knew I must desperately want to get out of here. In their opinion, nobody would choose to live where I do. 'There are no night clubs or movie theaters or anything to do,' they all said. So they assumed that I wanted to leave. They thought they were doing me a favor, but I like it here. I think I'm actually making a difference."

"But they can't just move you, can they?".

"Oh no. They used the excuse that I had been gone so long from the job. They told my school principal I must not be coming back, so basically I guess I got fired. I'm going to collect my things, then I'm quitting the Peace Corps. Those idiots in Tehran can't shove me around like this. I'm out of here."

By the time he returned with his possessions a few days later, Jim had calmed down. He decided to try and find another agricultural school at which to teach. I eventually learned that he found a position in the western part of the country. It was in the mountains and was a very green, very cool place, a world away from the desert heat and brown nothingness of Baluchistan.

Life in The Desert

The next several months were a routine of regularity. For breakfast, Fatima would bring fresh flat bread still warm from the oven from a nearby bakery and then brew tea for us. We would all go off to work in suits, except for Robert who dressed more casually. At 1 p.m. we returned for a meal of rice topped with meat, fish, or vegetables. After a nap we went back to work for a few hours, and then Jamal and I would usually go out for a sandwich and beer or take in a movie.

By April two more Iranians had moved into the house. One was Kareem, an accountant who worked with Jamal. The other was Sarkis, the civil engineer from my office.

The arrival of Sarkis meant there were five of us but only four bedrooms. To provide space for him, a wooden wall had to be built between the dining area and the former living room. Within a few weeks Jamal and I had covered the new wall with painted symbols and slogans just to liven things up.

Near our house was a large dry riverbed. Loads of trash were regularly dumped there by the households of the neighborhood and occasionally it would be burned. Also near the wash were several Baluch families, living in cardboard shacks on the banks of the riverbed. Sometimes a mentally retarded teenage boy would be seen running down the wash, his arms outstretched, pretending he was an airplane.

My time at work was generally unproductive since the government wasn't spending much money in the province. Despite earlier promises, funds did not arrive from the capital to build anything so our rainy trip to the south proved to be useless. I was told that the governor asked his bosses in Tehran not to send money to show them how frugal he was and, thus, impress his superiors. The result was we mostly sat around, not doing much.

The lack of anything to do at governmental jobs was very common in the country. A newspaper reported on the daily schedule for the Ministry of the Interior in Tehran, the agency for which I was working. "Interior Minister Mohammed Sam has totally banned tea-drinking by the staff of his ministry except between 9:30 to 10:30 and 2:30 to 3:30 in the afternoon. A story published in a magazine recently gave the office time-table of government employees as 8:30 to 9:30 arrival, 9:30 to 10:30 greeting colleagues and having tea, 10:30 to 11:30 attending meetings and having more tea, 11:30 to noon preparing for lunch, 12:00 to 1:00 lunch, 1:00 to 3:00 siesta, 3:00 to 4:00 p.m. preparing to return home." Those people were literally sleeping on the job.

At least in Zahedan we frequently discussed world issues. One of the newly arrived architects in the office wanted to know what the U.S. interest was in Vietnam and why my country had even gotten involved in the first place. He thought the war was sheer folly and kept insisting that I must be a draft dodger. That, in his opinion, was the only reason someone would volunteer to come to a remote place like Zahedan. I tried to explain that with a high lottery number I wasn't going to be drafted, but in a country where almost every male was required to serve in either the military or one of the Corps assistance groups, it was a concept I wasn't able to get across.

We also talked about the Palestinian/Israeli conflict. I outlined the American position as well as I could, even though I didn't agree with it. I offered a copy of *Exodus* to anyone who wanted another perspective on the situation, but my co-workers grasp of English wasn't good enough to allow them to read it.

After leaving the office in the afternoons, I would occasionally try teaching English to a variety of people. Many men asked for help, including some SAVAK secret police agents. After a few lessons, however, most of them would grow discouraged and give up.

Eventually, though, two men started taking lessons seriously and they both had the goal of studying outside the country. One was a doctor, and the other was Mohammed, a new accountant at the provincial engineering office. We would meet in my home once or twice a week and go through some easy lesson books. It was basic instruction, but the practice at speaking English was helpful to them.

Early in 1973, both men had learned enough English to apply for admission to take more advanced classes outside of Iran. The doctor was accepted to a program in the U.S. and Mohammed to one in England. When they received their notices of acceptance, we went out to the nightclub to celebrate. Their perseverance had paid off.

In the springtime heat, which soon exceeded 100 degrees on a daily basis, I mostly wore light suits to the office and shorts and t-shirts around the house. However, I also had a Baluchi set of clothes made so that I could be more presentable when company was visiting our home. My roommates insisted I not wear the balloon pants and long sleeve shirt outside the house since it wasn't acceptable for a "*mohandes*", or engineer in Persian, to be seen in tribal clothes. But when I wore them inside the walls of our courtyard, it quickly became apparent how comfortable they were in the desert climate.

Shortly after I returned from Pakistan and Afghanistan, the news came that Hassan-the-surveyor was to be reassigned. For some unknown reason, he apparently had political enemies in Tehran. He was accused of taking unauthorized leave for his own spring break and was ordered to Zabol as punishment. That was a demotion of the highest order, but there was nothing he could do about it. He needed the twice monthly paycheck and had no other opportunities, so off he went, along with Reza-the-draftsman, to open a small office. All I could conclude was that hard work and professional responsibility got you demoted in the Iranian bureaucracy.

To lessen the impact of the desert, I asked my parents to send some supplies. Kool-Aid was a big hit with my roommates, and the no-pest strips we received helped to keep the flies out of our rooms. Flies were about the only bugs we had to worry about since it was so dry in Zahedan that most insects just couldn't survive, which made sleeping outside all the more enjoyable.

My family also sent cookies which I would pass around the office and share at home. While there was a good bakery in Zahedan, the American recipes and different ingredients were interesting to my co-workers and friends. They eagerly awaited each package I received from Wisconsin.

During the warm months we continued our weekly visits to the nightclub. Occasionally the taxi driver taking us home would drop us at the main intersection in town, so he could get back to the club quicker to pick up another fare. Then we would walk the remaining five blocks, passed people sleeping on the sidewalk in the heat, by the military post watched over by an 18 year old sentry, and above the dry riverbed where at night wild dogs ran in packs and rummaged through the garage heaps there. With the risk of rabies very high, I was glad the dogs didn't come up onto the street.

One warm afternoon, the two architects from the office invited Sarkis and me to join them for lunch at their house. When we arrived and were shown into the dining area, an entire wall of the room was papered with *Playboy* pinups. I had been getting the magazine and let them keep the pictures, and this is how they had used them.

The loud "oohs" and "ahs" my roommates and co-workers expressed at seeing naked women was the standard response every time one of the *Playboy* issues appeared. Arriving in a plain brown wrapper, the magazine would have finally cleared customs, and the secret police had finished looking it over. That was a process, however, which sometimes took many months. Most of the men at work would quickly grab for the *Playboy* when I showed it to them and proclaim for all to hear what they would do if they only had a few minutes with this beauty or that.

Occasionally, visitors would stop in Zahedan on their way east or south. Sometimes Robert or I would invite a wandering world traveling couple waiting for a bus to join us for lunch. After these people left, Jamal would ask in all seriousness why he couldn't sleep with the women before they departed Zahedan. After all, he said, they were with a man they weren't married to. Thus, they must be promiscuous, so why couldn't he have them also?

Usually, however, it was some government official who would knock on our door unexpectedly. The solitude I had sought wasn't completely guaranteed, even in Zahedan. One group was from the Peace Corps English teacher program. They were headed into rural Baluchistan to look over the province for possible placement of future volunteers. That, though, never happened. Another man was a Fulbright scholar researching city planning and architecture in the country.

Our most impressive visitors, however, were a couple from Montreal. He was a professor at McGill University who had studied the lifestyle of the Baluch for years. Having lived with them for awhile and written about the experience, he was now returning with his wife to spend a year with a wandering tribe. It was a blistering hot July day when they arrived in Zahedan, and over lunch the professor described the daily schedule of survival that the tribal people had to follow.

"They have to be up before dawn to feed their animals, the children, and themselves. After the herd is milked, the men and boys take the flock out to graze while the women stay in camp making butter, sewing clothes, and doing other necessary chores. The entire tribe has to work together in order to survive. They work very hard."

"From what I've seen," one of my Persian roommates sarcastically said, "the Baluch spend their time napping under date palm trees, waiting for the fruit to ripen. When it falls off, they pick it up and eat it. It must be an enjoyable life."

"That's just not true," the professor shot back angrily. "Every member of the tribe has to perform multiple tasks in the early morning hours as well as late in the afternoon. That is the only way the group can survive the intense heat. In reality, in all of the time I have spent with them, I have never seen a lazy Baluch." From the look on his face, it was obvious my roommate didn't believe him.

Postcard From Corfu

Two friends of mine from Wisconsin, Suzanne and Linda, wrote to let me know they were going to be traveling through Europe for the summer. We arranged to meet in Rome in early August, but what we would do wasn't decided in advance, so I flew to Italy a week early and spent several days touring the city on foot. A guidebook showed me around, pointing out numerous sites and how to reach them by walking.

Unfortunately, before heading out to the catacombs, I didn't look at the map very closely. By the time I was miles outside of the city, my feet hurting, it was too late to turn back. I kept going and eventually limped around the underground tombs, enjoying the cool air of death. Then I found a bus back into town.

One evening at sunset I walked to the Spanish Steps, a gathering place for young travelers. A passing parade of people from all over the world marched along the sidewalk in front of the sitting congregation which was scattered across the long flight of steps. An Italian man soon sat down next to me, introduced himself, and asked where I was from. He began a one-sided conversation in broken English and by the time he got to the line, "Do you like boys?", I was leaving.

The week went by quickly, and the night before I was to meet my friends I went back to the Spanish Steps. Hundreds of college-aged travelers were there, sitting in the fading sunlight, watching other tourists go by.

Suzanne and Linda had arranged to meet me in front of the American Embassy the next day at noon. But there they were on a warm summer Roman night, two women in cutoffs and tank tops, walking down the street. One of them had a sign which read, "Looking for a ride to Greece". I asked if they were going my way to introduce myself as we hugged.

They had spent the summer, Suzanne immediately said, seeing Europe and wanted to end it on a Greek island. Based on that, we made some instantaneous decisions and decided to check out of our hotels and hurry to the train station to catch the midnight run to Brindisi. From there we planned to get a car ferry to Corfu.

While walking later toward the train station up a quiet dark street, the handle from my suitcase was tearing into my hand. The large suitcase was filled with small rugs and other gifts for my family. They would be dropped off with my brother and his wife when I met them in Zurich in ten days, but until then the extra weight just slowed me down.

Even at this late hour the second class car we boarded was full of people, and we had to split up just to find seats. Stuck between an elderly woman in black praying the rosary and a youngster that kept wiggling in fits of sleep, I soon excused myself and went to sit in the unlit corridor. It was cooler there, and the rush of reintroduction to western women and American ways was fogging my mind.

Suzanne soon joined me. After a few minutes of familiar chitchat, we fell quiet. Then she told me of her summer while I stared straight ahead as farm fields illuminated by a bright moon rushed by.

"It's been all right, I guess. Some highs and some lows. Linda has occasionally met a guy and gone off with him for a couple of days, leaving me by myself, which isn't the best. She's also gotten heavy into drugs a few times. But all and all, it's been O.K."

Sitting in the silent darkness, I could imagine the problems the two of them would have traveling together. Linda had a centerfold's body, a small town upbringing, and seemed in awe of many things. Suzanne couldn't compete with her looks, but knew a lot more about the ways of the world. A strange pair, maybe, but at least they were still friends after more than two months of travel.

We soon returned to our separate compartments, and after unsuccessfully making several attempts at sleep, the train finally arrived on the coast. The ferry wouldn't leave until the afternoon, so we had to pass the time in a city park, running off local men who thought Linda should be prime for gawking and pinching.

The ship departed for the Greek mainland via Corfu under a hot sun and humid Mediterranean sky. It was a large car ferry carrying families back to Greece, college kids east to their individual adventures, and us to a week on the beach. As the ship churned through the calm blue water, I lay in an airplane-type seat in the TV lounge, trying to soak in the culture of my former world which seemed so foreign to me now.

Around 2 a.m. the ship docked at Corfu and a few passengers got off. Walking down the gangplank while dragging my suitcase, I was trying to think of where we could stay. On the pier, Suzanne was already yelling that she had found a ride to a campground that would be perfect, so we hopped in the back of a pickup and drove off into the star filled night.

After arriving, we had to step over and around bodies to look for a place to spread out their sleeping bags. Having nothing to sleep on, I borrowed part of Linda's until she got cold and pulled it away from me. Later, while in the midst of a vivid dream, I awoke in a cold sweat. A pack of dogs went running through the camp, the sound of their approaching footsteps terrifying me. I covered my head to shield my face from their bites, but they just kept going.

Daylight showed us where we had come. It was a campground with a few acres of grass on a hillside that gently sloped to the sea. The narrow highway which circled the island was near the water, and on the other side of the pavement were a restaurant and bar on the sandy beach. A couple of dozen people lay scattered around the place, some in tents but most sleeping on the ground. We were miles from a town and in our own little western world. Two nights without much sleep did not leave a favorable first impression of the place with me.

The next week, however, proved to be therapeutic. On our first full night on the island, I found that a lot of the Greek cloudy and powerful liquor, ouzo, made the ground much softer and sleep quite a bit easier. In the days that followed, while Linda played heavy breathing roly-poly games in her sleeping bag with some Englishman, and Suzanne went off touring the island on a motorbike, I camped out under a tree and enjoyed my daily hangover.

To pass the time, one day I walked up into the nearby olive tree covered hills to a small whitewashed village which seemed to be deserted in the afternoon heat. The path I followed through the orchard looked out over a crystal clear aquamarine bay, two lovers skinny dipping in the isolated cove far below the hill.

Most of the time, though, I spent reading a copy of *Jane Eyre* someone had given me. The campground's loudspeaker blared out Top 40 music for much of the day, so to the tune of "Black is Black", I followed the exploits of life in long ago England.

Each evening was the same. Eat a meal at the restaurant, and then head for the bar to get drunk. The corkscrew in my Swiss Army knife was getting a workout as a few others and I shared bottles of ouzo or whatever else the bar had to offer.

In the morning the bright blue sky would reveal people walking around in next to no clothing, openly expressing their lust for one another. This was not what I was accustomed to in Iran, and it took some getting use to.

I didn't really see much of Suzanne or Linda. They had their own interests, I had my bottle and book, and that was satisfactory. But when we went to reserve tickets for the ship back to Italy, my fuzzy perceptions of a week of sunny harmony proved wrong.

After the ticket agent asked for money, Linda matter-of-factly announced she didn't have enough with her and would need a loan. That was the only spark that a week, and summer, of heat, humidity and personal tension needed to be set off. Suzanne lit into her about the constant borrowing and never paying back, about the repeated dependency and relying on their friendship to get bailed out. Linda just stood there in her suntanned beauty and let the words bounce off. By that evening's farewell dinner to our week on Corfu, however, they were laughing and talking with each other, friends once again.

The ship deposited us downhill and about one mile from the train station in Brindisi. By the time I had lugged the heavy suitcase up to the platform, my arms were aching and my throat needed a drink. A train to Rome soon appeared with people crammed into the cars, bodies occupying almost every space available to sit or stand. Suzanne and Linda managed to get on, but I shouted at them that I couldn't make it and would wait for the next train, so they got off and stayed with me. In an hour another train arrived and it had vacant seats.

On this train we were again split up in the crammed cars of summertime traveling Italians. By the next morning I did not know what had happened to Suzanne and Linda. They weren't in the compartment where last seen and by the time the train pulled into Naples, I assumed that our trip together was over. Heading north later, my thoughts were on the past week and how it had been an reintroduction back into my own culture.

The tracks into the Rome station are elevated above the city. Passengers look out at the backs of flats where humanity is pressed together or on old industrial buildings spewing smoke. From the daylight, trains enter a long, dark, cave-like terminal. After a walk down a light bulb lit platform, the traveler emerges into an enormous depot where the roof reaches to the sky, and sunlight rains down.

As I looked up at the great space, a female voice said, "So there you are". Suzanne and Linda had stayed on the train, but our paths hadn't crossed. I asked if they wanted anything from Iran, and both ordered sheepskin coats, at $10 a great deal for the cold snowy winters of Wisconsin. Heading for the platform marked Florence, I left them seated together on a bench making plans to go home.

After seeing the Uffizi Gallery and the magnificent bronze doors of Ghiberti, visiting Pisa and trying to soak in the significance of the Renaissance, I was going to Zurich to meet my brother and sister-in-law. As I lugged my suitcase through the dark streets of Florence heading for the station to catch a late night train north, I had to switch hands every ten steps. Softly cursing my decision to load it down with so many gifts, I slowly moved along.

The station was crowded with people but I quickly found the track where the train to Milan was scheduled to stop. There were only a few other people waiting, so I hoped I might be in luck and get a seat. When the train pulled in, however, it was immediately obvious I would have no such good fortune. People were standing and sitting in every compartment and hallway. There was hardly space to throw my suitcase on board and climb up after it. When I did, it was apparent that this hot, muggy night was not going to be spent sleeping, or even sitting. I did, though, have a choice of where to stand. One option was the small space at the end of the second class car, next to the toilet and in the company of about a dozen others. The alternative location had me standing almost by myself in the breeze on the swaying platform between the train cars. I chose the fresh air.

Rocking and bouncing as we went north, I counted the hours until Milan where I assumed the train would empty. Sometime after midnight the conductor appeared and looked into the car. When he saw that the corridor was jammed with sitting and standing people, he shrugged his shoulders and retraced his steps. No one was getting through that tightly packed crowd, and he wasn't going to try.

Shortly after dawn we arrived in Milan. As hoped, most of the people got off the train. I found a seat, stowed my suitcase, and closed my eyes. The Swiss border was a blur as I shoved my passport out at a security guard and tried to keep the sleep I had found going, but I didn't do very well.

After a few days touring Switzerland with my brother and his wife, they went off to the Olympics in Munich and I flew back to Tehran to visit Gerry. Before I returned to Zahedan, we were going to the annual Urban Planning conference in Isfahan, mostly to see the people we had been in training with the year before.

When Gerry and I arrived at the conference hotel, our former Persian teacher Fereshteh was sitting in the lobby, speaking with someone. She called out warmly, "Hello, David" as we walked in and I waved back. Over the next few days, however, we circled each other like a pair of wary animals, afraid to take a step forward. Our worlds were much different now, hers still in northern Tehran and mine now in Zahedan, and we never did get together.

Before breakfast one morning, a group of us at the conference was watching TV to pass the time. A news bulletin came on, but the announcers were talking rapidly and in Persian words none of us recognized. Over their heads, photos of someone holding a gun on someone else were shown, but we couldn't understand what was happening.

As the day went on, the terror in Munich with the hostage-taking and then killing of the Israeli athletes became more apparent. The Iranians attending the conference were as shocked as we were. When I returned to Zahedan a few days later, my co-workers and roommates expressed outrage at what had happened. The massacre was an unforgivable act of evil to all of them.

Sarkis

Sarkis moved in with us because his former roommate had gotten married, and the new couple decided to stay in the rented house. Sarkis was a civil engineer, a Christian in a land of Muslims, soft spoken, educated in Turkey, and very short. He was in his early thirties, had neatly kept graying hair, was well dressed, and assumed that he would never marry. Being confined in the outpost of Zahedan where there were very few other Christians didn't help. "I am stuck, Mister David," he would tell me with a long face and forlorn frown. "Perhaps if I was in Tehran my family there could find me someone and arrange things. But here, it is impossible." Despite his personal problems, he remained generally good-natured about our life in Zahedan.

Shortly after Sarkis moved in, Jamal started kidding him about his height, his dignified manner, his poor prospects for marriage, and his preference for plump prostitutes. I found Sarkis to be more open minded and tolerant than most of the others.

By the time I returned from Europe, Jamal's kidding had become harassment. It was constant and mean-spirited, and when told to stop, he just kept picking at Sarkis as if at a sore. American men would have thrown punches over this behavior, but Iranian males were physically meek and self-restrained. Fighting was just not their way. Instead, they generally loved poetry and could recite many verses of their favorite Persian poets by heart. Violence simply didn't seem to be in their character.

To escape Jamal's taunts, and to indulge his one great pleasure, Sarkis would go to the movies almost every night. He loved Indian fantasy films with their heroes of great fighting prowess and their leading ladies of incredible beauty. He lost himself for a few hours in the darkness of the theater to his poor hopes for marriage and his intolerable living arrangements.

Once in awhile I would join Sarkis for a movie. He told me he dreamed of finding a Christian woman as beautiful as those we saw on the screen. If she were tall, so much the better, he said. That way their children would be of normal height.

Outside the movie theater he tried to keep his spirits up as best he could. He was saving money, he told me, to buy the things he would require if he ever did get married. A middle-class Iranian man was expected to supply all of the furniture and other household items a newly married couple would need. Since that was very expensive, in order to save enough money, many men didn't marry until their late 20s or early 30s. Their brides would usually be teenage virgins found by the groom's family, and the new couple would have their muebles, or furniture, already purchased.

One evening as we sat in his room drinking beer, Sarkis told me a Persian joke. These were not very common in my experience, most laughter coming from everyday situations or slapstick comedy.

"A long time bachelor about to be married had finally saved up enough money to buy rooms full of the best furniture. He bought high quality living room pieces, nice bedroom furnishings, and other expensive items. Plus, he had made all of the other arrangements for his marriage. On his wedding night, however, he discovered his bride wasn't a virgin, so he urinated all over the new furniture."

As he told me this, Sarkis was holding his zipper, pointing it at a chair. He was bent over double in laughter, tears streaming down his face. At least, he said between joyful sobs, his fate might be better than that.

Upon my return to work after visiting Europe, the office's new boss sent me off to Zabol by myself. I discovered that a high ranking government official there had a son who wanted to practice his English, so for a few days I argued with the teenager over the U.S. loss in basketball at the Olympics and the prospects for the future of Iran. That quickly got tiring, though, so I left.

One of the main jobs I was concentrating on at work was redoing the Zahedan land use master plan. The colored map of the future city had been sent from Tehran and was prepared by someone who obviously had never set foot in Baluchistan. It had grand streets running where washes were, houses located on steep hillsides, and parks where housing already existed. People, however, constantly reminded me that it was the adopted plan for the city.

I had been trying for several months to convince the Mayor and City Council that the plan needed to be changed. I met with the Mayor a few times, and every time I entered his office, he would salute me and politely ask if I wanted tea. As a former military man, and appointed to his post, he didn't want to make any quick decisions that might upset someone, so the discussions about what to do about the plan dragged on and on.

Sarkis encouraged me to stick to my intentions to revise the plan. He insisted that because I was an outsider, people would listen to me and follow my advice. It was obvious the plan needed to be changed since many poor people would lose their homes if it were ever implemented. As time went by, however, I wondered if Sarkis was right about people listening to me.

When Ramadan began again, the wrapping paper coverings went up on the restaurant windows once more. Inside the walls of our house we continued our normal eating routine, but we did have to wait until after sundown to go drink beer.

The fasting month also affected our TV viewing. Sarkis had brought a set with him, and we would occasionally watch a variety show or sports program. But during Ramadan, especially on the holiest days, the only things broadcast were religious sermons or reenactments of the founding of the Shiite sect of Islam. We didn't bother to watch either.

Social Visits

By fall, Robert had moved out of the house. The government had finally allowed his wife to join him, and they rented an apartment. They would also soon be parents. Another engineer from my office moved in with us and quickly joined our lifestyle of drinking and male partying.

Robert and his wife seemed to be a strange couple. He was a quiet, easy going, beer drinking auto mechanic from upstate Wisconsin in his twenties. He still carried memories of his time in Vietnam but wouldn't talk about them much. Robert didn't know much Persian and didn't want to learn. He didn't particularly care for the food, the climate, or the government of the country, but he stayed.

She was in her late 30s and from a well-to-do Tehranian family. She spoke English perfectly, was highly educated, quite cosmopolitan, and desperately wanted to leave Iran. We never talked about whether she knew what his hometown of Superior, Wisconsin would be like if that is where they eventually settled.

One weekend our former roommate Kareem came for a visit from his new job in Zabol. He was the chief accountant in the Water Department office there, and the position was a promotion he couldn't pass up. He joyfully announced that he had become engaged to his 16 year old cousin from Shiraz. He was 25, and they would marry in two years when she finished high school. Everyone congratulated him, but Sarkis looked somewhat sad as he offered his good wishes.

About the same time, Iran's Prime Minister Amir Abbas Hoveyda flew to Zahedan. He was in town to kick off his political party's election campaign. The Parliament and city councils in Iran were elected while other offices were filled by appointment. Of course, the ruling party and the shah were synonymous, but a few loyal opponents were allowed to be elected. Baluchistan was one of the places that sent opposition party members to Parliament, and Hoveyda had come, we were told, to try and change that.

Everyone was given time off to go see the Prime Minister speak. One of the largest traffic circles in town had a stage built on it, and the streets nearby were closed. Bus after bus, each full of Baluchi tribal members, pulled into the city and parked as close to the square as they could. The Baluch were being brought to Zahedan from their desert homes specifically to hear the Prime Minister and to insure a large, attentive audience.

In a low but strong voice, Hoveyda spoke in simple terms of what needed to be done in Sistan and Baluchistan. His language was plain enough for both the tribal members and me to understand. Jobs and water were the two major issues facing the province, he said, and the country's new 5 year plan would address both.

According to the next day's Tehranian English language newspaper, "Hoveyda promised the people of this arid province that in less than five years their water and power problems would be solved". He was politically powerful, but that was a promise that couldn't be kept.

After his short speech, the Prime Minister was whisked off by the military men surrounding him, and everyone else went home. By the end of the year it was announced that tens of millions of dollars had been allocated for the province in the nation's upcoming 5 year budgetary plan. That meant some things might get built at last.

Several years later, when Hoveyda was imprisoned by the shah as a scapegoat for the country's problems and then executed by the fundamentalists after the revolution, I regretted the news. He had given me the impression of someone who really cared about his work. It was also said that he had been a moderating influence on the shah.

He was rumored to be a Bahai, however, a religious belief the Muslim fanatics would not tolerate. Plus he had looked the other way concerning many of the shah's excesses. He paid for his loyalty with his life, but that is the way a patriot would want it.

Also during the fall, we had a few visits from a representative of the U.S. consulate. He occasionally flew to Zahedan to visit an American interned in the local jail for drug smuggling. Over beers and whisky, this young government employee and I would compare lifestyles. He had western rules to live by and spoke a little Farsi, even though it wasn't encouraged by his bosses. He was very proud that in his interview for the position he had admitted to having used drugs. "And I still got the job," he proclaimed enthusiastically.

He stayed with us while in town and fit right into our social circle. During his second visit he asked if I could do him a favor. He had been told to remain in Zahedan to meet an elderly American woman who was flying solo most of the way around the world. He had other business obligations, however, that required him to be in Tehran, so he asked me to go out to the airport and see if the old world traveler needed anything.

On the appointed afternoon, Jamal and I took a taxi to the deserted terminal. After awhile a small aircraft appeared from the west and landed. A few airport workers ran to help the 82 year old woman out of the plane. As they did, they were muttering about how she didn't understand either their specific approach instructions given in English or proper flying procedures in general.

Mrs. Hart was a socially prominent Washingtonian who quickly announced that she had decided to spend the night in Zahedan. She asked us to take her to the best hotel in town. Not surprisingly, she found it unacceptable. It had small rooms and a shared bath with hole-in-the-floor toilet which didn't impress her. Since Sarkis was on a trip to the south, we invited her to stay with us.

It was a Friday, Fatima's day off, and Jamal and I bought sandwiches and beer for supper. Mrs. Hart joined us at our kitchen table and described her trip so far. It sounded like the U.S. government had been carefully chauffeuring her around the world, but she seemed pleased with her progress.

She also told me she planned on voting for Nixon in November. "My family would disown me if they knew since we've been Democrats for generations. But I like what he has been doing. His foreign policy initiatives have been good and we are getting out of Vietnam, if slowly."

"Plus, I just don't trust McGovern. It isn't only his changing Vice-Presidential candidates. It's his whole attitude. I just don't believe him."

"Mostly, though, I back Nixon because of what he has achieved in foreign affairs." That, I thought, was a strange way of putting things since we were sitting in a country where our government encouraged the shah's use of billions of dollars on U.S. military hardware while people starved. But I kept my mouth shut.

In the morning Mrs. Hart was off, flying east toward Pakistan, where she would be someone else's problem. A few years later I saw her on the television program "What's My Line" as a guest who had flown around the world, by herself. At least that is what she said.

About this same time the mayor of Charbahar dropped by the engineering office for a visit. He still had hopes of a better assignment, and we laughed over the weather problems in the spring. I gave him the German foot odor product he had asked me to buy for him in Europe. It was the least I could do to repay his hospitality.

While in Tehran on a business trip, I had dinner with one of my roommates and his parents. They were Jewish and had done financially well for themselves. Their son was a civil engineer and their daughter was in college. We discussed life in Iran from my perspective, what our home in the desert was like, and their hopes for their son to return to the capital in the near future. His family needed him to be nearer, they said, and Zahedan was not a good place to live.

During the urban planning conference in Isfahan, I had invited Jeff, Jim and Cindy, and the volunteers from Mashad to join me for Thanksgiving in Zahedan. All but Jeff could make it, so I spoke to

Fatima months in advance about the need to find and prepare a turkey or two. She assured me it would be taken care of and said I didn't have anything to worry about.

On a Thursday two weeks before the holiday, several of us from the house went to the airport to see someone off. The terminal lobby was as crowded and bustling as usual, the arrival and departure of the four-times-a-week plane being a very special social occasion for Zahedan's elite. Dozens of men milled around and women stood chatting while covering themselves with *chadors*. Before the plane arrived, the noisy terminal got suddenly quiet, very quiet. Everyone had turned to look at a group of seven obviously western women in shorts and t-shirts walking through the building toward the gift shop.

My companions quickly saw an opportunity. "Mister," they said excitingly, "you must go and introduce yourself. Then invite them to the nightclub this evening. We will take care of everything". I did, and they agreed that I would pick them up at the public campground where they were staying.

That afternoon a group of men from the office along with my room-mates gathered at our house. It was arranged that only seven of us would be seated with the ladies. There was nervousness among some of my co-workers about the social propriety of the situation, but everyone agreed to meet at the nightclub.

My boss and I went out in the office's Land Rover to the campground near the airport to pick the girls up. They crammed into the vehicle dressed in their best, and as we drove out into the country, they explained what they were doing in Zahedan.

"There are about 50 of us traveling on a tour from Istanbul to India and Nepal. Two buses full of folks. We're camping and cooking our way east."

"We spent the last week or so in Iran. Isfahan was great. Very beautiful, and the bazaar there is wonderful. This place, though, doesn't have much."

"We were only suppose to pass through here but the tour operators screwed up. They didn't get the right insurance or the proper permits for us to enter Pakistan. So we're stuck here for awhile, but they promise us it should only be a few more days."

"It's been three days so far with little for us to do. We sit around talking, smoke a little pot, play some cards and sometimes walk to the bazaar. But there sure isn't a lot to do here. That is why we went to the airport this morning, just to have something to do."

"Tonight should be fun. We had an excuse to put on our best clothes for a change, and we'll get to see the locals in a more personal way."

Jamal had arranged a table for 14, and as we sat down, every eye in the place was on us. While most of the Iranian women did not cover themselves in the nightclub, and music and drinking were part of the evening's entertainment, the presence of so many female western guests was definitely something out of the ordinary. Two of the men from my office who were to join us sat at another table instead. They refused the possible social ill-will which could result from being seen publicly associating with foreign women, so it was seven women and five men that made up our group.

They proved to be a diverse bunch of travelers. Two were sisters from Amsterdam, three were from Australia, one from South Africa and another from England. They were all young and out to see the world. They had enjoyed their few days in our town, liked dressing up for this evening, but wanted to get going again.

When the four-piece band began to play the same songs it did every week, one of them asked me if it would be proper to dance. Young children usually got on the stage and swung to the music but no one else ever did anything. So I said no, it wouldn't be the right thing to do. Jamal complained in Persian, only half-jokingly, that I was a coward for not dancing.

Over the next week I would run into some of the women as they walked around Zahedan. Obtaining the proper papers was taking much longer than expected, and they were getting very bored. Word soon spread through our office that at least one of them was sharing a bed with a local government official.

Some of my co-workers had dreams of the same pleasant situation happening to them. One afternoon my boss, with a wily grin on his mustached face, asked me to invite three of the women over to his house for an evening of entertainment with him, his roommate, and myself. "Maybe they'll stay the night," he hoped out loud, but I found a polite way of avoiding his request.

Eventually the needed forms arrived and the group was ready to move on. Jamal and I visited the campground the evening before they left. The women and their traveling companions were sitting around getting drunk and talking about what they would be doing over the next month. It reminded me of my stay on Corfu, but these people were from a world which I had left behind for awhile. As we parted, I did not regret my lifestyle.

That same week a kitten took up residence in our garage. I left milk out for it, but Fatima strongly objected, saying that food should be for people, not stray animals. It was hard to argue with that philosophy, but I kept feeding the cat anyway until it disappeared a few days later.

In most places in Iran, domestic animals were treated terribly. Occasionally in Tehran or a few other large cities, dogs as pets would be seen. It was much more common, however, to see animal abuse, especially by young children.

I always assumed this harsh treatment was due to the risk of disease, but seeing children pelt a dog with stones or hit it with sticks was not pleasant. The poor animal, bony from malnutrition and usually covered with scabs, would yelp in terror as the kids beat it mercilessly.

In Zahedan dogs ran in wild packs, and no one I knew had a pet. At night, in the moonlit darkness, a gang of dogs could sometimes be seen trotting in the wash or burrowing through a garbage pile. They scared me, but I felt sorry for them at the same time.

A week before Thanksgiving, two small turkeys were shipped from Zabol, and Fatima locked them in the garage. Each day they were fed breadcrumbs, and their gobbles got to be quickly commonplace. Jim and Cindy appeared at our door late one evening along with the other urban planning Peace Corps couple from Kerman. The next day the two volunteers from Mashad arrived, weary from a rough overnight bus trip over a bumpy dirt road.

On Thursday morning my friends went out to see the sights of Zahedan. There weren't many, but it kept them occupied for a few hours. While they were gone, Fatima corralled the turkeys into the courtyard and with a sharp knife gently slit their throats. As blood flowed down their necks into a pan, she carefully laid their heads on the ground, and they closed their eyes for the last time.

The birds' feathers were soon removed, and within minutes they were cooking in a large pan on top of the stove. Dinner for twelve was served on a sunny but chilly afternoon in the courtyard. As we ate, the Americans tried to explain the meaning of the holiday and the significance of the festive decorations my mother had sent. But after my experiment with green beer and spaghetti on St. Patrick's Day, my roommates knew that the country I came from had some strange celebrations. This was just another of them.

A few weeks later, the U.S. consulate employee returned to Zahedan. He brought along a good bottle of scotch, and Robert, he and I drank it all in one evening. We laughed about Mrs. Hart and her "solo" trip around the world. We also mocked the State Department's discouragement of its employees learning Persian. As the level in the bottle dropped, we talked louder and louder about how we would change things when we were in charge.

By the end of the evening, my lack of female companionship had become the main topic of conversation. "What do you do here? These local ladies must be off limits? So what do you do?" the consulate employee asked.

"Read a lot. Pass me the bottle please."

"Listen, you're going to be in Tehran for New Year's Eve, right? I'll see what I can do about fixing you up. There are some American women who work at the Embassy or who live in the compound that I'll give a call. I'll try to get you a date." He did, but he couldn't.

The News

While every evening the BBC overseas radio service brought me the news from a western perspective, another view of things was provided by the Iranian media. Some simple basic ground rules about it were known by everyone. The shah had to be praised and was never criticized or even questioned. Communism was illegal and was not to be discussed.

The role of SAVAK, the secret police agency, was not a subject for conversation either. People would occasionally whisper to me about them, and every group of any size was rumored to have at least one informant in it. I was told that their treatment for trouble makers, or even suspected malcontents, was usually very harsh.

One newspaper story I saw made this point clearly. A western woman traveling in rural Iran was arrested by SAVAK on suspicion of being a communist. According to the article, among the evidence against her was that she was photographing things tourists usually weren't interested in.

Because of the fear of being overheard, even among close friends political talk was very limited. As was discussion of anything controversial, like the frequent university student demonstrations in Tehran or the shah's extravagant lifestyle. They just weren't spoken about by anyone I knew.

Who the SAVAK informer was in our office was a subject of some speculation on my part. I had no proof, but suspected the accountant that Sarkis had once lived with. This man would periodically ask me pointed questions about my views on things like the shah, and he usually didn't participate in office functions. But I never knew if he was a spy for SAVAK or not.

Iraq was another subject that could only be discussed in unfavorable terms. Their government was the enemy and had been for centuries. The people of Iraq were considered victims of the Baghdad regime, and Ahmad Hassan al-Bakr, the ruler, was portrayed as a lackey of the Russians.

Religion wasn't a topic talked about much either, but it didn't seem to be a major subject of interest anyway. The middle-class men I associated with were not religious at all. In Zahedan, it only appeared that poor people and *mullahs* were faithful followers of Islam; everyone else just kind of went along with it.

With clear cut rules for what was acceptable, Iranian newspapers published consistently glowing articles about his majesty and the wonderful things happening in the country. The television news programs I would occasionally see on Sarkis' set were also a cheering section for the government. They often showed this or that departmental minister inaugurating this beneficial project or launching that worthwhile cause. Nothing negative ever seemed to show up.

The "everything is getting better because of the shah" philosophy was omnipresent even as most of the needs of the people of Sistan and Baluchistan province were ignored. For me it reached its peak when a Parliamentary representative from Baluchistan wrote a letter to the editor of the Tehranian English language newspaper. Responding to an article about the province which had been, I thought, overly flattering, A.M. Kashfi said Iran would "certainly see the day when Baluchistan will be a developed province and gain its role in the Persian Gulf in all fields including attracting tourists, businessmen and new industries in the rapidly spiraling progress of the area, in keeping with the development plans of his Imperial Majesty".

The shah himself would occasionally grant an interview, but they always had easy questions, lacked probing inquiries, and certainly contained no criticism. In a January conversation with some foreign writers, the shah said about military preparedness, "even though Iran today might not be considered a formidable military power I do not recommend anyone to try and meddle against us and that, especially, not in five years' time". That, of course, was shortly before he was driven from power, and the war with Iraq began.

In the same interview, the shah said of disloyal groups in the country, "What you see in our country is an opposition class. I mean, they are guided terrorists. We know where they come from to commit murder and go. They kill even those who raise their hands to surrender-those who attempt no resistance. We see elements like that among our students in America and Germany and I consider them to be the off-spring of an unholy alliance between extremists of both Right and Left."

Communism, he added, "is against the law in our country. Therefore, those who preach communism and pursue its objectives are sent before military tribunals. It is an entirely legal process and nothing can be done about it." Where the line was drawn between communists and left-leaning liberals who might criticize him, he didn't say.

His hope, the shah outlined in the article, was for the creation of a Great Civilization in Iran. "In our Great Civilization, that will begin in 11 years time at the end of two five year plans, there will be no illiteracy and there will be every possibility for the people to express their views. We shall certainly come to have all that you have in Europe and America today. Whether that is good or bad is a different matter." Those eleven years would be up in 1983, several years after he had been forced from his throne and died of cancer while being hounded from country to country by his political and religious enemies.

In the media at least, the shah, or king of kings as he was referred to in Persian, was the country. As a special newspaper supplement published on his birthday summarized about the time in 1953 when he had been driven from Iran for a few days by a populist uprising before being returned to power by a C.I.A. orchestrated effort, "What followed makes very interesting reading to historians as it concerns a nation's devotion to its Monarch who, through ages, has come to be regarded not only as the head of state but also as the embodiment of all national aspirations. It was genuinely believed by the vast majority of Iranians that Iran without the Shah would be a body without a head." With the revolution in 1979, of course, the head of the country would be replaced, becoming a *mullah* instead of a monarch.

In addition to his views on the Great Civilization which he hoped would be achieved in the future, in another newspaper interview the shah expressed thoughts on the changes occurring in Iran. These changes, whether women not wearing *chadors* in the large cities to the rebellion of college students against intellectual oppression to the western ways adopted by many young people, were affecting much of daily life in the capital, if not the country.

The shah said, "While we believe in the utmost respect for individual freedom, that is to say, in a democratic regime, we also know that such freedom is tenable in so far as it does not involve impinging upon the freedom of others." Concerning his own role, he added in a November speech, "Our regime is not a so-called dictatorship, nor one that dictates the private life of the individual." The reality of the country, of course, was much different.

His wife went further in discussing the rapid changes occurring in the country and the role that she and her husband played in guiding them. In an extensive interview published in June, she talked about these changes. The article included a picture of her looking like the modern woman she was. Her long flowing dark hair was there for all to see, even though it was the belief of many Iranians that a woman should be covered.

The Empress' understanding, like her husband's, was that opposition to their rule was from both the extreme left and right. After discussing communist opponents, she said, "The opposition on the other side came from those with conservative ideas, the supposedly 'religious' ones-because our own religion, I must say, very much favors the masses and is very socialistic in some ways."

This comment was based on her knowledge that some religious leaders were strongly opposed to the shah's social policies. It was said that these programs had negatively impacted the economic well-being of large land owning *mullahs* and Islamic religious institutions. The Westernization of the country was also seen by these clerics as tearing up the historic social fabric of the nation, leading to a sense of unease and uncertainty. Thus, many *mullahs* and others involved with religion were opposed to the "White Revolution". At least that is what the shah and his wife believed.

Concerning the role of women in society, the queen said that she favored the women's liberation movement. Then she added, "You know, many of the laws passed here in favor of women could have given rise to problems which have been largely avoided because these laws were part of the social revolution affecting most of the population."

With increasing economic prosperity, however, she also saw the potential for problems. "I hope that as our country becomes a developed nation it will preserve its clearcut individuality…I would like us to try to preserve our national character, our traditional hospitality which may tend to disappear with increased tourism and material progress… we must try to preserve the natural kindness of our people toward foreigners. Iran has never had racial or religious problems: let us retain this human quality and make sure that money, that essential tool for development, does not bring with it decadence and corruption."

The article, however, ended on a cautionary note. The empress talked of the danger of unkept promises and the problems they could cause. "Because promises made to them [prior to the 1963 "White Revolution"] were never kept, so naturally the people became pessimistic, negative. But for some years now people have been able to see for themselves that things are being done and they are coming out of this negative state of mind. But a serious setback now would be very dangerous, for it would then be very difficult to overcome their discouragement. We must keep our people's confidence and dare not awaken hopes that cannot be fulfilled."

A few years later, the growing expectations of the country collided with a high rate of inflation caused by booming oil prices. With many basic commodities, including the price of rice, beyond the means of more and more people, the hopes the empress talked about had been dashed. The result, as history showed, was that her prophecy was accurate.

Christmas in Kerman

In early December, Sarkis moved out of the house. He could no longer tolerate Jamal's constant harassment and went to live with the two architects from our office. He asked if I wanted to join them, but I declined since I didn't care for one of the men. Besides, I only had six more months left to stay in Zahedan, so I would remain where I was.

The move wouldn't be all negative for him, Sarkis told me as he packed his belongings. Not only was he tired of Jamal, but the quality of prostitute would be much higher at his new home. The architects could afford better than the poor Baluchi women Jamal solicited. He would miss Fatima's cooking though, Sarkis said.

I hadn't made Christmas in Yazd in 1971, but this year was going to be different. Jim and Cindy were hosting a party in Kerman for a large group and I was committed to going. Before I did, Christmas cards arrived from the U.S., from some of my Peace Corps friends, and one came from recently re-elected President Richard Nixon. While most of the cards were hung in our living room, that one I threw away.

The all day bus trip to Kerman was as rough as ever. In the middle of the desert the army had set up a roadblock looking for drugs and contraband. When we stopped, two young rifle-toting soldiers got on and slowly walked down the aisle, glancing at everyone. While all the passengers sat in silent nervousness, they poked bags in the overhead racks and looked suspiciously at some of the Baluch men. Standing right in front of me, the soldiers had inquisitive expressions on their faces about my presence but decided to keep going. Within a few minutes the bus was bouncing along again.

The Iranian military took itself very seriously, and some of its precautions were certainly amusing to me. Along dirt roads, far from any city, military outposts could be seen. Usually some trucks, jeeps and other vehicles were parked near barracks, the compound enclosed by a chain link fence. On a circular sign next to the road would be a camera with a red line through it. The outpost might be hundreds of yards away, but the army wanted to let people know that pictures of its equipment were not allowed.

By late evening on the 23rd, my taxi pulled up in front of Jim and Cindy's house. A small pre-Christmas party was just ending with beer bottles scattered around the floor and cigarette smoke still filling the room.

"Could you believe what he said in front of a SAVAK agent?" Cindy asked her husband as she cleaned up their living room. "Everyone knows that old guy has worked as an informer for years." Drinking a beer to get the dust out of my mouth, I wondered what had happened. They told me that one of their Iranian neighbors had gotten very drunk and started shooting his mouth off about his drug usage and selling.

All of his talk had been in front of a white bearded, well-dressed older gentleman who had an air of eloquence about him. He was the same man who had helped me when I stopped in Kerman on my way to Zahedan. That he worked for SAVAK was not in doubt any longer to the foreigners he associated with. What would happen to the loose lipped neighbor remained to be seen.

Christmas Eve day was spent exploring Kerman, a city with a wonderful covered bazaar, numerous exquisite mosques, and an ancient city center. As I crawled over the arched mud walls of some ruins near the bazaar entrance looking for picture angles, veiled women were walking below me, all of us underneath a crystal blue but cold sky.

While I had chosen to take photographs, many of the men staying with Jim and Cindy went off to a traditional public bathhouse. When they returned, Jim was ecstatic about the experience. "They take this rough pad and rub it all over you. The dead skin comes off in sheets. It looks scary, but doesn't really hurt. Plus you know you're really clean."

As night fell, the temperature started to drop. A Christmas Eve mass being held at a small Episcopal Church had a congregation of several Peace Corps people, their Iranian friends, and a few strangers. Our poor attempts at singing carols were mostly off key, but the look of joy on the minister's face showed his holiday present had arrived a day early. To have the tiny chapel located in the middle of a vast Muslim desert mostly filled on a special day made this occasion memorable for him.

The sky had been clear and deep black with a galaxy of stars illuminating the streets of the dark city when we walked to church. As we left to return to Jim and Cindy's, however, a few snowflakes were falling from the suddenly gray night. The branch of a fir would be our tree in their living room and decorations were made by hand. A string of popcorn was added for a ribbon of white. Outside, a thin layer of snow covered the ground as we stopped for the day.

First light on Christmas morning showed that a blanket of snow covered the city. The large mud domes next door, which at one time were used to store ice through the summer, now looked like giant sugar-coated beehives. After exchanging presents, we were offered menus by our hosts from which to choose our holiday breakfast.

We passed the day telling stories and talking about the future. After lunch and a nap, we walked over to the house where the Christmas party was to be held. Folks filtered in, and by dusk it was packed with Americans, Iranians, men, women, spouses, lovers, and lots of people I didn't know. Eating, drinking, and talking were going on everywhere, and the feeling of family was present.

It was a typical party really, but the similar shared experiences, the knowing what other volunteers were going through in this strange land, gave it extra meaning. The time of year, the continuation of the Christmas tradition of a gathering of family and friends that I had brought with me from Wisconsin, was something special.

The snow was gone, but it had turned very cold by the time we went back to Jim and Cindy's. As we walked along, pounding our arms together to keep warm, my thoughts were with those people in Zahedan who lived in cardboard boxes and palm frond huts. How they would survive this hard freeze remained to be seen.

Upon my return to Zahedan, it was obvious that the frigid temperatures had taken a toll. People were huddled around small campfires, and they tried to make it through the night that way. Our house was cold but provided shelter, and at least we had kerosene heaters in each room to keep the frost out.

It got so cold that one night a mouse crawled out of a hole in the mud wall next to my bed and got under the blankets with me. The sensation of his little legs moving down my body woke me with a frightened start. I don't know which of us was more scared as I threw off the covers and he scrambled furiously to get back to his hole in the wall.

It snowed twice over the next week. The tea man at the office said he had never seen snow in his 50 years in the province. The courtyard of our house was several inches deep in white powder. The landlord had to hire someone to get on the roof to shovel off the snow. That much moisture and weight wouldn't be good for the mud bricks and simple arches which held up the ceilings of each room. Along the riverbank, the Baluch huts were covered in white, their occupants defenseless against the freezing temperatures.

It was so cold that the slow drip coming out of the faucet in the sink next to our toilet froze solidly into a sparkling icicle. During the day it melted, but for several nights would magically turn into a crystal stalactite again.

Within 10 days the snow had all disappeared, but the cold lasted for weeks. Before the winter was over, many people had frozen to death throughout the province. The winter of '72 would go down in memory as the year it snowed and froze in Zahedan and throughout Baluchistan.

1973

1973

Johnny Walker Black Label

As I sat at my desk on a chilly January morning finishing a simple cross-word puzzle, Housein the tea man came running to fetch me. "Mister, come quickly, you have a telephone call in the reception area," he yelled several times as he raced across the courtyard. Since it was very rare for anyone to call me, and because Housein said it was an English speaker on the line, I was afraid of bad news when I picked up the receiver.

"Mr. Devine, this is Jay Stoker of the American Embassy," I heard in a strong, very professional voice. "I am in Zahedan for a few days with my wife and was wondering if we could have lunch with you today? Would it be all right if we came by your office and picked you up about one?" I assured him it was, but shook my head in bewilderment as I returned to my desk.

Contact with the American Embassy staff was highly unusual, especially when they just showed up unannounced. Peace Corps people ridiculed them for not knowing the language, not caring about the country or the people, and being ignorant of Iran's history. All they were good for was an occasional western dinner and cheap American beer, both of which were served in the Embassy's dining room. Other than that, most of us stayed away from them.

Mr. Stoker arrived right on time in a brand new Land Rover. He was a big, bearded man in his thirties and introduced me to his petite wife. As I climbed into the back seat, he asked where we should go. "Please take us somewhere I don't have to eat mutton," his wife pleaded, so I suggested the airport restaurant.

Sitting at a table which overlooked the empty runway, Stoker explained what they were doing in Zahedan. He worked for the economic section of the Embassy and was touring the southeastern part of the country to check on possible development projects. He would be talking with local government officials, but was also interested in my views of the province and the potential it might have.

"I'll be talking with various Iranians about their thoughts on these issues. I'm meeting with the governor and his staff tomorrow morning, but I'd also like to hear what you think. How much of the province have you seen, and what do you see as the economic future for Baluchistan?"

Not having considered that question much, since future possibilities didn't mean a lot to me given current problems, I was stumbling for an answer when the waiter appeared. As we ordered, it was obvious that Stoker's Persian was excellent, but that his wife didn't know five words of the language. She was able to get chicken and thanked me profusely for the recommendation of a place to eat. "We have lived in Tehran for over a year, and I have never eaten mutton. It would make me sick, and I don't want that to happen," she said in all seriousness.

In a country where the primary meat was mutton, her diet was certainly an accomplishment. Despite that, I invited them to our house the next day to sample mutton cooked by an expert, Fatima. Mrs. Stoker reluctantly agreed, but said she wouldn't like it.

As we ate lunch in the almost empty airport restaurant, Stoker asked me again about what I had seen of Baluchistan and what I thought the future might hold for the province. He also wanted to know what I knew about the fighting in the south.

"All I know about that is what I hear on the BBC," I replied. "Seems that the Iraqis are supplying some of the Baluchi tribesmen with weapons, and there is a guerrilla campaign going on with the intention of creating a greater Baluchistan nation. From the old military fort I saw in Iranshahr, it appears like this fighting has been waged for almost a century. But we were able to drive wherever we wanted when we were there, so it can't be too serious. What I hear on the radio though, it sounds like the Iranian government thinks it is."

After paying the bill, they drove me home. Before I lay down for my daily nap, I wondered again why someone from the Embassy would care about my opinions on such important subjects.

The next day, the Stokers arrived for lunch bearing gifts. He had been to talk with the governor and other high ranking officials and had taken them bottles of Johnny Walker black label as tokens of his appreciation for their time. This was a highly prized drink everywhere in Iran, almost impossible to get in Zahedan, and very expensive. He had two bottles left and offered them to me. I gladly accepted.

As we ate, and both of them complimented Fatima on her delicious cooking, we talked about what he had heard. "The officials here don't know many details of the fighting in the south," Stoker said. "There have been some casualties on both sides, but most of the information is very sketchy."

"It is obvious though," he continued, "that they and the people in Tehran are very worried about the fighting. The talk of a new country being formed out of parts of Iran and Pakistan definitely has them concerned. The Iraqi involvement in helping the rebels adds to the problem. But they don't seem to know what to do about the situation."

The Baluch had once controlled much of Pakistan and some of far eastern Iran. Jim-the-farmer and I had visited the former kingdom's capital at Hyderabad, and its imperial buildings and grand streets showed that this was a tribe with a proud history. Today, the Pakistani branch of the Baluch people was ruled by chieftains who apparently rarely cooperated with each other. In Iran, the tribal structure had been replaced by the indifference of governing Persian bureaucrats.

The Iranian Baluch were divided into city and desert dwellers. Those that had moved into urban areas were primarily low paid domestic help, construction workers, or employed in other menial jobs. Many of the Baluch who still roamed the desert continued to shepherd flocks of sheep and camels across the international border looking for grazing land.

Both groups were basically ignored by the Iranian government unless they caused trouble. As Muhammad Sardar Khah Baluch wrote in his book, *History of Baluch Race and Baluchistan*, which I had purchased in Pakistan, "The Baluch race since the dawn of history, till the present age has been looked down on as an alien race by the Persian rulers, and their territory ever remained a neglected part of the Persian dominion."

My response to Stoker's question about why the Iranian officials would be worried about Baluchistan was that it was probably to protect the potential mineral wealth, not concern about the Baluch people, that interested them. The province was thought to contain vast natural resources which someday could be exploited. As we talked, Jamal sat trying to decipher our conversation and would nod his head knowingly when a word of English he understood was spoken.

That night we opened one of the bottles of scotch, and my room-mates wanted to know what these people were doing in town. "Strangers come with expensive gifts. You talk to them very quickly in your own language. What is this about Mister David?" Jamal asked.

"Oh, he probably works for the C.I.A.," I replied nonchalantly, "and is collecting information about the fighting in Baluchistan. But all I know is what I hear on the radio, so that can't be news to him."

"You're kidding, Mister. The C.I.A.? Like in the movies?"

"I'm serious. I just don't know why they'd want to talk to me."

While in Kerman for Christmas, I had heard that C.I.A. agents were approaching volunteers for information. The staff of the Peace Corps had vigorously complained to the Embassy, but obviously the practice continued. With Richard Helms, the former director of the C.I.A. being the newly appointed ambassador to Iran, that wasn't surprising.

As we sipper our drinks, I thought to myself that if I had known something important, I probably would have told it in exchange for the liquor anyway. It certainly was smooth and excellent.

Work

The first fifteen months of my stay in Zahedan had produced very little in the way of results on the job. I had, however, learned the language well, along with the customs and behavior of middle-class Iranian bachelors. I just didn't accomplish very much at work since there hadn't been much to do.

Rumors spread through the engineering office that the governor had notified his superiors in Tehran that Sistan and Baluchistan province didn't need any financial help. He said this, I was told, so that he could impress the shah. At the same time, though, the governor was accused by some of my co-workers of pocketing much of the money that did make it to the region.

There was no way of telling whether this was true, but our office certainly didn't do very much. Early in 1973, however, that changed. A new governor came to the province with an attitude of building things, improving things, getting things going. Whether this was due to the troubles with the Baluch in the south or because the new man wanted to make a name for himself by implementing projects didn't matter to us. We started working.

Our first job under the new governor was to find another location for the office. Being on a main street in town was the only criteria. By February a second story complex across from the girl's high school had been rented. Over a weekend, all of the furniture and equipment were moved, and on a Saturday morning we occupied the new space.

Within a few weeks, a significant disadvantage of the new location became apparent. One evening, severe winds off the desert whipped up a huge dust storm. By the next morning the entire office, all the plans, all the desks, all of everything, was covered in a thin layer of dirt. Large windows might give an excellent view of the teenage girls on the playground across the street, but they couldn't keep the blowing dust out the way the thick mud windowless walls of the old building had.

Our new street side view did show me parts of Iranian life that I hadn't been exposed to before. One morning the funeral procession of an army officer passed by. He had been killed the previous day in fighting to the south and a large group of walking mourners followed the plain wooden coffin, the dead man's photograph riding on top of it.

On a religious holiday which celebrated the centuries old martyrdom of one of the Shiite sect of Islam's most holy men, I went in to work on Zahedan's land use master plan. The people in Tehran now wanted it revised quickly, and I was trying to accommodate them. Below me, hundreds of mostly poor men and boys wearing black shirts paraded by, methodically chanting as they rhythmically struck themselves on the back with tire chains. They would continue this procession of self-flagellation for hours, some of them tearing their backs up severely enough to require medical treatment.

A newspaper article on this practice in the capital said, "The processions in central Tehran were relatively tame, but somewhere south of Cyrus Avenue our bus was jammed next to a writhing crowd of black clad young men. As a group they had lost all cohesion and fell against the sides of the stalled vehicles, chanting almost incoherently, beating their bared breasts spasmodically and falling on top of each other, drawn on now less by will than by uncontrollable emotion."

To work on Zahedan's land use master plan was one of the reasons I had come to town, but until this time the issue had been mostly ignored. I had fooled around with some revisions but done nothing serious. In early 1973, however, the Ministry of the Interior in Tehran decided they wanted it redone, which was welcome news since the current plan had obviously been laid out by someone who had never been to Zahedan and didn't care about what they were doing.

Using the best air photos I could get and supplementing them with my own crude photographs taken from a small plane, I tried to devise a scheme for the future city which took the existing situation into account. Assuming the population projections for the community were correct, even though I considered them wildly inflated, I was trying to design a future city for almost 100,000 people.

The importance of that job didn't seem at all out of place for a young, inexperienced American. After Christmas I had brought several books back with me from Kerman, my favorite being *A Connecticut Yankee in King Arthur's Court.* The point Mark Twain made about being "THE BOSS" in a strange land and the impact that could have on others seemed like a lesson I was living daily.

One morning a Baluchi man came into the office and asked to see me. In simple Farsi terms, he asked what was to become of his house. With tears in his eyes, he said he understood it was to be demolished to make room for a road.

"I am a poor man, Mister. I can not afford to build a new home. My house is all I have. What will happen to my family if we are forced to move?"

Looking at the current plan, the man pointed on the colored map to where his house was, right in the middle of a proposed multi-lane land-scaped boulevard. In reality, though, it was next to a dry wash which would make the road virtually impossible to build. In the calmest tone possible, I told him I intended to try and change the plan. If successful, his house would be saved. But if the government was willing to build roads by moving camels like Hassan-the-surveyor had done in Negur, how could a poor family's house stand in the way of a new wide street in Zahedan?

In addition to revising the master plan, I was also given the job of designing the layout for two housing projects. One of them was to be built in Iranshahr, the other in Zahedan. The dwellings were intended for low-income Baluch and Persian families, but because the units were going to be new, and have subsidized rents, decently paid government workers were clamoring for the chance to move in also.

In deciding on a design for these projects, I took several factors into account. The straight line pattern of Iranian residential streets, laid out precisely along a north-south or east-west axis, was something which I found uninteresting. Almost every place you went in the country, one or two story mud brick homes would border the street, the only openings to the homes being the front doors. Family life was lived inside, around the courtyard and kitchen table. Meeting neighbors took place at the bazaar or on a main street while out for a walk, usually not in front of a house.

One potential modern day problem with traditional Persian land use planning was where to park the growing number of automobiles. While it wasn't an issue in Zahedan yet, in major Iranian cities pedestrians had to squeeze down narrow streets to get by cars parked in front of homes. Since many of these residential alleys were only about 12 feet wide, it didn't leave much room for anything else.

Combining these issues, the typical straight compass coordinate streets, the lack of any outdoor space for social interaction, and the intrusion of the automobile, I tried to come up with a subdivision layout which was different. I started by running the alleys for Zahedan's 48 unit housing project on an angle from the main street while keeping the rays of the sun in mind. I then arranged three houses in a row and offset each grouping to create a twisting pattern of homes. This setback area would also be a place which would be in the shade most of the day, making for easier streetside conversation.

To accommodate the automobile, I designed two small parking lots on either end of the development. Not wanting people to drive to their front doors, I made the alleys narrow enough that this would be impractical. I questioned the feasibility of keeping cars completely out of the residential area, but my co-workers told me the plan could work.

My concepts were in many respects a rejection of the traditional method of Iranian city planning. Persians had been building livable cities in the desert for many centuries, but I was trying to improve on their customs. While it looked interesting on paper, it probably wouldn't work when built. It was really just a foolish idea of a young westerner trying to leave his mark.

A few months after the design was finished, and only a week before I was to leave Zahedan, Sarkis told me to get into the office's Land Rover. We drove out to the edge of town where a crew of men was working, building homes. The general contractor came over to talk to us and he had my plan in his hands. On the ground were chalk and string lines showing where the alleys and homes were to be constructed. They were all at an angle from the main street, just as I had drawn. "Mister," the contractor said, "this is the strangest looking place I have ever built. We will see what becomes of it."

Breakup

By late February, Jamal's behavior toward Fatima was out of control. Her young daughter would accompany her each day, and after work Jamal always wanted to play with the child. At first this had seemed innocent enough, but his constant insistence on playing with the girl, even when she didn't want to, had led Fatima to ask him to stay away from her daughter entirely.

This aggravated Jamal like a bug bite beneath his belt. He was the only one among us who had no prospects of leaving Zahedan and that bothered him immensely. His high school education, lack of family connections, and aggressive approach to life meant that his hopes of returning to his native Shiraz were minimal. Meanwhile, the rest of us in the house were all making future plans to depart permanently.

To vent his frustration, Jamal had first made Sarkis' life miserable. When he left, Jamal went after the maid. She was disobedient, he said, and would not listen to him. She was our servant and had to obey us, he insisted. She might be stealing, he added, and we should all be concerned. It finally reached the point where I was appointed as the one person in the house to speak with Fatima. Everyone else was to leave her alone entirely.

That didn't work either. Jamal needed someone to boss around and Fatima was his selected target, but she wouldn't budge. He might want to play with her daughter before lunch everyday, but she wouldn't have it. It got to the point that one evening, after some heavy drinking in our courtyard, I suggested that to settle things, maybe we should just fire Fatima the next day.

"It would be too bad since she's a great cook, but if that is what you want, we'll get rid of her," I said after taking a long swig of beer. "We can always find somebody else, so tomorrow she goes."

"No," Jamal replied contritely, "that won't be necessary. I will leave her alone. She is an excellent cook, and it would be a shame to lose her."

"Are you sure? I'll do it if you want," I said earnestly because I was tired of the constant arguing.

"No, Mister David. It will be all right."

Peace prevailed in the house for awhile. Then, during breakfast one day, I asked my roommates what they wanted for lunch. "Cabbage stew," Jamal exclaimed excitedly. It was a specialty of Fatima's, and one of his favorites. "We haven't had it in quite some time, and I would really like it," he said.

I left them and went next door to the kitchen. It was obvious that Fatima had heard what had been said because she whispered that she didn't think any cabbages were available in the bazaar. Based on that, I told her to look, and if not, she should fix something else.

Jamal heard this and was livid. With a crimson turning face, he yelled that she just wanted to spite him, and there were plenty of cabbages available. I was fed up with this petty bickering and screamed back, "Fine. We'll go to the bazaar right now, and if we find cabbages, we fire her. If not, you will apologize and leave her alone for good." He agreed, and we stormed out of the house together, our two shocked roommates still in their pajamas looking dumbfounded.

Before we had gone 100 yards, Jamal turned around and said he didn't have time to go to the bazaar. He had to get ready for work and would talk to me later. Left standing on the bridge which crossed the dry streambed near our house, my Irish temper was running over. I decided that I had taken enough of his nonsense. Cabbages or not, I instantly concluded I would be sleeping somewhere else by nightfall.

As I walked quickly to the bazaar, a raging anger was pressing at my temples, ready to explode. Looking for cabbages but not seeing any, I inquired of one green grocer and he said he didn't have any.

At work thirty minutes later my temper was still boiling and I asked Sarkis if his invitation to join him in his new house still stood. He said it did, so I ran home and told Fatima to get her nephew Ali to help me move my things. Then, as calmly as possible, I added that she could join me if she wished. She thanked me for the opportunity and said she would.

By noon my few possessions were loaded on a small wooden push-cart and my room was empty. I was sitting in the courtyard, waiting for lunch to be served, when Jamal came storming in. He had a paper sack and threw it harmlessly at me from across the reflecting pool. "See, Mister," he screamed as two cabbages rolled along the ground.

In quiet, diplomatic terms, one of my other roommates tried to talk me out of leaving. He asked me to give it a few weeks to see if things didn't get better. He said we had financial arrangements, like who owned the refrigerator and stove, which needed to be worked out. He added that Jamal had promised to leave Fatima and her daughter alone for good.

"No, I've had enough of him," I yelled for all to hear. Anyone who wouldn't take five minutes to walk to the bazaar to finally decide something that had been festering for months I didn't want to be associated with anymore. "After lunch I am gone from here, and Fatima is coming with me." We ate a very quiet meal together, and it wasn't cabbage stew.

Within a month, Jamal had returned to the boarding house where he was living when I first met him. The two others in the house had departed for Tehran, not to return. They had new jobs, and Zahedan was just a memory for them. My new roommates welcomed Fatima and me into their house and were glad to have found a really good cook instead of having to eat restaurant food every day. Jamal never understood why I left, always thinking it was because of the cabbages.

Another Spring Break

For the Iranian New Year's holiday in March, Mohammed, the accountant from the office to whom I had been teaching English, and I decided to go to the beach. Bandar Abbas, the city near where the Gulf of Oman pinches together to become the Persian Gulf, had become a coastal destination for college students from Tehran. They were looking for a change of pace from their studies, and it was as close to my Daytona Beach experiences of a few years before as I was going to find in Iran.

The bouncing bus ride to Kerman was still rough, but south from there to the coast the two lane road was a paved highway. As we neared the ocean, desert scenery was left behind, and the bus passed palm trees and rolling sandy hills. By nightfall we were in a small rented circular hut of bamboo walls, palm frond ceiling and dirt floor, camping near the water.

Mohammed liked the heat and humidity, and the next morning went off to find some Tehranian girls. Several groups of well-to-do female college students from the capital were in Bandar Abbas for the holiday, and they spent the day lying on the beach, acting just like the western women they were trying to emulate.

I didn't get along with the climate, so instead walked to the bazaar. It was a relatively new building without any charm and was filled mostly with imported and smuggled goods from the south side of the Gulf.

Near the bazaar I ran into a contingent of Peace Corps volunteers who had also come to the coast for the holiday. We drank our lunch together in a nearby bar and traded stories of our exploits. One of them told tales about Margaret, the lone single woman from our training group. It was rumored she was skinny dipping with Iranian men and passing her body around from one to another in the small town she lived in. That, we agreed, was not in the best interest of understanding between our two cultures.

That evening Mohammed had a date, so I joined the other volunteers for a trip out to the local oil company restaurant. It served western food, and we were looking for some cold American beer. They had that, and a table full of American oil workers besides.

These guys were earning lots of money for doing their job, but all they could do was complain about the place. One of them explained how stupid a merchant was in the bazaar. "I just wanted some shoe laces and asked him for them. He looked at me like I was an idiot. I think they're stupid idiots who just like to make our lives miserable. I don't know why I came here," the man wondered as he downed another whiskey.

We inquired if he or any of the rest of them knew some Persian. "Nah, why would we want to know that? It's a stupid language for stupid people who would just as soon cut our throats and cheat us while they're doing it. I can't wait to get out of here." We quickly left them behind, absorbed in their bottles and their own misery.

The next day Mohammed and I took a small tour boat out to an offshore island where retailers specialized in selling imported merchandise. Most of the stuff was cheap plastic goods and toys. It was like shopping at a K-Mart on the beach, covered tables set up in the sand. The middle-class Iranians loved it. They were buying things just like Americans at a discount store clearance sale.

As our boat bounced through the waves returning to the mainland, I looked over an English language newspaper purchased on the island. A big, bold headline proclaimed that Iran was about to purchase $2 billion worth of military hardware from the U.S. The country's oil money would pay for the airplanes and other equipment. I didn't think that would do much for the average Baluch family, but then again it wasn't supposed to.

The economy of Iran depended upon oil sales, and the future for the industry looked bright. Whether the increase in profits would somehow benefit the majority of the country's people, however, remained to be seen.

Early in 1973 the latest 5 year budgetary plan for Iran had been released by the government. It called for massive increases in social spending, more infrastructure improvements, and additional agricultural production. The ability to implement the ideas, however, had to be proven.

The goal of the financial plan, according to a newspaper editorial endorsing it, was to create the kind of country the shah dreamed of. "He dreams, and has always been dreaming, of a country that sees not only to the material needs of its people but, more importantly, to its spiritual needs, its cultural needs, and its moral needs so that material gains become the means to a society where human values come first."

But the plan also proposed something unusual in a nation ruled by a free spending dictator. He skied in Switzerland, vacationed in France, lived lavishly, and didn't seem to mind that people knew about it.

Despite that, the budgetary plan suggested, "Observance of a revolutionary spirit, introduction of rigorous economy, campaigning against luxuries as a matter of national policy in all government spending and private life. This would require creation of a new approach to life and new social values together with special legislation to prevent waste and destruction of national wealth." How that policy would affect the shah's extravagant lifestyle wasn't mentioned in the newspaper article.

Just after the end of the five years covered by the 1973 spending plan, the shah was driven from the country. A different kind of revolutionary spirit from that anticipated would control Iran. The shah's dreams would have turned into his nightmares by then.

To begin implementing the 5 year plan, the government announced an annual budget of $10 billion with 28 percent being devoted to military expenses. According to the Prime Minister, even more was needed

for defense, but that would have to await the training of additional personnel. While the traditionally poor relationship with Iraq was an obvious military threat to the country, the push by Richard Nixon, Henry
Kissinger, and the U.S. government to make Iran a regional policeman
was also playing a major role in budgetary decisions.

As our boat neared the shore, I looked around. Would these people
be better off in five years under the proposed budgetary plan or not?
History, I decided, could determine that.

The water front boulevard of Bandar Abbas where our boat docked
provided a perfect pedestrian promenade for the city. Walking, being
seen by others, and stopping to talk with friends, was a major Iranian
past time. They had their homes and courtyards for privacy, but when
Iranian families went out walking, they wanted to see others and be
seen. Teenage girls would stroll arm in arm while couples slowly pushed
baby carriages. Even though Bandar Abbas had an Arab look and feel to
it, the Persian tradition of the promenade was obviously strong.

On the wide decorative sidewalk next to the ocean, small trinkets and
other goods were laid out on blankets looked over by dark skinned,
headdress wearing businessmen. Some Arabic women along the sidewalk were completely covered, black insect-like masks hiding their faces
from view. College aged girls from Tehran visiting Bandar Abbas for the
holiday were in shorts and tank tops as they paraded down the street. A
warm, salty breeze blew across the boulevard as we headed back to the
campground.

Before dinner, Mohammed and I went to the public bath to wash off
our sweat. Unlike the one in Charbahar, these showers had fresh running water. Like all the other baths I used in the country, though, it was
clean, cheap, and had lots of hot water.

On our way north the following day, Mohammed updated me on his
plans to enroll in an English training course in Brighton, England. Once
his knowledge of the language was better, he wanted to apply to a

University in the U.S. While many Iranian men proclaimed they sought the same thing, Mohammed had the drive and intelligence to pull it off.

He also told me that my fellow workers all thought I must be working for the C.I.A. "Mister, look at it from our viewpoint. Why else would someone from a rich country like yours come out to a poor, terrible place like Zahedan? We all want to leave, and yet you stayed. So there must be something keeping you there. Is that right, Mister?"

I could only chuckle. No matter what I said, or how often I expressed my delight at living in Zahedan, they would never believe me.

We parted in Kerman. Mohammed was headed to Tehran for a few days and I was returning home. While waiting several hours for the east bound bus, I wandered through the bazaar looking for things to take back to Wisconsin. An elderly rug merchant in an out-of-the-way shop offered me tea, and as I sipped it, he showed me his inventory. From a chest high pile of carpets, his young assistant would pull down one and then another, some finely woven with silk and others crudely made.

One of the rugs caught my attention and I asked about it. "This one," he said, "I am selling for someone else, so the price is fixed. It is a used carpet, but as you can see, is in good shape. It is a tribal rug from south of here and the price is reasonable." It was different from many with its flashy colors and animal designs and the cost was affordable.

But this was Iran where no price was ever fixed, so I offered him about sixty percent of what he was asking. "I told you, it is on consignment and I really can take nothing less," the old man said politely. I replied that I didn't need the rug but would pay him eighty percent of his price. This rug seller, however, wasn't budging.

"Look," I said in exasperation, "I have a long bus trip ahead of me and don't really have any room for this rug. Besides, it's not in very good shape and is worn in spots. Look at those bare areas. Plus, I am in your country trying to help out, and this is the thanks I get? Let's just compromise and I'll give you 90 percent of what you wanted." But he wouldn't take anything less than his original asking price.

That was incredible. I wanted the rug, but I certainly didn't want to pay the full price. I walked outside for a minute, looked at my suitcase and bus ticket pretending I was thinking of leaving, returned, and made my final offer. "I'll buy it, but you must come off the first price. It just isn't Iranian," I pleaded. So he threw in a small prayer rug as a gift and we shook hands on the deal.

The afternoon bus for Zahedan was full when it left Kerman. The desert was very warm even though it was only March, and the barren scenery was as tantalizing as ever. The absence of vegetation, of wildlife, of anything, gave the desert a picturesque solitude which was very attractive to me.

Just before sunset we stopped in a remote spot to pick up two bearded Baluchi men who were crouching by the side of the dirt road waiting for a ride. They each had small duffel bags thrown over their shoulders and looked relieved when they got on board. Since there were no seats available, they sat in the aisle, bouncing along with the rest of us. Soon, one of them threw up, and the odor of his vomit quickly filled the bus. "It's probably his first bus trip," one of the Persians on board yelled, and he was undoubtedly correct. As the stream of light green stinking ooze made its way down the aisle, I thought about how I was going to miss this place, and these people.

North for The Weekend

My daily routine in Zahedan continued even as I was preparing to leave for good. Before I did, however, I had some decisions to make. What would be done with my few belongings had to be decided. How the things I was keeping would be shipped to Tehran and then on to the U.S. needed to be determined. When I would actually leave Zahedan was also a question that had to be answered.

But daily life went on. One morning, Fatima's husband came to the house with her. He was an elderly, white bearded Baluchi man, much older than she was. He had a doctor's appointment and was going to wait in the kitchen until the office opened.

At lunch, one of my roommates expressed great surprise at the age difference between Fatima and her husband. "Why, the man is so old, I doubt he can have sex anymore," he proclaimed. Then he added in all seriousness, "She must be very unhappy. We should consider offering to service her so she can relax."

Sarkis and I simultaneously burst out with loud complaints that this was truly a disgusting suggestion. In reply, our roommate said it was a genuine proposal, made in Fatima's best interest. Nothing came of it, however, and a few weeks later this architect had left Zahedan permanently.

A short time later, Essie, the urban planning program director, visited again. He was in town to determine if another volunteer should be sent to Zahedan to replace me. My offered opinion was that if future work projects would be guaranteed in writing, the idea was worth pursuing. If that wouldn't or couldn't be done, then no one should be sent.

My roommates and I took Essie out to the nightclub for supper the evening of his arrival. Over drinks, we discussed what I would be doing in the future, and why I had moved.

"It just didn't work out. Basically it boiled down to me having to choose between Jamal and Fatima, so I took the home cooked meals."

"You guys seemed to get along well when I was here last year. Sorry to here about it. Oh look, here comes Jamal now."

In his most condescending swagger, Jamal came over to our table. He and Essie had a short, intense conversation which I couldn't hear. After Jamal left, Essie said, "He thinks you moved out because of some cabbages. What is that all about?"

"You don't want to know," I said turning back to my beer.

In a letter to me after his trip, Essie wrote of the positive changes he had been told about in the engineering office. Of course, he heard them from the new boss, a man who was great at avoiding work while taking credit for what others did. Essie also pointed out that the Peace Corps was about different cultures getting to know one another. He acknowledged my concerns about the position but was obviously leaning toward sending another volunteer. It was his job security, after all.

A month before I was to leave Zahedan, my co-worker Jafar asked me to join him for a trip to his hometown of Birjand. It was located a few hundred miles north, half way to Mashad over a dirt road. We took a Land Rover and the trip was easy. Birjand was on the edge of the desert but was an irrigated agricultural area that had trees and grain and livestock.

One of the reasons I decided to go was to see Paul, a Peace Corps English teacher I knew. We had met in Hamadan in 1971, and both of us were now getting ready to leave the country. I wanted to see him and discuss what his experiences as an American Jew living in a Muslim country had been like.

We met for dinner at Jafar's family home, and Paul was invited to stay for the weekend. He agreed to keep me company, and we talked about his life in Birjand. It had been a fairly typical bachelor experience, and Paul was satisfied with his time spent in Iran.

His religion really wasn't an issue with Iranians, and one of my former roommates, who was also Jewish, had openly made his faith known to people. Such acceptance was not the standard with all other religious groups, like the Bahai's. They were considered infidels, but nothing seemed to be done to them under the shah. Perhaps that was because Bahai's avoided mentioning their beliefs in public and had to practice their religion in closely guarded secrecy.

People sometimes talked about how the head of SAVAK was a Bahai, but that was the worst thing I ever heard said of them. After the revolution, however, hundreds of Bahai's were persecuted and martyred by the fundamentalists because of their religion.

Women were the most obvious targets of discrimination in Iran in the early 1970s. Late one afternoon in Tehran I had seen a perfect example of it. An attractive uncovered woman walking down the street had been pinched on her rear by a young man. That was a common everyday occurrence throughout the country. Instead of shrugging it off, however, she decked the guy. As he lay on the sidewalk, a large crowd quickly forming around them, the woman was standing over him, screaming Persian obscenities. "I hope your father burns in hell! I have just come back from America, and this is how I am treated! You stupid bastard!"

During our training period, a young black American auto mechanic volunteer learning the language with the Peace Corps group in Isfahan visited us in Karaj. He and I went to a small store near our house to buy some things. As the shopkeeper added up the price, he spoke to his son, not knowing we understood what he was saying. "Look at him, just like a monkey. Why doesn't he go back to the jungle where he came from?" The other volunteer and I both remained silent, but a few weeks later he had left the country.

White western men were mostly ignored by this harsh behavior, except in the religious centers. In Mashad, teenagers threw stones and spit at Jim-the-farmer and me because we weren't Muslims. In general, though, Caucasian American men were treated as if they were Iranian.

The occasional pebble tossing group of children in Zahedan was tolerable to me since it was harmless and ineffective behavior. Besides, I assumed Iranians in the United States might sometimes be treated strangely because of their religion and customs.

Once in awhile, however, the frustrations caused by Persian discrimination toward others could cause Americans to boil over. In Birjand I shared with Paul a Peace Corps story making the rounds among volunteers throughout the country. It concerned the last night spent in Tehran by a departing volunteer from Hawaii. He had given two years trying to help people and had to tolerate in silence some occasional crude talk about his Japanese ancestry.

To celebrate his pending departure, a group of fellow volunteers had taken him out, and they all got quite drunk. As they walked home, weaving their way down Tehran's dark streets, an Iranian teenager passed them on the sidewalk and muttered "Slant eyes" to the Hawaiian. Of course, he didn't know the Americans could understand him. They grabbed the guy, dragged him into an alley, and knocked a few of his teeth out.

By the time the proper authorities were notified the next day, the volunteer was somewhere over Turkey, flying west. The Peace Corps did end up paying for the required dental work, but those of us who had experienced this type of name calling applauded the sentence which had been handed down.

While his religion had been a non-issue for Paul, the lack of attention to his requests for support from the Peace Corps office in Tehran was a problem, as it had been for me. I had written a critical letter to the country director about his failure to endorse Essie's idea for an all-volunteer conference. He had replied with a reasoned response about potential security problems, but that didn't satisfy me. I sent off a blistering letter asking what he did on the job, why he got so much money when the volunteers did all the work, and other such things. In my mind, I was questioning why Americans were coming to the country on a volunteer basis when the Iranian government could afford to pay them much more. If Iran had $2 billion for jet fighters, I knew they could come up with a few million dollars for U.S. English teachers, auto mechanics, and urban planners.

When I told Paul about these letters, he laughed heartily. He said the Peace Corps staff in Tehran would pass them around the office and get a good chuckle out of the critical comments.

Of course, this wasn't the first time I had questioned the administration of the program. At the final meeting of the 1972 urban planning conference in Isfahan, Essie innocently asked what I thought of the sessions. I was blunt and undiplomatic as usual. I liked seeing everyone and said so, but as for helping with my job, the two days had been a waste of my time. Based on these types of reactions, the staff in Tehran was less than enthusiastic about me.

The next morning Paul, Jafar and I drove out to a small village of mud brick homes crawling up a hillside. It was where Jafar's family had originally come from, and which they still basically owned. It was a typical Iranian rural settlement of one centrally located water faucet for everyone, a tiny stream where people would bathe, and rug making by women and children while the men worked in the farm fields.

There was a schoolhouse in the village, and the children were learning to read and write. Their small fingers might be used to weave the tight knots of carpets after class, but for most of the day they sat studying. If this was a symbol of the shah's "White Revolution" to try and change the country, I thought it seemed to be going in the right direction, if slowly.

The shah's 12 point program for improving Iran, the "White Revolution", was celebrating its 10th anniversary in 1973. The national media was giving the event extensive coverage, documenting how life had been altered. For all the successes the press showed, however, conditions for many of the country's rural people hadn't changed very rapidly.

Among the major goals of this non-violent "Revolution" were the ending of the landlord-peasant relationship by providing land to small farmers. It also included giving the vote and other rights to women, and the creation of the Service Corps.

According to the shah, the purpose of these changes was to, "build in this part of the world with your cooperation a country which will equal the most advanced anywhere in the world. Our country will be a free one where free men and free women shall live and through the Iranian genius we shall build it in a productive and useful atmosphere, away from all kinds of evil. The creative ability of this country which has been the secret of its survival shall be reflected better and in a greater measure because now the fetters of slavery have been broken and 75 percent of the population of this country which had lived in slavery has been granted the bounty of freedom."

By slavery the shah meant the feudal system of land ownership which had previously existed. The "White Revolution" mostly ended that practice, and many rural people now worked for themselves on their own land instead of for a wealthy landlord.

A vote was held on the proposals in January of 1963. Not surprisingly, the reported results were 5,589,7112 in favor, or 99.9 percent, and 4,115 against. For the first time, women had been allowed to vote, even though their ballots didn't count because the new laws wouldn't take effect until after the election.

The changes brought about by the "White Revolution" were truly monumental for some Iranian women. As one said in a newspaper article marking the 10th anniversary, "before January, 1963, Iranian women were classed along with the insane, the mentally incapacitated, criminals and the like, but now thanks to the Revolution, they have attained the full rights to which they are justly entitled."

Another woman, an employee of the Tehranian municipality, indicated in the story that, "had it not been for the White Revolution, she would not now be sitting behind her desk, nor would she be able or have much to say about what constitutes women's rights".

While some of the social policies of the "White Revolution" did not substantially alter life throughout the rural parts of the country or in small towns like Zahedan, they were having a tremendous impact in the major cities. Resistance to them from displaced landowners and some clerics still existed 10 years later, but change was obvious.

That evening in Birjand, Paul and I talked with Jafar's family about our experiences in Iran. Both of us spoke Persian well enough to be comfortable in this situation, and we were accustomed to being in the spotlight. As we drank beer while leaning on floor pillows scattered around the room, he and I told them of our lives and how things were different from where we came from.

One of the lessons I had learned well, I said, was how to bargain, and the role it played in their society. A very proud moment had come for me a few weeks earlier. It was a lasting memory which I would take with me from Iran.

I had been in the Zahedan bazaar with Essie. He was an Iranian who had been educated in the U.S. and had become very Americanized while there. He had seen a camel-skin lamp from Pakistan which he greatly admired, but the shop keeper was asking far too much, so Essie left empty handed.

I spent a minute examining the lamp and then made an offer. The merchant countered, and we had an intense five minutes of negotiation. By the time I departed, I had the lamp at about one-half the price he had quoted Essie. The shopkeeper said that I was "as hard as an elbow" when it came to bargaining. That was a real Persian compliment which I enjoyed immensely. Jafar's family nodded in polite approval as I finished my story.

The following day, Jafar and I drove back to Zahedan, my last trip in the area over. As we rode through the desert, we discussed my time in Iran, the people I had worked with, and the experiences I had.

I reminded him of his refusal to sign the letter I needed before I could leave Iran to visit Pakistan. He asked for my forgiveness, saying that as an interior decorator he wasn't comfortable with ever being the boss of an engineering office, even if only on a temporary basis.

Then I said, "In many ways, your country and mine are very different. Your food, your lifestyles, and your habits and customs are not like America's. You give much more importance to family and traditional values than we do. We treasure personal freedom and liberty. Yours is a gentle, peaceful country. Mine is a aggressive, violent one."

"Like in the movies, Mister David. You have cowboys and gangsters."

"The movies are make believe, Jafar. My country isn't like that, but sometimes we act as if it is. Just like some of the men here treat women terribly and can be real jerks. But most men aren't like that. They are genuinely caring, sensitive, peace loving people."

"Our countries and cultures are very different, aren't they?"

"Yes they are. And it is important to keep those cultural differences in mind when talking about either place," I said.

As we drove into Zahedan, going by the small space ship-shaped billboard that advertised a brand of cooking oil, Jafar asked me what I would remember most about his country. "The people, I think," I said while trying to fight back the tears.

Leaving Home

One of my roommates was scheduled to depart Zahedan a week before I did. He was moving to the far western part of the country to become the head of a provincial engineering office in a place not affectionately known as "behind the mountain". It was a remote, cold location without much work, but the move was a step up for him professionally, so he took it.

While he was the man who had suggested we needed to "service" Fatima, he was also the most serious thinker in the office. We would discuss Vietnam, Iranian foreign policy, and race relations in the U.S., sometimes in heated conversations. He was more open, and articulate, with his opinions than the others I worked with. He wasn't afraid of criticizing his own government, but he wouldn't talk about the shah. That was too dangerous a subject, even for him.

He said he envied my ability to travel, partially because he had lost his. During his university student days in Tehran he had participated in demonstrations against the government and, as a result, would never be issued a passport. He wanted to visit western Europe to see the architecture he had heard and read about, but could not. Instead, the best he could do was go "behind the mountain".

His last weeks in Zahedan had been frantic. He was a 30 year old college graduate carrying on a telephone romance with a high school student. He had never talked to her in person since face-to-face communication between them would not have been tolerated in Zahedan. Instead, they would talk for hours each evening, since this house, unlike my previous residence, had a telephone.

One night, while we were sitting around the living room, Sarkis and I inquired what the girl was like. "Oh, Mister, she has beautiful eyes," my roommate said. "You should meet one of her friends. They are all very nice."

When the telephone rang, saying with a smirk that maybe I would meet one of the girls the American way, I rushed over and picked up the receiver. After a young voice said, "This is Shahla," I responded, "Want to go to a movie tomorrow night?". She was a friend of my roommate's romantic interest who prided herself on her English. Her quick reply was, "No, I don't think so. It wouldn't be the proper thing to do." With that I turned the phone over.

To see the girls in person, one Friday afternoon my roommate excitedly gathered the men from the house together and drove us to the bazaar. There we walked up and down, passed the shops and stalls while his *chador* covered girlfriend and her companions walked the other way. The two phone lovers made eyes at each other, and when we returned home, he talked like a 15 year old in heat. It was, I thought, ridiculous.

His going away party and mine were combined and held at the nightclub. A large crowd of men turned out on a weeknight and the liquor flowed freely. We had the place almost to ourselves, and everyone was telling stories and getting drunk.

One of the guests told the tale of how he had invited me to his house for lunch shortly after I arrived in Zahedan. "Mister didn't want to have our whore," he said between laughs, "insisting he didn't appreciate being tenth in line."

Meanwhile, my roommate was out in the restaurant garden, finally able to spend some private time with his phone friend. He was leaving early in the morning and what they did was between them, and her father.

The party eventually moved to our house and carried on late into the night. With music coming from an old record player, drunk dancing men with outstretched arms slowly circled each other, snapping their fingers and wailing loudly along with the Iranian tunes of love and despair. The departing architect lay on a bed, passed out from the liquor. Someone asked me to dance, and I politely declined, citing that in my country it wasn't proper to dance with another man.

The next evening Sarkis took me to the home of a Christian family he knew. Over mud thick coffee and rosewater flavored sweets, he moaned on about his fate. "If I was in Tehran, maybe something might be worked out. My family could help me there. But in this place, what chance do I have for finding someone to marry? I just may have to settle for a Muslim woman. My father would disown me, but what choice do I have?"

During the next week I arranged to sell most of my belongings. The remainder I loosely packed in the old refrigerator box for shipping to Tehran. I also had to send the gifts my co-workers had given me: a small inlaid table from Pakistan, a carved cigarette dispenser, and some other wooden items were all wrapped carefully.

At work I kept getting asked where I was going and what I would be doing. Most of my plans were uncertain, but two things I knew. My parents and brother would be flying to Tehran in a few weeks to join me for some travel around the country. Then in August I had to be in Tucson to enter graduate school in the urban planning program at the University of Arizona.

My co-workers insisted on helping with the arrangements for my parents visit. "Mister," one of them said, "we must treat them like they are part of our family, because they are. You are one of us. I will have my brother in Shiraz make reservations for you at the best hotel, and he will guide you around the city. It is the least I can do."

Another man, a native of Isfahan, demanded that his family reserve a room for us at the Shah Abbas, an internationally known hotel. I couldn't refuse. The Persian custom was to help travelers and friends. My acceptance of their assistance was the Iranian thing to do.

By this time my revisions to the Zahedan master plan were completed. I recommended the future city grow onto undeveloped land, not consume existing structures. It would be up to others, however, to try and work the changes through the bureaucratic maze needed for approval.

A few nights before leaving, I was packing the refrigerator box when the phone rang. Being alone in the house, I answered. In a slow, dreary voice, a man said, "Mister, this is Reza-the-draftsman. Is Sarkis there?" When I said he wasn't, Reza mumbled, "Tell him I have eaten hashish and am going to die. Tell him I appreciate everything he and you have done for me. Say goodbye for me."

Thinking as quickly as possible, I asked where he was and told him that Sarkis would call shortly. Reza was a well-known drunk and manic depressive who had been banished to Zabol with Hassan-the-surveyor. Shortly after we returned from the rainy trip to Charbahar, Reza had become a problem in Zahedan. He would show up at work red-eyed and disoriented on many mornings, so exiling him was the chosen solution. But he had returned to town a few days before for a vacation.

Sarkis soon appeared, and I frantically blurted out what Reza had said. "Don't worry, Mister, this isn't the first time this has happened. I'll go see what I can do." An hour later Sarkis was back. He had taken Reza to the hospital where his stomach was pumped. "They'll keep him overnight just in case. He'll be O.K. for now. The only real solution, though, is to find him a wife and get him out of here. He hates this place and can't accept living in either Zabol or Zahedan. I'll try my best. This latest episode just might help."

The old refrigerator box had to serve one last function, as a moving crate for my things. Even though the cardboard was deteriorated, I loaded rugs, travel posters, gifts for my family, and much more into it. After haphazardly stringing some flimsy rope around the middle, I had it hauled down to a freight moving company. When I saw it leave town the next day, sitting on top of a truck full of well-made wooden boxes, I hoped it would survive in one piece over that long road to Tehran.

My wooden bed, the radio/cassette player, and some other miscellaneous items I sold to a merchant in the bazaar. I had developed a case of bedbugs about a month before my departure and used DDT power to try and get rid of them. That didn't work, so I started sleeping on the floor. Somehow I forgot to mention the bugs when I sold the bed.

Finally, my turn to leave came. Fatima cooked my favorite meal of a meaty dark pomegranate sauce to put over rice for my last lunch in Zahedan. After inhaling it, I visited with her for a few minutes. She was scheduled to have surgery but had it delayed until after I was gone. Her daughter was clinging to her *chador*, peeking at me once in awhile and giggling. I thanked Fatima for all she had done for me and gave her two months salary as a parting gift. She wished me well and with that I left her to clean up the dishes.

Later in the afternoon, Sarkis and some guests of his were visited by a prostitute. She was the same woman who had been at the house I had gone to for lunch shortly after arriving in town.

After the other men left, I talked with her. She was young and attractive, but her husband had deserted her. Everyone knew, however, that her father would kill her if he ever found out what she was doing, so she had to sneak around and make excuses for her long absences from home.

Even though she was childless, she had turned to prostitution in order to buy things. She had expensive tastes, but Sarkis said she was doing well financially.

I asked to take her picture, and in a soft, shy voice she replied, "Mister, you know that many Muslim men don't like to have photographs of their women taken. Some of them think it steals our souls."

"But I am leaving tomorrow, and no one will ever see it. Besides, you know those ideas are ridiculous. It can be your going away present to me."

"All right, but you must never show it to anyone here. I could get into a lot of trouble." We went into the courtyard and I snapped a picture. It showed an attractive, well dressed young woman wearing makeup and looking nervous. After the camera clicked, she threw a *chador* over her head and went on her way.

My last evening in Zahedan was spent talking with Sarkis. He had adopted a miniature desert deer as a pet and it was running around in the courtyard. "Mister, that animal may be the only family I ever have," he sighed, "so I'll give it the best life I can."

We discussed what I had learned in Iran, and the memories I would take with me. My impressions, I said, were of a country of caring people that took some getting use to. Persian culture and social standards were much different than what I was accustomed to, but the people were generally kind, concerned about those less fortunate, and certainly they had treated me well. Iranians had their faults like everybody else, I concluded, but I would not forget their generosity toward me.

I complained, however, about not learning the language well enough. Sarkis replied, "Mister David, you speak Farsi more fluently than any foreigner I have ever known." I knew he was being polite, but that really felt good.

I had decided to fly to Kerman, not wanting to face the bouncy bus trip one more time. On the appointed morning, every man from the office joined me at the airport. I went down the line, exchanging kisses on the cheek, bidding farewell, telling them I would never forget them. Tears were streaming down my face when one of them said, "Mister, don't worry. We will never forget you either. You are as Iranian as any of us."

My plans were to stay with Jim and Cindy for a few days, but when the taxi dropped me off at their house, the door was locked, no one home. I had made arrangements with them well in advance and wondered what could have happened.

Riding back into town, I had the driver drop me at the entrance to the bazaar. I knew the other Peace Corps couple that worked in the

Kerman engineering office lived somewhere nearby, but I hadn't been to their home and didn't really have a good idea of exactly where it was. I was going to ask a merchant where the foreigners lived when the kindly looking, white-haired, older gentleman approached me from out of the crowd. He asked if I needed assistance. Even if he was a secret police agent, it was uncanny how he could appear at just the right time. Of course, he knew precisely where the young Americans lived.

After a few days in Kerman, I returned to Yazd to revisit Jeff. I had been told that he had been burglarized a few weeks before. Several carpets he was using, but had not yet purchased, had been stolen. Since he couldn't afford to pay for all of the rugs, he had become very conscious of the chance of losing things.

Theft was not a common problem in Iran, but it could occur. We might have had a lock on our front door in Zahedan, but a strong kick would have knocked the flimsy wooden thing down. The chances of that happening, however, were minimal, as was the possibility of someone climbing over the courtyard wall. Armed robbery was also very rare, so we never worried much about having things stolen in Baluchistan.

In Jeff's house I found that most of the cockroaches were gone. A few still crawled out of the hole-in-the-floor toilet, but the kitchen, the bedrooms, and even the courtyard were rid of them. Jeff would be leaving in a few months himself, so the roaches would probably be reclaiming their former territory soon.

When I boarded the bus to depart for Tehran, Jeff asked where I carried my travel money. I pointed up to the roof, indicating my suitcase. "Get it down, right now!" he loudly insisted, acting like a mother sending a disobedient child off to school. "You will keep your money on you. That's all there is to it," he ordered. So I meekly complied.

A week later in Tehran I was staying with Gerry, my Peace Corps college classmate from Wisconsin, when Jamal and his girlfriend from Shiraz appeared unexpectedly at the door. Jamal had been to some parties at Gerry's apartment and remembered the place. We had started to patch up our friendship in Zahedan, but it was never really the same. Occasionally he would come by my office, and we would go to a movie or to drink a beer. It occurred to me that I might be the only one in Zahedan he could do that with, and I felt sorry for him.

"Do you know that Robert and his wife and son left Zahedan about the time I did?" I asked after some small talk. "They are staying with her parents in Tehran and have invited me on a blind date tonight. If you'd like, you two could join us. Here is a map to their house, and we are meeting at six. Can you make it?"

"I think so," Jamal replied in a hesitating manner. "We will try." But I never saw him again, perhaps because he thought they would have been imposing on our get-together.

Robert's wife wanted me to meet her cousin, a high school senior. She and I had little to talk about, but Robert, his wife, and I went on and on about what they were going to do. Robert wanted to head back to northern Wisconsin, but getting permission for his wife to permanently leave the country would be difficult. "Maybe we'll just stay here for a year until she is eligible to retire. I can get a job doing something, but I don't really like it here in the big city," he said, in English.

His wife, who spoke English very well, replied to me in Farsi, "Something will work out. I want to go to America, but we'll have to work with the authorities. But it will be O.K."

The next few days I spent visiting friends and going to parties. One was for the religious mechanic who had explained on the flight over to Iran how he was going to convert the masses. He was marrying an Iranian woman, and they were going to live in Tehran. His proselytizing days were over, he said.

The day after that party, two Iranian women who had been there came to Gerry's apartment for a visit. Wearing shorts and a t-shirt, I sat talking to them in English, discussing the nightclubs of Tehran. I had come a long way from Zahedan in only a few days.

I also visited with Jim and Cindy. He had come down with a case of hepatitis right after their springtime trip to Afghanistan and had been air evacuated to Tehran. Staying at the Peace Corps director's house, he was doing well but was very weak. He did, however, promise to recover.

After more than a week, the possessions I had shipped from Zahedan still hadn't arrived in Tehran and I was beginning to worry. I called Sarkis to ask for his assistance in finding out what had happened to them. The next day I called back, and he told me they had been sent to a different freight office than the one originally planned. But, he said, they were in Tehran. Then he added, "Mister David, we miss you already. Everyone here wishes you would come back."

West from The East

Before leaving Iran, I wanted to visit its western provinces. They had cool, green land, with farm fields and mountain towns populated by Kurds and other tribal people. It was a long way from Baluchistan both geographically and socially.

After spending a few days in Tabriz exploring the bazaar and other sites, I boarded a minibus for Sanandaj. It would be an overnight trip and we stopped late in the evening at a small village. The driver pointed out a two story rooming house where men could stay. I paid a few coins to the desk clerk, and he whispered that I should go up the stairs. There was one large room with cots in straight rows. Most of the beds were occupied and I tried to make my way silently through the maze, doing my best not to bump into anyone in the dark.

Sanandaj was a mid-sized city which some people had told me was the loveliest in Iran. I found parks and boulevards, brisk air, a few church-like looking mosques, and not much to see or do.

While sitting in the main city park at dusk one evening, watching school children in neat blue and white uniforms walk home each carrying an armful of books, I was approached by a soldier. The army had a post across the street and he wanted to know what I was doing, sitting there. When I told him in his own language that I was traveling after having been in Iran for two years, he wished me a safe journey and left.

The van to Kermanshah the next day was filled with Kurds. The men sat silently while uncovered women dressed in colorful flowing robes made of sparkling material and with gold jewelry hanging on their heads gossiped away. Persian was their second language, so we communicated well. The women talked to me about my time in the country and what I would be doing in the future. When one of the men wanted to ask a question, his wife sharply rebuked him, keeping him in his place.

In Kermanshah I found Jim-the-farmer. He had moved to the area upon being driven from Baluchistan after our New Year's holiday trip to Pakistan and Afghanistan. He said he'd enjoyed himself in this new location. It wasn't the desert, and he didn't teach only tribal people, but he had found someplace with a climate much like central Wisconsin, where he was from.

Once back in Tehran, I went to the American Embassy to take Jay Stoker up on an offer he had made while in Zahedan months before. He promised to buy me lunch in the embassy restaurant if I contacted him, so I called to see if he had the time. He did, and the next day I was shown into his small, cluttered office.

While finishing up some paperwork he asked how I was. I replied that things were fine and I would be interested in seeing the report he had written on Baluchistan. "You know, that's classified information," was his answer, but he showed it to me anyway. It had nothing in it that a general knowledge of the province combined with listening to the BBC wouldn't have revealed.

According to Tehranian newspaper reports, Iraq's involvement with trying to cause trouble throughout greater Baluchistan had been shown conclusively a few months earlier. An arms shipment intended for the rebels in Pakistan was discovered in Iraqi diplomatic mail pouches. In response, the two offended governments in Tehran and Islamabad had expressed suitable outrage.

In the crowded embassy restaurant, as all-beef hamburgers and fried chicken were served to well dressed Americans, Stoker and I talked about the conditions of living in Iran. U.S. government personnel, he said, were discouraged from learning the language. Apparently that was the policy because it was the State Department's hope not to have its employees get too close to the natives. Plus, embassy workers tended to stick together anyway, so many of them had very little contact with Iranians. Stoker was one of only a handful of Americans at the embassy who even spoke the language. "That's a shame," I said. "There is a lot they could learn if they could just talk to the people."

Sitting at a nearby table were a group of Peace Corps volunteers, including Paul from Birjand. They nodded their heads and smiled at me as Stoker and I left the restaurant.

That night, Robert, his wife, her cousin, and I went to see a movie. Our first get-together had mostly excluded the teenager, so I wanted to try again. But she was a high school student who didn't have much to say, especially with her cousin and I doing most of the talking.

At the end of the film I asked if she wanted to go with me for a drink at an English-style pub. She politely reminded me that it wouldn't be a proper thing to do without her cousin and Robert joining us. Thus, the evening concluded with them dropping me in front of Gerry's apartment and then riding off in a taxi.

A few days later I was at the Tehran airport, waiting to meet my parents and brother for a week long tour of the country. After they registered at their four star central city hotel, I went to collect my bags from Gerry's place in order to stay with them.

The taxi driver I hailed quickly found that I spoke his language. He asked if I wanted to join him in picking up prostitutes, that he knew where some good ones were. I declined the offer, but as we drove along he pointed out to me this pair of *chador* covered women walking the street or those waving for a ride that could be had for a price.

For dinner I took my family to Ray's, a basement bar and restaurant where the beer was on tap and the pizza made to order. The next evening we dined with Robert and his wife at an Iranian restaurant she recommended. It was up in the northern part of the city, and the unmetered taxi ride was costly.

When I flagged down a cab to return to the center of town, Robert's wife suggested I bargain over the price. Robert moaned that wasn't necessary, but she said, "David knows, that is the Iranian way of doing things".

On a bus tour of the city the next day, between the guide's commentary I talked with my parents about the different parts of Tehran. In the south were crowded streets, donkey-drawn carts, central water taps, in essence a large village. The people who lived in southern Tehran upheld the traditional lifestyle of the country, and their numbers were increasing rapidly as vast urbanization occurred.

The center of Tehran was the commercial and office core of the city. It was also where the American Embassy was located. To the north were the homes, shops, hotels and nightclubs of the affluent. It was there, up at the base of the mountain, that the shah lived.

According to one newspaper article I read, "The traditional lifestyle seems to be found only in an ever dwindling group of villagers and first-generation migrants to the cities who have not yet adopted 'Western' ways through education and affluence." Whether that was true or not the future would determine. In 1973, the cultural divide in Tehran symbolized the material and spiritual split which was occurring throughout the country.

After flying to Shiraz and being escorted around the city by my co-worker's brother, my family and I took a taxi ride out to Persepolis. This trip included a tour of the tents which had been used in the shah's celebration of the Persian monarchy. Two years before when I had visited the site, the emphasis had been on the ruins, the high stone columns and magnificent carvings of the ancient palace. Now the tourists' attention was also turned to the encampment where heads of state had slept and dined. As we toured the tents, the memory returned of the little naked boy playing in the dirt on the road from Zabol while a fly slowly walked across his unblinking eye.

We also flew to Isfahan, and Gerry suggested I join him for a beer at the hotel where he was staying. Jim and Cindy, Essie and he were all involved with a new training group of Peace Corps urban planners that would be spending the summer there.

I walked over from the Shah Abbas Hotel and found them on the patio. They were talking of where new volunteers could be placed and asked if I thought someone should go to Zahedan. "Only if there is a commitment of work, and I doubt you'll get that. If you don't, don't send anyone," I said bluntly.

That certainly was not what Essie wanted to hear. He squirmed in his seat and looked like he wanted to argue, but didn't. While he remained silent, he was obviously uncomfortable with my opinion. Feeling out-of-place, I quickly drank my beer and left.

The Shah Abbas was an internationally known hotel built in an old caravan rest stop. The rooms were small and plain, but the magnificent lobby, courtyard, and hallways gave an overall feeling of opulence.

The hotel's outdoor patio restaurant was highly rated, and my family and I found a table for dinner under a sky full of stars. After being seated, I told them what I knew of the history of Isfahan and the importance of its architecture.

After a long wait, our orders still hadn't been taken. I called the waiter over and in the harshest Persian terms possible let him know that the service was unacceptable. He couldn't treat foreigners that way, I said, and he would take our orders immediately.

Our food was soon in front of us. I explained to my parents that my critical words were the Iranian way of doing things. Waiters were told in no uncertain terms when service was poor, but were tipped well when it was good.

The next day we toured the bazaar and magnificent central square. Walking through historic but almost empty mosques, the beauty of Persian architecture was obvious.

We also went to see the Sio Se Pol bridge, an ancient monument of 33 arches spanning the Zayande Rud River. Near the bridge some cars had driven down the riverbank, through a strip of marshy reeds, and right into the tiny meandering stream. The drivers were throwing water on the vehicles, rinsing them off at a sort of free car wash.

A few days later my family was on an early morning flight out of the country. After they left, I made a last quick check on my belongings. They were ready to go, and so was I. My anticipated itinerary was to travel to Istanbul and then decide how I would spend the summer going overland through Europe.

Two months later, after the charter plane I was on had landed at JFK, my plans were to take a bus from New York to Madison. As I entered the lobby of the terminal, however, and looked around at a place, and a people, I hadn't seen in over two years, thoughts of another overnight trip just weren't appealing.

A telephone call quickly told me what the plane fare would be, so I checked my wallet and decided to spend what cash was left. A bus ride to La Guardia, a late-night flight, and a taxi got me to my parents' house by midnight, almost broke.

The next week is a blur of memories—revisiting the college bar that my crowd had hung out in, going to the A&W of our high school days, visiting with Linda, who looked bored but beautiful behind the counter at a liquor store where she was working, giving her and Suzanne the sheepskin coats they had ordered a year earlier in Rome, sitting at a party in my parents' backyard with the two women and some others from our college days who had traveled the world. A few feet away, those from our group that had stayed in Madison talked and drank beer together, their conversation basically the same as it had been in 1971.

The bus ride I took to Tucson was tougher than expected. It was two days of little sleep, eating in dirty restaurants, and sitting in terminals next to dozing drunks and grinning but toothless panhandlers. The scenery went from farmland to prairie, oil wells to desert scrub. By the time we reached El Paso at 4 a.m. on the second day, I was mentally exhausted. Tucson was still 8 hours away, but at least I knew I would make it. After finally arriving, a taxi took me to the dorm where I had arranged to live, and I collapsed onto my bunk bed.

I wrote Mohammed, the English-learning accountant from the office in Zahedan, shortly after I settled in. We had gotten together twice when I was in England and he had reminded me then of his hopes of enrolling at a university in the U.S. He responded to my first letter and said he understood I wanted to help him find a place to study, but I didn't receive a reply to my next letter.

While in Munich I had run into Paul from Birjand and he told me about Bell Helicopter wanting to hire former Peace Corps volunteers to teach English in Isfahan. He indicated that for those Americans that wanted it, luxury housing would be provided in a suburb of the city.

In response to my inquiry about a job, the company offered to fly me to Los Angeles for an interview. The work consisted of teaching Iranians how to read a maintenance manual for repairing military helicopters. The pay was good, but I declined the opportunity. It just wouldn't have been the same.

I had Robert's address in Superior, Wisconsin but didn't send him a letter since he was probably still in Iran. Many months later I looked in my address book. There was Robert's listing, but for some unknown reason I decided not to write him and never did.

For the summer of 1974 I obtained an internship job at a regional planning agency outside of Milwaukee. One of the staff members unexpectedly turned out to be my college and Peace Corps friend Gerry. Over the next twenty-five years we would sometimes get together when I went back to Wisconsin or he would come to Tucson.

In 1980 and 1986 I stayed for a day with Jim and Cindy and their two children in Los Angeles. The other Jim had returned to his family's farm in central Wisconsin. When I visited with him and his new wife a few years after our experiences in Baluchistan and Pakistan, a child was on the way, and there were cows to be milked.

In 1987 I saw Jeff in Boston. We talked about the difficulty of having a serious conversation with many Americans. Most of our countrymen seemed to be preoccupied with television, sports, and the weather. Iranians, we agreed, were more informed about what was going on in the world and were more interested in discussing international issues.

During a trip to Philadelphia in early 2001, I went looking for the Hotel Sylvania. Thirty years after I had left it for Iran, the building was still there. But according to a resident, it had been converted to apartments many years before.

A few months after I left Zahedan, another volunteer was sent there, but he lasted only a short time. Whether it was because of the lack of work or not I never heard.

The Peace Corps stayed in Iran until 1976. It left, I was told, in a dispute over how much the Iranian government would pay toward supporting the program. It was just as well. When the shah fell in early 1979, all of those Americans scattered around the country would have been at great risk from the fundamentalist revolution.

One day in the fall of 1973, a letter from Sarkis arrived in Tucson. He wanted me to know that life was wonderful. His family in Tehran had found a Christian girl for him to marry. Now he was going to have a family of his own. A photograph was also in the envelope. Two short people were smiling for the camera, their bright white wedding clothes lighting up the interior of a dark church. He was obviously twice as old as she was.

Sarkis finished his letter by writing, "Mister, you must come visit us. We are waiting for you." It was the last I heard from him.